Rhetorical Philosophy and Theory
Series Editor, David Blakesley

Other Books in the Rhetorical Philosophy and Theory Series

Unending
Conversations

For Tom

To our own unending
conversation. May it
last as long as we do.

Best,
Greig

Unending Conversations

New Writings by
and about Kenneth Burke

Edited by
**Greig Henderson and
David Cratis Williams**

Southern Illinois University Press
Carbondale and Edwardsville

Library of Congress Cataloging-in-Publication Data

Unending conversations : new writings by and about Kenneth Burke /
    edited by Greig Henderson and David Cratis Williams.
        p.   cm. — (Rhetorical philosophy and theory)
    Includes bibliographical references and index.
    1. Burke, Kenneth, 1897—Contributions in philosophy of rhetoric.
    2. Rhetoric—Philosophy. 3. Criticism. I. Henderson, Greig E. II.
    Williams, David Cratis, 1955-. III. Series.
    P301.U54 2001
    818'.5209—dc21   00-030978

    ISBN 0-8093-2352-4 (alk. paper)
    ISBN 0-8093-2353-2 (pbk. : alk. paper)

The paper used in this publication meets the minimum requirements of
American National Standard for Information Sciences—Permanence of Paper
for Printed Library Materials, ANSI Z39.48-1992. ⊗

Contents

Preface

Unending Conversations: New Writings by and about Kenneth Burke takes its title from one of Burke's most famous topoi: the drama of human life as an unending conversation.

> Where does the drama get its materials? From the "unending conversation" that is going on at the point of history when we are born. Imagine that you enter a parlor. You come late. When you arrive, others have long preceded you, and they are engaged in a heated discussion, a discussion too heated for them to pause and tell you exactly what it is about. In fact, the discussion had already begun long before any of them had got there, so that no one present is qualified to retrace for you all that had gone before. You listen for a while, until you decide that you have caught the tenor of the argument; then you put in your oar. Someone answers, you answer him; another comes to your defense; another aligns himself against you, to either the embarrassment or gratification of your opponent, depending upon the quality of your ally's assistance. However, the discussion is interminable. The hour grows late, you must depart. And you do depart, with the discussion still vigorously in progress. (*PLF* 110–11)

Though Kenneth Burke has departed, the discussion of his contribution to twentieth-century thought is still vigorously in progress, and this volume of essays seeks to contribute to the ongoing conversation by featuring essays by Burkean scholars and by Burke himself.

Part One, "Dialectics of Expression, Communication, and Transcendence," deals with the dramatistic view of poetic form and literary symbolism that is to be found in two of Burke's unpublished manuscripts—"Poetics, Dramatistically Considered" (PDC) and "A Symbolic of Motives" (SM). Following a "Textual Introduction" to these two manuscripts, substantial excerpts from each comprise the second and third chapters. The fourth chapter charts the complicated relationship between the two works.

From what we can tell, the twelve chapters of PDC were completed by 1958, though the bulk of the manuscript was written in the early 1950s. (Please see chapter 1, Williams's "Textual Introduction," and chapter 4, Rueckert's essay on PDC and SM, for further details.) With the exception of minor textual corrections, such as those involving obvious typographical errors and spelling consistency, the sections from PDC and SM are printed precisely as Burke wrote them, without benefit of the final revisions and clarifications to which Burke routinely subjected his drafts prior to publication.

For reasons elaborated in the "Textual Introduction," our selections from PDC include chapters 1, 2, 7, 10, and 11. In " 'Poetic,' 'Aesthetic,' and 'Artistic' " the point of departure is Aristotle's *Poetics*, and Burke argues that "the direct approach to art is through its nature not as knowledge, but as a species of action (symbolic action)." Aristotle, he goes on to say, does not even use the word "truth" and merely requires that a tragedy be "plausible." "Though the six 'parts' of tragedy are 'inductively' derivable from the systematic observing of particular tragic specimens," Burke concludes, "there can be too much stress upon the empirical nature of Aristotle's observations" and too little on the fact that the six parts "are *deductively* derivable from the logic of the Dramatistic terminology itself." In "Logic of the Terms," he pursues this idea further, contending that "you best get an insight into the genius of Aristotle's analysis if you note that his terms are not merely a set of shrewd observations connected with one another by 'and' (there is plot *and* character *and* thought, etc.). Rather, these terms all share a common Dramatistic logic (if action, *therefore* plot, *therefore* character, *therefore* choice, *therefore* passion, etc.)." Burke's "business of carving out a Poetics" centers on the belief that "a Dramatistic analysis of drama provides a set of purely empirical observations connectable by 'and' while at the same time the logic of the terminology is under the sign of 'therefore,' with all the terms spun from the genius of a common generating principle . . . the term 'act.' " This incipient "logologic" adumbrates the manuscript's later argument that dramatic catharsis, dialectical transcendence, and entelechial fulfillment are interrelated aspects of a work's symbolic action.

In viewing form as the psychology of an audience whose expectations are aroused and fulfilled—though not without some frustrations along the way, for such are the complications of sophisticated works of art—"Form" isolates "the entelechial principle" as an essential aspect of poetic development, entelechy, of course, being Aristotle's term for a thing's internal principle of motivation, its incentive to attain the kind of perfection appropriate to the kind of thing it is. "If the beginning of a work is viewed as setting up potentialities which are fulfilled at later stages in the work," Burke writes, "in this sense the beginning can be thought of as matter that is subsequently actualized. The beginning, we might say, has 'the makings' of an ending. . . . And much is gained by making us conscious that each step in a process can be viewed as requiring its own particular kind of finishedness." He also shows how the motives of self-expression, communication, and consummation interinanimate each other. The argument in this chapter harks back to *Counter-Statement* and its elaboration of the fourfold nature of form—progressive (syllogistic or qualitative), repetitive, conventional, and incidental—as well as points forward to what one would now call reader-response criticism. Burke's linking audience expectancy with "the formal principle of consummatory self-consistency" is a creative synthesis of reception aesthetics and critical formalism that goes well beyond the limits of each.

" 'Beyond' Catharsis" suggests that "a certain kind of poetry gets certain of its effects by allusion (not just superficial allusion, but profound allusion) to certain religious practices that preceded it" and that such allusion is not "merely a matter of 'origins' but an *intrinsic aspect of the poetry itself.*" Those readers who would see giving critical weight to such allusions as an instance of genetic fallacy fail to realize that neither the intrinsic nor the extrinsic can be isolated in its elemental purity, that both are dialectical concepts, each of which must be defined in terms of the other. Considering the similarities and differences between Greek "cathartic" tragedy, Plutarch's "biography of admiration," and Corneille's "theatre of admiration," the rest of the chapter explores the interconnections among dramatic catharsis, dialectical transcendence, and entelechial fulfillment, construing each to be an instance of "beyonding."

Finally, in "Platonic Transcendence," Burke notes that although " 'transcendence' and 'catharsis' may often be used as synonyms, there is also a sense in which a purely dialectical cleansing is better described as 'transcendence,' while 'catharsis' better applies to dramatic cleansing by tears or laughter." Consequently, Burke compares and contrasts the nature and function of such dialectical cleansing in, among others, Plato, Marx, and Nietzsche.

The selection from *A Symbolic of Motives* is a wide-ranging and freewheeling discussion of individuation and amplification in James Joyce, Ernest Hemingway, Virginia Woolf, Dante, and William Carlos Williams, and of the language of "thisness" in Aquinas, Duns Scotus, Goethe, Hegel, E. M. Forster, and Shakespeare. The extended treatment of Woolf's *Mrs. Dalloway* is particularly insightful in its illumination

of "the unresolved issue of homosexual and heterosexual love that repeatedly recurs in Mrs. Woolf's fiction" and the resultant "tangle of
motives both social and sexual." Burke's expert tracking of the motif
of ascent and descent, especially as it connects to the many textual instances of "plunging," pays off handsomely and illustrates nicely his
practice of "indexing" works by determining what goes with what
(identifications), what versus what (agons), what leads to what (progressions), and what becomes what (transformations). In his essay on
"A Symbolic of Motives" and "Poetics, Dramatistically Considered,"
William H. Rueckert examines Burke's usage of indexing and joycing
(pun analysis) and delineates the relationship between *A Rhetoric of
Motives,* "A Symbolic of Motives," "Poetics, Dramatistically Considered," and *Language as Symbolic Action.* He also develops a theory as
to why "Symbolic" was abandoned and never published as a book. (See
also "Textual Introduction.")

Part Two, "Criticism, Symbolicity, and Tropology," focuses on
Burke's interrelated theories of form, dialectics, and language and their
relation to criticism and philosophy. The first essay in this section shows
how many of the concerns addressed in Burke's work on poetics look
back to Burke's first book of criticism, *Counter-Statement,* and look forward to the reader-response criticism of Wolfgang Iser and Stanley Fish;
the subsequent essays examine, respectively, symbolicity and Burke's
place in contemporary theory, and tropology and the dialectical relationship between Burke's dramatistic pentad (act, agent, scene, agency,
purpose) and his four master tropes (metaphor, metonymy, synecdoche,
irony).

In "A Rhetoric of Form: The Early Burke and Reader-Response Criticism," Greig Henderson takes up some of the issues raised in "Poetics,
Dramatistically Considered" concerning audience expectancy and considerations of form. Its central contention is that the three nonaesthetic
essays from *Counter-Statement*—"Psychology and Form," "Lexicon
Rhetoricae," and "Applications of Terminology"—together compose a
version of reader-response criticism that is proleptic of discussions to
come not only in *Poetics,* but also in the works of later critics such as
Wolfgang Iser and Stanley Fish.

In "Screening Symbolicity: Kenneth Burke and Contemporary Theory," Thomas Carmichael also provides a context for understanding
Burke's contribution to the "unending conversation," citing the same
celebrated passage that prefaces this introduction. Examining Burke's
relation to thinkers such as Paul de Man, Jacques Derrida, Stanley Fish,
Fredric Jameson, Jean-François Lyotard, and Richard Rorty, Carmichael maintains that Burke's sense of our embeddedness within this

unending conversation not only "directs us toward both the historical situation of rhetoric and the ways in which all discursive practices are caught up in an infinite play of signification, but also serves to remind us of the complex network of continuities and affiliations that links his position . . . with the project of contemporary theory." According to Carmichael, Burke is a skeptical and anti-foundationalist thinker whose edifying philosophy is at its best when it resists the temptation of being overly systematic.

Robert Wess's "Pentadic Terms and Master Tropes: Ontology of the Act and Epistemology of the Trope in *A Grammar of Motives*" is a dense and subtle analysis of the relation between the ontology of the act inscribed in the text proper of Burke's *Grammar* and the epistemology of the trope inscribed in one of its appendixes, "Four Master Tropes." Questioning "whether it is even possible to divide ontology from epistemology, not just in Burke's discourse but in discourse in general," Wess concludes "not that Burke's epistemology subverts his ontology but rather that it is its counterpart." Even if ontology is the senior member, the two are "partners rather than mutually exclusive antagonists." The real, for Wess, is a rhetorical topos with multiple expressions, and the topos, "a discursive site in the unending conversation," "mediates between truth (ontology) and our access to it (epistemology)." Burke writes "from a position within the conversation to expose multiple pentadic differences among the conversants."

Part Three, "Transcendence and the Theological Motive," deals with transcendence and questions of its implications for the theological motive in general and Burke's theological inclinations and influences in particular. In "The Many Voices of Kenneth Burke, Theologian and Prophet, as Revealed in His Letters to Me," Wayne Booth mines a correspondence with Burke that began in 1971 to amass evidence for the contention that Burke, his own protestations notwithstanding, does more than use theology as a vehicle for providing insight into the nature of language itself as a motive. Even though Burke insists that logology (words about words) is a resolutely secular orientation that discovers in theology (words about God) the terministic compulsion and perfectionism that propel all discourse, Booth maintains that the self-styled logologist is at times a closet theologian, his quest for god-terms betraying a displaced and disguised quest for the absolute. In making this argument, Booth isolates eight voices in Burke's writing:

- the voice "of the self-reproaching egotist who was never fully satisfied . . . with *anyone's* efforts to sum him up";
- the voice of "self-criticism";

xiv   Preface

- the voice of the comedian;
- the voice "of an old man lamenting his aging and thinking about death";
- the voice "of an unrelenting literary scholar" who was
  sometimes a "skeptical prober," a "system-smasher,"
  and sometimes a "confident system-builder," an "absolutist";
- the voice of the poet;
- the voice of "the religious inquirer";
- the voice of the logologist, prophet, and theologian.

The essay also makes mention of a short 1981 article by Burke entitled
"Sensation, Memory, Imitation/and Story." Then on the editorial board
of *Critical Inquiry,* Booth rejected the article, much to Burke's chagrin.
The incident is discussed in the essay, and Booth includes the article as
an appendix, which is reproduced here as a separate chapter. Booth reports that the text of "Sensation, Memory, Imitation/and Story" is "a literal transcription of KB's typescript, with a few corrections of typos
and occasional printing in brackets of his original version."

In "Kenneth Burke and Mary Baker Eddy," Michael Feehan discusses Burke's astonishing revelation in a 1983 interview that rather
than rebounding from a naive kind of Marxism in *Permanence and
Change* (1935), he was rebounding from what he had "learned as a
Christian Scientist." His "drastic confession" was that he "secularized"
ideas derived from Mary Baker Eddy, especially ideas concerning all
that "psychogenic illness stuff." Just as Eddy's *Science and Health* is
a sacralization of mesmerism, Burke's *Permanence and Change* is a
secularization of Christian Science. Feehan establishes a connection between key Burkean terms—piety, propriety, pliancy, perspective by incongruity, rebirth, conversion, identification—and their Christian Science counterparts—reversal, faith, translation. Whereas Burke focuses
on ideological conversion, secularizing the sacred to create new linkages, orientations, and perspectives, Eddy focuses on religious conversion, sacralizing the secular to translate the material into the spiritual.
What both have in common is the translation principle itself.

Unending Conversations invokes and pluralizes Burke's topos of
the conversation in the hope that the different voices with their different topoi will bring us closer to the logos that Burke hails in his poem
"Dialectician's Prayer," part of which reads:

And may we have neither the mania of the One
Nor the delirium of the Many—
But both the Union and the Diversity—

The Title and the manifold details that arise
As that Title is restated
In the narrative of History.

To salute both the Union and the Diversity, we believe, is the right spirit
in which to honor the first centenary of Kenneth Burke. To him we
dedicate this volume.

Acknowledgments

This volume is the product of many minds and many hands, even aside from those of the editors and authors. We would like to extend our deep appreciation to the Kenneth Burke Literary Trust, and to Anthony and Michael Burke personally, for permission to publish selections from Kenneth Burke's "Poetics, Dramatistically Considered" and "A Symbolic of Motives" as well as his essay "Sensation, Memory, Imitation/and Story." And we thank William H. Rueckert and Wayne C. Booth, respectively, for making these manuscripts available to us initially.

David Cratis Williams wishes to thank the Newberry Library for a fellowship that enabled portions of the research for his essay. Special appreciation is extended to Robert Cowley for permission to quote from letters in the Malcolm Cowley Papers in the Newberry Library, Chicago, and from letters in the Beinecke Library at Yale University and to the Burke Literary Trust for permission to cite Burke's letters. Thanks are also extended to the Special Collections staffs at the Newberry and the Beinecke for their cheerful assistance.

The Department of English at the University of Toronto provided tremendous support for this project, including providing a "base of operations" for both editors during the early stages of the editing process. To them we owe a debt of gratitude, with a special note of appreciation to the chair, Brian Corman.

In various ways, the authors of the works that constitute this volume are all—to employ a standard Burke term—"linked" to the Kenneth Burke Society, an organization dedicated to co-haggling, in the words of its eponymous "founder." In 1996, the Third Triennial Conference of the Kenneth Burke Society marked what would have been the start of Burke's 100th year with a "Centennial Celebration." This volume is intended as a parallel gesture to that conference. As we are now posed in the interregnum between not just centuries—as was of course also the case at the time of Burke's birth—but also millennia, it is perhaps all the more appropriate to employ centennial and millennial metaphors in thinking of Burke. A man of the twentieth century, almost literally spanning its expanse, Burke has an influence that is perhaps at its strongest ever as we leave the twentieth century and move into the twenty-first. Soon it can be said with full accuracy that Burke's influence touches two millennia. That leaves him just one behind Aristotle.

Abbreviations

ACR	"Auscultation, Creation, and Revision"
ATH	*Attitudes Toward History*
CS	*Counter-Statement*
GM	*A Grammar of Motives*
LASA	*Language as Symbolic Action*
PC	*Permanence and Change*
PDC	"Poetics, Dramatistically Considered" (manuscript)
PLF	*The Philosophy of Literary Form*
RM	*A Rhetoric of Motives*
RR	*The Rhetoric of Religion*
SM	"A Symbolic of Motives" (manuscript)

Part One

Dialectics of Expression, Communication, and Transcendence

1

Toward Rounding Out
the *Motivorum Trilogy:*
A Textual Introduction

David Cratis Williams

The selections from Kenneth Burke contained in the first part of this volume are from one of Burke's most productive, yet, curiously, least studied periods: the 1950s. In many respects these selections, drawn from unpublished manuscripts entitled "Poetics, Dramatistically Considered" (PDC) and "A Symbolic of Motives" (SM), stand alone; in a larger sense, however, they should be viewed as parts of a much larger project in which Burke was engaged at least incipiently albeit at times inchoately from the 1930s on. If his first book of critical essays, *Counter-Statement* (1931), documents Burke's shift in emphasis from "self-expression" to "communication," from an "art for art's sake" aesthetic to "considerations wholly outside the realm of literature proper," then, as Burke himself suggests, his second published volume of critical thought, *Permanence and Change* (1935), might be viewed as an "outgrowth" of the first in that it "in effect takes up where *Counter-Statement* left off" (*PC* 3d ed., "Afterword" 314, 302–3). Originally entitled "Treatise on Communication" (and changed only after the publisher objected that it sounded too much "like a textbook on telegraphy"), *Permanence and Change* widened Burke's orbit of speculations "to include a concern with problems of motivation in general" ("Curriculum Criticum" 214). It was "followed" in 1937 by *Attitudes Toward History,* which Burke saw as a further extension of his concerns with communication and motivation: "Thinking of kind rather than degree, we might say that P&C is to ATH as Plato's *Republic* is to his *Laws.* That is, just as the *Republic* deals with an ideal State, and his

Laws deals with a real one, so P&C thinks of communication in terms of ideal cooperation, whereas ATH would characterize tactics and patterns of conflict typical of actual human associations" ("Curriculum Criticum" 216). Although Burke greeted the 1940s with the publication of *The Philosophy of Literary Form* (1941), largely a collection of previously published essays and reviews, he was simultaneously pursuing the trajectory of *Permanence and Change* and *Attitudes Toward History.* He had begun the 1930s taking copious notes on "corporate devices whereby business enterprisers had contrived to build up empires by purely financial manipulations"; he now broadened his notes to include "all sorts of tactics whereby people sought to outwit themselves and one another in social intercourse (tactics ranging from world-shaking diplomatic maneuvers down to the minutiae of drawing-room repartee, social 'cat-fights,' bland insults, and the like." "The notion," he later recalled, "was that this 'post-Machiavellian' lore should be treated in a book 'On Human Relations' designed to round out the concerns of P&C and ATH" ("Curriculum Criticum" 214, 217).

But his efforts resulted not in a "rounding out" in tripartite form of the trajectories of *Permanence and Change* and *Attitudes Toward History;* rather, as he worked through his notes on "devices," he discovered the need first to answer the question, "What must we be prepared to look for, when anyone is saying why anybody did anything?" His work then shifted to a manuscript, initially entitled "On the Imputing of Motives," which attempted to answer this question ("Curriculum Criticum" 218). The entanglements, however, soon far exceeded even this revised plan, and the design transmuted into a new "trilogy," one that perhaps most properly should be viewed as growing out of the dismal world situation of the 1930s and '40s. Beginning with what had evolved from "On the Imputing of Motives" into *A Grammar of Motives* (1945), Burke undertook to write a trilogy on human motives roughly parallel to Aristotle's trilogy concerning logic, rhetoric, and poetics, but with his stress upon motives and symbolic action Burke proposed a "dramatized" treatment of the topics. In addition, in keeping with his stated motto for both *A Grammar* and dramatism in general, *Ad bellum purificandum,* Burke's trilogy on motives had an explicit political, perhaps more broadly a humanitarian, motive of its own: he hoped to foster analytic, critical, and ultimately philosophical appreciation of the resources and nature of language that, in Burke's understanding, culminated too frequently in conflict, scapegoating, and war.[1] Only by understanding symbolic action and human motives—which is to say, understanding how humans use and are used by language— can we improve human relations and reduce the prospects for additional conflicts on the scale of the Second World War, conflicts that, with the "progress" of weapons technology, could literally obliterate humanity itself. Thus arose what Burke would come to call his *Motivorum Trilogy*. The book jacket to Prentice-Hall's 1945 edition of *A Grammar* touted it as "the first volume of Kenneth Burke's *magnum opus:* a trilogy of books on human relations. It will be followed by *A Rhetoric of Motives* planned for publication in 1947 and by *A Symbolic of Motives* in 1948."

Again things did not work out quite as planned, and the project designed for the forties defined much of Burke's work through the fifties and lingered (maybe malingered) thereafter, forever unfinished; indeed, now, over fifty years after the announcement of the trilogy, sections of two unfinished versions of "A Symbolic of Motives" are published for the first time. This essay will chart the evolution of the *Motivorum Trilogy* and will situate these "new" selections published here within that evolution. We begin by reviewing Burke's design for the trilogy, sketching briefly what is known of the relationship between what became the 391-page PDC and what became the 269-page SM (deferring most of the discussion of SM to Rueckert's essay, "Kenneth Burke's 'Symbolic of Motives' and 'Poetics, Dramatistically Considered'"), following which we will delve into the task of "placing" PDC relative to Burke's published essays (and hence also placing the mostly previously unpublished selections contained herein relative to those sections of PDC that are published, either directly or in substantially similar form). Finally, we will return to the topic of the *Motivorum Trilogy* and "A Symbolic of Motives."

In the *Motivorum Trilogy*, Burke proposed to offer a rounded theory of human motivation, and it was pursuit of this well-roundedness that, as an entelechial quest, guided his work through many permutations in the following years, stretching into decades. In moving from primarily literary concerns to a broader orbit of questions, Burke embarked upon his journey into what he came to call, starting with *A Grammar*, "Dramatism." The "'Dramatistic' step," he suggested in *Dramatism and Development* (1972), is "from specific literary analysis to the consideration of human motivation in general" (21). Burke later reconstructed his initial design for this consideration of human motivation, recalling, "I had first planned a trilogy: (1) universal relationships, as in my *Grammar of Motives;* (2) partisan relationships, and their modes of real or apparent transcending, as in my *Rhetoric of Motives;* and (3) a *Symbolic of Motives*, the study of individual identity." He emphasized the "place" of the "Symbolic": "This third volume would include both poetic and ethical dimensions, inasmuch as both the character of the individual poem and the character of the individual person embody 'equations' (explicit or implicit assumptions as to what fits with what)" ("Curriculum Criticum: An Addendum" 222). But as he worked to enact this plan, he found himself pulled in many unanticipated directions, and transformations in the initial scheme began almost immediately.

Even as Burke awaited publication of *A Grammar* in 1945, he was hard at work on *A Rhetoric*. On November 19, 1945, he wrote to his close friend William Carlos Williams, "Have been batting away at the Rhetoric (It will become, I guess, a study devoted to showing how deep and ubiquitous are the roots of war in the universal scene and the human psyche—a study extending our meditations on the war of words.)" "I am convinced," he added, that the "trilogy can build up a fairly comprehensive abstract of human relations" (Nov. 19, 1945, Beinecke Library, Yale University, hereafter designated BL). But as he worked on *A Rhetoric,* the focus expanded. By 1949 he began to suspect that he had two volumes under way, as he indicated in a letter to lifelong friend, confidant, and critical conscience Malcolm Cowley: "Am hoping, within the next month at the outside, to get the first volume of the Rhetoric completely revised. (Did I tell you it grew into two quite sizable tomes? The second not quite finished.)" (Jan. 3, 1949, Newberry Library, hereafter designated NB). The "second" volume was now what Burke had referred to as rhetorical "devices"; it constituted at least in part the compendium of examples of partisan appeals that Burke had been collecting since the 1930s (see Burke to Williams, June 9, 1948, BL). Although ultimately not included in *A Rhetoric,* the "devices" continued to hover around the edges of the *Motivorum* project, reappearing periodically as a part of the design for the "Symbolic."

It was 1950 before *A Rhetoric of Motives* finally followed *A Grammar,* at which point Burke began to work seriously on the third and "concluding" element of the trilogy, "A Symbolic of Motives." In *A Rhetoric of Motives* he had promised, "our third volume, *Symbolic of Motives,* should be built about *identity* as titular or ancestral term, the 'first' to which all other terms could be reduced and from which they could be derived or generated, as from a common spirit. The thing's *identity* would here be its uniqueness as an entity in itself and by itself, a demarcated unit having its own peculiar structure" (21). Or, "The *Symbolic* should deal with unique individuals, each in its own peculiarly constructed act, or form. The unique 'constitutions' being capable of treatment in isolation, the *Symbolic* should consider them primarily in their capacity as singulars" (21–22). In placing its stress upon the singular, which is to say upon the unified whole, the realm of the "Symbolic" is a harmonized, fundamentally cooperative realm; Burke writes,

> The *Symbolic* should be at peace, in that individual sub-
> stances, or entities, or constituted acts are there considered
> in their uniqueness, hence outside the realm of conflict. For
> individual universes, as such, do not compete. Each merely
> *is,* being its own self-sufficient realm of discourse. And the
> *Symbolic* thus considers each thing as a set of inter-related
> terms all conspiring to round out their identity as partici-
> pants in a common substance of meaning. An individual
> does in actuality compete with other individuals. But within
> the rules of Symbolic, the individual is treated merely as a
> self-subsistent unit proclaiming its peculiar nature. It is "at
> peace," in that its terms *cooperate* in modifying one an-
> other. (*RM* 22–23)

The form par excellence most peculiar to, and expressive of, the individual qua individual is the lyric: In *A Grammar,* Burke suggests a "wa-
vering distinction between the dramatic and the lyrical. If Aristotle's
world is essentially a dramatic one, his God (as a pure act identical with
perfect rest) is essentially lyrical" (245). That is, "the lyrical attitude is
rather the kind of rest that is the summation or culmination of action,
transcending overt action by *symbolically* encompassing its end" (245).
Considering the "Symbolic" as under the sign of the lyrical may help in
distinguishing its projected role in Burke's tripartite theory of motives.

It was this plan that guided Burke's work when he began in 1950
to write the "Symbolic," but again things did not turn out quite as
planned. For one thing, he began to have dreams about his dramatistic
theories of motivation, dreams in which he came to realize that he was
associating each of his five children with one of the terms of his pentad
(Burke to Cowley, Nov. 16, 1950, NB). (In later years, after he had
"hexed" the pentad with a sixth term, "attitude," this association led
to a joke in the Burke household in which they awaited the arrival of
that bastard son, Attitude). Additionally, he continued a pattern evident in his own poetic and critical production since at least his novel
Towards a Better Life (1932) and *Permanence and Change* (1935): he
experienced psychosomatic symptoms unique to each project. Relative
to the *Motivorum* project proper, he tells Cowley, "as regards my great
Migratory Symptom, the project seems to have developed thus: For the
Grammar, high blood pressure; for the Devices portions of Rhetoric
(still unpublished), a stinging, ringing left ear; for the aspects of the
Rhetoric that lean towards 'pure persuasion,' a laggard heart, and when
I got to the middle paragraph on 'suspended animation,' p. 294, I just
about melted away; and now, for the Symbolic (or at least, the Poetics
section of the Symbolic), a really sustained battle with gaspo-gaggo-

gulpo symptom . . . " (Nov. 16, 1950, NB). Along this line, it was not uncommon for Burke to refer to his "Red Ear Ache" when discussing informally the second volume of his trilogy (See Burke to Cowley, Aug. 4, 1950, NB). Reflections on these aspects of symbolic action that bind together in some fashion deliberate symbolic constructions with dream-state associations and psycho-physical manifestations led Burke to again broaden his orbit and transform his design:

> Why all this? Well, such considerations belong at one point or another in the Symbolic, if I can contrive to find the strategic (diplomatic) way of presenting them. I may as well admit: No matter how much I modify or qualify, the Symbolic is in essence an "ego" realm, dealing with "identities" in their uniqueness. And that's why the study of Symbol-using as Somnambulism finally brings us back to the clinical use of the self, as test case. Mainly, I have notes on White Oxen and Turds a Beddy Love,[2] which I think of using, for at least one long chapter. Thus: first section, on Poetics proper; second section, Symbolic, of the "dream" in general, on man's life as first rough draft of a poem; and then, why not, for a rounding-out, to put the two together, a long chapter detailing the major points as regards our discoveries about our own sentences, by a critic who is *revenant* to himself as fictioneer? (Burke to Cowley, Nov. 16, 1950, NB)

Having now conceived of the "Symbolic" in two sections, one on poetics and one vaguely called "Symbol-using as Somnambulism," he plunged into his new manuscript in inauguration of the new year, 1951.

Work on the poetics section began productively. Burke wrote to Cowley on January 6, "At present, am writing *a long essay* built around my comments on Aristotle's Poetics, 'Dramatistically Considered.' It's a me-and-Aristotle sort of thing. This morning's assignment: To have our say on his term 'mimesis,' and how it has been misunderstood (primarily owing to 'scientistic' dislocations)" (NB). And Burke's essay was indeed long—both in length and in coming (although he does publish "A Dramatistic View of Imitation" in 1952). The "essay" soon outgrew its design, and Burke was launched on what became "Poetics, Dramatistically Considered."

His work in the opening months of 1951 must have approached a fevered pitch (consistent with his association between physical symptoms and intellectual, critical, or artistic projects). On February 1, he told Cowley, "Meanwhile, I continue with my me-and-Aristotle chapter, which, after interruptions due to some fantastic ailments, is now btw. 16 and 18 thousand words along the way." And the "essay" had by now spawned several "sections" that, as will be seen when we consider the text of PDC itself, were in themselves becoming substantial essays (and soon in many instances "gazette" articles). Burke continued: "So far: (1) Logic of the Terms; (2) Imitation; (3) Purgation; (4) Pity, Fear, Pride. In another couple of pages, section four should be complete. Looks as though the entire item should be at least 25,000 words. And I do believe I'm getting some of my best stuff said with minimum pain to the reader" (NB). His momentum carried him forward. On February 6, he sent Cowley a postcard asking for information about cats, specifically, "Do you happen to know whether there really is a species of cat called 'Cheshire'?" He explained, "A point I am making in my present section of the Poetics essay wd. be a bit stronger if there were no such species, though I can scrabble along anyhow" (NB). Burke's discussion of *Alice in Wonderland* appears in his essays on "The Thinking of the Body."

By March he crows to Cowley that work on his "Symbolic" is racing onward: " . . . this note is but a pretext to trumpet, to throw back my head and blow, blow, blow": "Have . . . smacked out another 25,000 words. And at this stage at least, I think they're hitting on all cylinders. Also, whereas I was frightened by the Monster chapter that wrote itself [probably "The Thinking of the Body"],[3] these next pages, to my great relief, required no slight effort. (incl. a 34-page, single-spaced index of Oresteia)." And he adds, in his cultivated spirit of self-righteousness, "The paragraphs in my Outline, summing up the contents of this section on Poetics, now amounts to 48 single-spaced pages. Surely, at least, I am allowed to blow about my own *industry*, especially since it generally implies nothing—but!" (Mar. 15, 1951, NB).

By the following year, "gazette" articles (Burke's terminology for his essays published in periodic journals) began appearing derived from his work on his Poetics; these articles will be discussed later in their relationship to the eventual manuscript, "Poetics, Dramatistically Considered." However, it is worth noting in the current discussion that as Burke began to publish pieces of his evolving Poetics in the early 1950s, he frequently offered headnotes or textual references to suggest where the essay might fit in relation to his book in progress. These notes and references sharpen the picture of a fractured development of the "Symbolic" that emerges in his correspondence. It is thus intriguing to note that from among Burke's articles from this period in the early 1950s, none that we have seen are identified as being from "A Symbolic of Motives"; indeed, to our knowledge, after *A Rhetoric*, Burke tends not to refer in his publications to *"A Symbolic"* by name at all until into the 1960s (although he continues to do so frequently in his correspondence).

This may suggest that by the time of the publication of the flurry of essays written in the opening months of 1951 he was no longer certain of the trajectory of the "Symbolic": was it one book or two? If two, which essays belonged in which book? For whatever reason, it is manifestly evident that Burke carefully avoided *naming* in publication the book on which he was working; for instance, in his 1952 essay "Form and Persecution in the *Oresteia,*" Burke neatly evades the issue by indicating simply that the essay is "from a book now in progress" (377). A similar tack is taken in "A 'Dramatistic' View of 'Imitation'" (1952), which is identified obliquely as "from a much longer essay" on poetics (229).

The headnotes also reveal to some extent Burke's struggle to find a thematic and, specifically, a structural coherence among his growing pile of poetics essays. "Form and Persecution in the *Oresteia*" (1952) begins with an acknowledgment that the "essay is a rewritten version of a longer section" from his "book now in progress"; moreover, his description of what "immediately preceded" the "matters considered in these pages" suggests differences both from what he had suggested to Cowley in February of 1951 and from the eventual structure of PDC (the beginning of which, in fact, mirrors closely the structure Burke had conveyed initially to Cowley). In "Form and Persecution," Burke broke down those "matters" into the following sections:

> (a) a section designed to show that the meaning of "imitation" in drama has become "scientistically" obscured, by failure to approach Aristotle's concept of *mimesis* through his concept of the *entelechy,* with its peculiar stress upon "fulfillment"; (b) a section on "allusion" in Greek tragedy, the gaining of dramatic forcefulness and stylistic dignity by allusion to contemporary situations and to religious rites; (c) a section on "civic tensions," for the *ad interim* resolving of which by poetic means Greek tragedy was "cathartically" designed. (377)

Section (a) no doubt corresponded closely with the chapter "Imitation (Mimesis)" in PDC, which was published—in substantially the same form—as "A 'Dramatistic' View of 'Imitation'" in *Accent* in the autumn of 1952. Although the themes announced in (b) and (c) are discussed in the text of PDC, there are not sections focused on these matters per se. As Burke proceeds to explain his headnote to "Form and Persecution," these considerations all culminate in "the problem of poetic 'catharsis,'" which is what took him to a "step-by-step analysis of Aeschylus' *Orestes* trilogy" (377). Here, as well as elsewhere, he comes upon "allusive" qualities of tragedy, allusive on several levels, including the personal, the civic, and the mythic or supernatural. "At this point in our inquiry," he announces, "a kind of calamity occurred. Since 'catharsis' also has analogues with bodily processes, we asked how 'pity,' 'fear,' and 'pride' might figure, when translated into bodily terms" (378). Burke had already written a version of "The Thinking of the Body" (or, as he had told Cowley, it had written itself) by the time of the publication "Form and Persecution," and despite the advertised "calamity" of his situation, he was confident that completion of his book on poetics, if not the entire *Motivorum* project, was at hand.

Even as these articles were being prepared for publication, Burke thinks the end is in sight, as he tells Cowley in March of 1952, "Nearly everything cleared away now until summer. So, for final swing at the Symbolic, in hopes I can finish it off before going to Indiana" for a speaking engagement (Mar. 24, 1952, NB). He most probably was referring to the poetics section, including the psycho-physiologically slanted "The Thinking of the Body." The "Devices" discussion, however, would again have to wait. "I have been holding" off on "my catalogue of 'Devices,'" Burke writes Cowley on March 25, 1952, "until I was finished with the 'denser' portions of my stuff on motives. But I have a lot of them done, typed, and even tentatively codified" (NB). But his very industry—that of which he had trumpeted so loudly to Cowley—in pursuit of the trajectories of symbolic action before him, the "'denser' stuff," soon led him yet again to overshoot the designs for the "Poetics" and, perhaps ultimately, the entire "Symbolic" project. His lucubration led him into systematic consideration of *the negative,* considerations that irreversibly transformed his *Motivorum* project as they issued in the developmental line that led him toward what he came to identify, notably in *The Rhetoric of Religion* (1961), as "logology."

Initially, however, Burke saw the negative as an integral part of the evolving "Symbolic," albeit a part that would perforce reshape the design of the project. In early April 1952, as he was writing his "tour de force anent the Negative," he gushed to Cowley, "Dawlink, you'd be sooprized what you can do with the Negative and what the Negative can do for you, once you start hanging around that corner every evening (like a drugstore cowboy). . . . This thing is terrif, Malcolm." Indeed, he saw it as the "piece de resistance for the Symbolic" (Apr. 10, 1952, NB). And, again, the orbit expanded; by the beginning of 1953, as he awaited the appearance of his essays on the negative in serial form in the *Quarterly Journal of Speech,* he told Cowley, "I consider them the keystone of my Motivorum project" (Jan. 16, 1953, NB). And, again, the design for the *Motivorum* project itself transformed. On September 15, 1954, Burke wrote to Cowley:

Plans are to begin next week on the finishing of my Sin-
Ballix. (Psst: I'm telling myself don't just finish up one book
Burke but two. Wadda form! "Substance" for the Grammar.
"Identification" for the Rhetoric. "Catharsis" for the Poetics. And for the Ethics—Character, Personality—the Great
Lore of No-No, Huh-uh, Mustn't, and the ways of life that
congeal about it, or shatter around it. But alas, there are
cracks in the symmetry, too. For "Identification" had to
share with "Persuasion" in the Rhetoric. And "Catharsis"
must share with "Identity" in the Poetics. And "Identity"
also o'er-flows into the Ethics, which furthermore quoth the
raven should contain our lore of the Devices, Burke on de
virtues and de vices, plus alas also our tentative glimpses at
"channels of affinity," which might be our late way of getting around to the Goethean concern with Wahlverwandt-
schaften). (NB)

He could not keep to his tripartite design; the project had begun to divide. "At some stage along the way," Burke recalled in "Curriculum
Criticism: An Addendum," "I saw this third volume splitting in two"
(222). A glimpse of this fracture in process can be gleaned from Burke's
1953 description of the project in his initial "Curriculum Criticum," a
new afterword to the second edition of *Counter-Statement* (also reprinted in the 1966 third edition): *"A Symbolic of Motives* is now in
progress. These three *Motivorum* books deal with linguistic structures
in their *logical, rhetorical,* and *poetic* dimensions respectively. And they
will require a fourth volume, probably specifically entitled "On Human
Relations," stressing the *ethical* dimension of language" (218; see also
"On Catharsis" 340; Wess 245).

    In the anticipated transformation of Burke's trilogy to a tetralogy,
the design of the "Symbolic" proper began to focus closely upon the
domain of the poetic, presumably leaving other considerations to "On
Human Relations." Burke continues his explanation in the 1953 "Curriculum Criticum":

    The *Symbolic* will seek to treat of further problems that
    have to do with the intrinsic analysis of texts. The whole
    project aims to round out an analysis of language in keeping
    with the author's favorite notion that, man being the specifi-
    cally language-using animal, an approach to human motiva-
    tions should be made through the analysis of language. It
    seeks for observations that, while central to the study of any
    given expression in its internality, also have reference to

human quandaries and human foibles generally. The project
begins in and never far departs from (since it never wants to
depart from) the Aristotelian notion of poetry as *catharsis*.
(218–19)

Again, however, the situation quickly becomes more complicated. The
proposed "On Human Relations" apparently never was written; however, Burke wrote not one but two manuscripts that begin in and hover
around "the Aristotelian notion of poetry as *catharsis*": "Poetics, Dramatistically Considered" and "A Symbolic of Motives."

By the mid-1950s, with the design now clearly two volumes, one
on poetics and one on ethics (presumably focusing on the Negative
and the "Devices"), Burke again turned to the task of completing
the poetics. On May 18, 1955, he wrote Cowley in the spirit of self-
chastisement, "I simply must get to work on the finishing of my Symbolic, before it finishes me" (NB). By June, having written but not yet
revised a new section, a "big item in my godam Symbolic," on Emerson's "long essay on Nature," he despairs that the end, while in sight,
appears no closer for his efforts: "My own book continues in the stage
it has been in for at least 2 years; namely: five weeks from completion"
(Burke to Cowley, June 27, 1955, NB). And some seven months later,
with the Symbolic still languishing, Burke turned his immediate attention to preparations for his teaching duties at Bennington for the spring
term of 1956: he began work "indexing" Virginia Woolf's *Mrs. Dalloway* (Burke to Cowley, Feb. 6, 1956, NB).

When he came back to the Symbolic, he did so with an altered emphasis: he tended to speak not so much of "finishing" the manuscript
directly but rather of "revising" the still unfinished project, perhaps re-
casting his earlier material in a manner that he conceived of as more
consistently compatible with the tetralogy design. On September 17,
1956, he wrote Cowley of his plans to take a post-Christmas trip to
Florida for a couple of months, adding, "I hope to get my Symbolic
definitely revised before the first of the year. Then I'll take with us [to
Florida] my notes for the fourth book (the damned trilogy having become a godam tetralogy)" (NB). But by November, back in Andover
and recuperating from the hernia surgery that was to provide the immediate impetus for the short story "The Anaesthetic Revelation of
Herone Liddell," Burke was still working on his dramatistic consideration of catharsis: "I'm happy to announce that, after a fantastic amt. of
trouble, I think I have my definitive general chapter on 'Catharsis' going
well." He planned to get that chapter "out of the road," take time off
to prepare a talk scheduled in December, and then "try to line up a
devil of a troublous chapter on litry criticism in general—and from then

on I think that the major part of my work on the present volume will be minor revision, editing, etc." (Burke to Cowley, "first Monday before the first Tuesday," Nov. 1956, NB). Instead, he wrote the autobiographical "Revelation of Herone Liddell," after which he wrote Cowley from Florida: "My Wahrheit und Dichtung 'Revelation' having cleansed me along those lines, I am now ready to resume my work on Catharsis, for my book" (Jan. 30, 1957, NB). But his work proceeded slowly. In February, he reported still "picking away at the Catharsis problem" (Burke to Cowley, Feb. 22, 1957, NB), and on March 17 he wrote Cowley, "I began the day by a stint on Catharsis that I feel quite cleansed about. . . . Now Alky Hour" (NB). Despite such progress on catharsis, Burke's book on poetics—perhaps complicated anew by reconsideration concerning "The Thinking of the Body" (see Burke to Cowley, Mar. 3, 1957, NB), perhaps further entangled by major "indexing" projects such as that involving *Mrs. Dalloway*, perhaps ensnarled structurally and conceptually by wrinkles arising from the negative, or perhaps any number of other possible perhapses—the book remained unfinished through the summer of 1957. That autumn, though, Burke began a lengthy fellowship at the Center for Advanced Study in the Behavioral Sciences at Stanford. Here, he thought, surely he would finally complete his Poetics.

There is no question that Burke both enjoyed his months at the Center immensely (frequently referring to it as "paradise" in later years) and worked diligently while there. The work focused around his Poetics; in late December, he wrote Cowley that he was "spending the major part of my time trying to knock my book, etc., into shape" (Dec. 29, 1957, NB). But he did not finish; indeed, it may well have been during his stay at the Center that what survives as PDC was both "completed" and put aside and that what was to become *The Rhetoric of Religion* was, in essence, begun. Toward the end of his stay, Burke felt that he had both a new trajectory for the project and the force of momentum:

> Not much over five weeks to go here. So I want to work like fury, to get a maximum amt. of my Poetics into shape for multilithing. Book may take a form quite different from my original intentions. But the gravitational center remains the same: Catharsis, via the goat. As for the various analyses of particular works or authors I have published in gazettes (pieces of a few thousand words each): I may not use them at all, but simply offer them as a separate volume. (Burke to Cowley, Apr. 22, 1958, NB)

Forswearing any concerns about the desires of his publisher for the *Motivorum Trilogy*, Burke proceeds to tell Cowley of his new plans: "Book will involve three theories of catharsis, (and its problems); and still will be concerned with three major analyses: The Oresteia, Augustine's Confessions, first three chapters of Genesis" (Apr. 22, 1958, NB). Three years later, as he was awaiting publication of *The Rhetoric of Religion,* built around three essays including the ones on Augustine's *Confessions* and on the first three chapters of Genesis (followed by a "satyr play" between the Lord and the Devil), Burke wrote to Cowley, who was himself beginning a stint at Stanford's Center for Advanced Study in the Behavioral Sciences, "Nobody ever got more out of that place than I did. Two-thirds of the book that is coming out this June were done there, along with the Poetics Ms (of which you have a multilithed copy), though much of that work was revision" (Mar. 1, 1961, NB).

By the time he left Stanford around the first of June 1958, Burke had completed and "multilithed" a substantial portion of his Poetics, the portion that survives today as "Poetics, Dramatistically Considered." But he was not completely comfortable with it. As will be seen when we consider the text itself, the manuscript remains in some ways incomplete. Moreover, Burke was not certain that it was in the appropriate final form. As he told Cowley, in preparation for shipping him "a chunk of Poetics," "In particular, I am trying to decide about the advisability of retaining the long blow-by-blow description of the Oresteia. So, if you ever happen to feel like looking at any of the Ms., and have any bleats to communicate, I'd be grateful for the info. As you will note, the enterprise is still not finished. Also, I shall probably add an appendix containing some of my essays already published in magazines" (postcard, Burke to Cowley, postmarked June 13, 1958, NB). When he arrived in Indiana for the six-week summer session, he brought PDC with him, along with the now separate essays on Genesis and St. Augustine, as well as one on E. M. Forster's *Passage to India* (Burke to Cowley, July 29, 1958, NB), and he freely distributed the multilithed copies of PDC to students in his seminar as well as to professional colleagues, notably William H. Rueckert and Henry Sams (see Rueckert, *Kenneth Burke and the Drama of Human Relations* 231, 290; Wess 243).[4] Even after he left Indiana in late July 1958, however, Burke remained uncertain of precisely what to do with the substantial—yet still incomplete—manuscript; Indiana, however, did not suffer these same uncertainties. Burke "left a copy with the Library there—and some months later a student of mine wrote to announce that he found it disassembled, with the other side of the pages being used as scratch paper by the staff. I forthwith vowed to get that one down somehow in history" (Burke to Cowley, Aug. 31, 1965, NB; see also Rueckert, *Kenneth Burke and the Drama of Human Relations* 231).

It seems probable that Burke's uncertainty relative to PDC concerned the relationships among poetics (and catharsis), the negative, and, increasingly, the bevy of concerns that galvanized as "logology." Indeed, carried forward by the trajectories of the essays on the first chapter of Genesis and on St. Augustine, Burke concentrated his efforts during the tail end of the 1950s not on poetics at all but rather on logology. And his gazette articles from the period, including those drawn fairly directly from the text of PDC, again reflect some indecision about his book in progress: in "On Catharsis, or Resolution" (1959), for instance, Burke is coy, identifying the article as simply "part of a Poetics" (337). And indeed, his next book, his first of theory and criticism since *A Rhetoric of Motives* in 1950, was not the long-trumpeted "Symbolic" or even a more narrowly defined poetics but rather *The Rhetoric of Religion* (1961). On June 23, 1960, after discussing a mutual friend's health problems and detailing his own latest health concerns, Burke rather lamely informs Cowley, "Today, in a way, I guess I finished a book, though I'm not sure that I'll use this last section in the book. It's a dialogue btw. The Lord and Satan, in which both of them talk suspiciously alike, because both of them talk suspiciously like one K. Burke, in a mood of weighty academic levity" (NB). A few days later Burke elaborates, "The book is an extension of three talks I gave at Drew about three years ago. Tentatively, I think of calling it by the title of the first, 'On Words and The Word,' possibly with the winsome, best-seller subtitle, 'Studies in Logology'" (Burke to Cowley, July 20, 1960, NB). *The Rhetoric of Religion,* and the logological orientation that it ushered in, clearly is located within the broad orbit of Burke's concerns with human motives, and for many—if not in fact virtually all—readers of Burke, *The Rhetoric of Religion* has come to stand in the place of the never published "Symbolic."[5]

Burke himself, however, never felt that *Rhetoric of Religion* in any way replaced or rendered irrelevant the place of the poetic in his *Motivorum* project. Immediately after guessing that he had finished a book, Burke told Cowley, in a tone of rather subdued resignation, "Well, ennihow, it's done—so I can plague myself in other ways, such as reverting to my Poetics, into which this Logology stuff intruded, or out of which it protruded, though in a way that required separate treatment" (June 23, 1960, NB). No doubt his initial hope was that, with the intrusions/protrusions of logology out of the way, he could simply wrap up PDC. And indeed, with the publication of "Catharsis—Second View" (1961), drawn from the PDC manuscript, Burke refers in print to PDC by title for the first and perhaps only time, permitting the editors to identify the essay as a "chapter from the forthcoming book by Mr. Burke, *Poetics, Dramatistically Considered*" (107).

But when he returned to the "Poetics," it was with a difference, one marked not so much by the spirit of either wrapping up the text of PDC or of minor revision or amendment; rather, at least in some senses, he started over. Indeed, at the time he signed a contract with Beacon Press for the publication of *The Rhetoric of Religion,* he declined their offer "to sign for the Poetics on the same terms," concerned that "the manuscript is not in the same degree of readiness" (Burke to Cowley, Jan. 7, 1961, NB).

In 1961, following his resignation from his teaching position at Bennington College, Burke pursued his quest to complete the *Motivorum* sequence of books. "[W]hat I most dote on," he confided to Cowley, "is the idea of just cleaning up the Motivorum project and going abroad with nothing but an Italian dictionary . . . " (Feb. 16, 1961, NB). Although his pace evidently did not reach the fevered pitch that characterized his initial plunge into poetics in 1951, he seemingly made steady progress. On October 4, 1961, he reports to Cowley, "Just now, I'm in the thick of revision on my Poetics Ms., trying if poss. to get it done by the time the whistles blow at New Year's. I now have about 120 pages (typewritten) definitely done. Though I had intended to *cut,* this 'abridgment' has brought me to p. 38 of the multilithed version, a copy of which I once sent you." And even though his "abridgment" had thus far constituted an extension, he remained optimistic that the end was very near: "However, I dare promise myself that such perversity won't continue to prevail. Most of the delay is due to the fact that I have added new materials which I had originally intended to put at the end" (NB). It seems fairly certain that this "abridgment" eventually evolved into what we have today as "A Symbolic of Motives." "Poetics, Dramatistically Considered" ends with the chapter "The Poetic Motive," which is the note on which SM begins, and "Catharsis (First View)" begins on page 38 of PDC while chapter 8 of SM, "Catharsis (Civic Aspect)," begins on page 134 of the extant manuscript, reasonably close, given a little textual tinkering over the years, to the "about 120 pages" Burke mentioned to Cowley. Subsequent textual references in Burke's publications reinforce this inference, as we shall see.

Despite his optimism, the revised "Poetics" was not polished off with dispatch; indeed, by spring of 1962 Burke seems to despair somewhat. He wanted to finish the project, to round out the *Motivorum* sequence of dialectic, rhetoric, and poetics, at least, but progress was slow. And, increasingly, he found himself enticed by teaching and lecture offers, offers that could sustain him financially in ways that his royalties never did, or ever promised to. On April 18, 1962, he tells Cowley, "The godam Poetics is NOT finished. A whole, as they say, spate (or do I mean cowflop?) of invitations for me to peddle my wares turned up—and I didn't have the character to turn them down" (NB). It was another year before he thought that he had created an opening in his schedule sufficient to allow him to wrap up the project: on September 23, 1963, he writes Cowley that he has almost completed compiling his new "book of verse," after which he will "pitch into finishing the Poetics. Except for a couple of days in Tex-ass, I have no lecturing or teaching duties until late January. So I do dare hope that I can really get the Poetics off my chest for good" (NB). Yet what was by now the burden of the poetics remained unrelieved, and in "The Unburned Bridges of Poetics, or, How to Keep Poetry Pure?" (1964), which draws heavily from the opening chapter of PDC, Burke fails to mention PDC, his Poetics, the "Symbolic," or, however vaguely, any such book in progress, inviting the inference that perhaps Burke had by then "burned his bridges" to the PDC manuscript.

In fact, of course, the poetics still weighed heavily upon him, although most of the burden now probably derived from the relatively new, unfinished draft, SM. During the early summer of 1964, as he was pushing in preparation for a visiting appointment at the University of California at Santa Barbara, he lamented, "My only sorrow is that I may not get the godam Poetics wholly disentangled before I must goid up my lirns and sally forth" (Burke to Cowley, May 13, 1964, NB). But entangled it remained as Burke sallied forth to Santa Barbara, and on to Arizona, Texas, and other destinations as well; in the meantime, the University of California Press encouraged him to pull together a volume based on his various "yipings" on the "Academic Circuit" (see Burke to Cowley, Feb. 1, 1965, NB). By August of 1965, Burke feels that he is close to completing the new book—not the poetics, but the book of essays that was published as *Language as Symbolic Action* (1966)—and then he can turn his attentions back to the poetics; he writes Cowley, "Tomorrow, bing-bing-bing, every morning, to finish up the book of essays (I'm leaving them as is, but think of adding transitions nsech.) Godwillens, it should take a month at the outside. Then I can get back and wrestle full-time with my Poetics." And he clearly catalogs the multilithed version of the poetics that he had sent Cowley following his stay at the Center for Advanced Study at Stanford in 1957, the version that has survived as PDC and from which our selections are drawn, as the "first draft" (Aug. 31, 1965, NB).

The publication of the collected volume, *Language as Symbolic Action,* offered additional indications that PDC had been set aside in favor of the "abridged" revision we suspect is SM. For one thing, the new volume of essays included with very few changes "Form and Persecution in the *Oresteia,*" an essay first published in 1952 and, as we will see in the discussion of the text of PDC, a truncated version of the PDC essay of similar title. Telling among the changes, however, is the following rewrite of the opening sentence: "This essay is a rewritten version of a longer section in a book *that has since undergone much revision"* (125; emphasis added). And, indeed, the table of contents for SM does not include the Oresteia essay. Moreover, other essays that are integral parts of PDC, but less obviously so SM, are also included in *Language as Symbolic Action*. In the reprint of "The Thinking of the Body," for instance, Burke retains the editorial introduction to it from the *Psychoanalytic Review* (1962), which indicates the essay was written "in connection with" his book on the Poetics (308). However, in the *Psychoanalytic Review* article, Burke includes the following in a footnote to a discussion of the "Demonic trinity": "This refers to an earlier section in my forthcoming book, where I treat pity, fear, and pride as 'spiritual' analogues of the genital, urethral, and anal images respectively, though the correspondences are not exact." He then directs the reader to his treatment of fright and the urinary in Coleridge in "On Catharsis, or Resolution" (34). In the version of the essay in *Language as Symbolic Action,* the footnote is identical, with the somewhat telling exception of the first line: "This refers to pages where I treat pity, fear, and pride as 'spiritual' analogues of the genital, urethral, and anal images respectively, though the correspondences are not exact" (315). There is the subsequent reference to "On Catharsis," but no mention of a "forthcoming book." Yet there is good reason to believe that Burke still maintained aspirations for this revised poetics, even though his next book projects were to be his second volume of poetry, *Collected Poems, 1915–1967* (1968), and his expanded collection of short stories, *The Complete White Oxen: Collected Short Fiction of Kenneth Burke* (1968).

Devastated by the death of his beloved wife Libbie in May 1969, Burke slowly turned back toward what he came to call his "Unfinished Biz" in the hopes of "rounding out" his position before his own death, and looming most prominently was the poetics, the long awaited "Symbolic of Motives." Making arrangements to go to the writers' colony at Yaddo for the winter months of 1970, where his old adversary from the literary wars of the 1930s, Granville Hicks, was the interim administrator, he hoped to "really get into the swing of things": "Above all, what I'd like to do is clear away my Poetics definitively. (It's largely but a job of editing and typing now . . .)" (Burke to Cowley, Sept. 25, 1969, NB). He planned take a car because, as he explained to Cowley on October 17, 1969, "I expect to be using quite a batch of books and MSS, finishing my Sin-Ballix Motivorum" (NB). His letters to Cowley written during his stay at Yaddo, however, fail to mention his poetics or the Motivorum project at all, and while it is clear that the three-month stay was of great value to him personally during that most difficult time, it is not clear that he was able to focus his energies productively upon his work.

In his later years, after Libbie's death, Burke became a truly peri-patetic scholar, accepting short teaching appointments or scholar-in-residencies, and sustaining himself primarily through a rigorous sched-ule of campus lectures. Although this lifestyle was conducive to his continued productivity in journal articles, in the "gazettes," as he rou-tinely turned his talks into publications (thereby "giving away the store" on a particular topic or angle and obligating himself to continue gener-ating new talks), it was not conducive to him finishing his longer proj-ects. His only new book from this period, *Dramatism and Development* (1972), is a slightly edited compilation of two lectures that Burke deliv-ered at Clark University in the Heinz Werner lecture series. In those essays, Burke is no longer touting any forthcoming book; in the essay "Biology, Psychology, Words" he charts his own development from *Counter-Statement* through *Language as Symbolic Action,* yet never mentions either of his long, unpublished manuscripts, articles derived from them, or plans to revisit the topics (11–32).

Nonetheless, he kept aspiring. Writing from Princeton on March 16, 1973, Burke tells Cowley that he has been discussing pulling to-gether all of his Shakespeare essays, "plus my hitherto unpublished notes on William Himself. Nor should that take long. And I'm gwanna sit down and finally edit the other two MSS that have already piled up" (NB), presumably on "Devices" and the poetics, most likely the "abridged" version we call SM. Yet on May 11, 1973, he suggested a different order of priorities in a letter to Cowley, "Jobs for now until the leaves fall: To do a topical index for the new edition of PLF; to do final editing on my Devices MS; to put my Shakespeare stuff together, for a collection thus specifically slanted" (NB).

It is not altogether clear that Burke ever completely abandoned the idea of publishing a volume under the title "A Symbolic of Motives," although his design for what such a book might contain obviously shifted considerably during the thirty-plus years over which he contem-plated the volume. As late as 1978, Burke still had aspirations to round out his *Motivorum,* but it remained for him a much tangled project. On May 30, he wrote Cowley, "I shd. finish the editing of my third Mo-tivorum book. But the goddam line has turned up some further twists, which I have been twirling about somewhat" (NB). By June, he seems prepared to bracket the "new twists" out of the Motivorum proper, even though his immediate interest seems to be to pursue the twists and snarls. He tells Cowley, "And I'm vexed by the fact that my new twists engross me for a Last Phase, yet precisely now I should settle down and clear away my third Motivorum volume" (June 27, 1978, NB). And, with a bit greater specificity about the twists, he reiterates his own mo-tivational quandary in July: "I am now tinkering with . . . 'Nature,

Symbolism, Counter-Nature,' when I should be clearing away my final editorial obligations, quite trivial in comparison, for FINALIZING my third Motivorum volume, to incl. the possible fourth" (Burke to Cowley, July 20, 1978, NB). And he offers in print his plan to finish the "Symbolic": as Rueckert observes, the headnote for Burke's "summer 1978 article in *Critical Inquiry* entitled '(Nonsymbolic) Motion/ (Symbolic) Action' says that 'Kenneth Burke is now developing the implications of the position stated in the present essay. He is also editing his "Symbolic of Motives," a work designed to complement his *Grammar of Motives* and *Rhetoric of Motives*'" (*Encounters With Kenneth Burke* 180). The "version of the 'Symbolic'" which Burke proposed in 1978, however, "bears little resemblance to the 'Symbolic' as he wrote it between 1950 and the early sixties, but consists of yet another omnibus grab-bag collection of essays written over a forty-year period and would resemble, as a book, *The Philosophy of Literary Form* and *Language as Symbolic Action*" (Rueckert, *Encounters With Kenneth Burke* 182).

We draw our selections for this volume from these two unpublished Burke manuscripts, "Poetics, Dramatistically Considered" and "A Symbolic of Motives." In this section, we will "place" these manuscripts in relation to Burke's published essays from the 1950s and the early 1960s, including those subsequently collected in *Language as Symbolic Action* and the Hyman readers, in the process "locating" the selections published herein relative both to Burke's articles from the period and to the manuscripts in themselves. "Poetics, Dramatistically Considered" and "A Symbolic of Motives" are necessarily intertwined texts; each is a product of Burke's extracted effort to complete his trilogy (or tetralogy). Yet they exist distinctly, separately, and in ambiguous relation to each other; moreover, neither is manifestly finished, and neither matches precisely either the "Symbolic" that Burke promised in the early announcements of the design of the *Motivorum* trilogy or in the later permutations of the project into either a tetralogy or an "omnibus grab-bag." What we have, then, is a bit of a curiosity. Let us sort out what we can.

What we consider as the "final" draft of Burke's "Poetics, Dramatistically Considered," from which the selections published in this volume are drawn, was a product of his 1957–58 stay at the Center for Advanced Study in the Behavioral Sciences at Stanford. In what follows, we will offer the reader a "roadmap" to PDC, indicating both the design of the final manuscript and the publications that emanated from it; simultaneously, of course, we will also be charting what portions *have not* been published previously. It is from the essentially unpublished sections of PDC that, as a general rule, we have drawn our selections for this volume.

The design of PDC includes twelve unnumbered, titled "chapters" (our term), only one of which is further subdivided, in addition to the "missing" sections noted below. The existing chapters are, in the order presented:

"Poetic," "Aesthetic," and "Artistic"

Logic of the Terms

Imitation (Mimesis)

Catharsis (First View)

Pity, Fear, Pride

The Thinking of the Body

Form

The Orestes Trilogy

"Beyond" Catharsis

Catharsis (Second View)
    Vagaries of Love and Pity
    Fragmentation

Platonic Transcendence

The Poetic Motive

The table of contents of the manuscript concludes parenthetically: "Still missing: Section on Comic Catharsis; further references to individual works, illustrating various observations by specific examples; batch of footnotes indicating various other developments; appendix reprinting various related essays by the author, already published in periodicals." How significantly these missing sections would elucidate, alter, or modify the claims advanced in the manuscript can remain only a matter for speculation: neither the section on comic catharsis nor, presumably, the relevant "further references" and associated footnotes were ever written.[6] Moreover, reprints of published "related essays"—if one could with confidence identify which such essays to include—would if nothing else add extensively to the length of the volume, thereby compounding the difficulties attendant to interpreting the manuscript as a coherent whole. If one were, somewhat arbitrarily, to restrict such published "related essays" to only those articles (as contrasted with book sections) *referred to* by Burke in the "final" text of PDC, the list is formidable: "Three Definitions" (1951), "Othello: An Essay to Illustrate a Method" (1951), "The Anaesthetic Revelation of Herone Liddell" (1957), and "On the First Three Chapters of Genesis" (1958).[7] Despite these obvious limitations, PDC should not be viewed as an inchoate collection of essays. Indeed, Rueckert argues elsewhere in this volume "that Burke's *Symbolic of Motives,* his often mentioned and discussed but never published book, which was to have been Burke's dramatistic poetics to go with his grammar and rhetoric is, for all intents and purposes, a finished, completed work which could now be assembled, probably in two volumes, under the double titles of this essay," "Poetics, Dramatistically Considered" and "A Symbolic of Motives."

Of the essays that do comprise PDC proper, "The Thinking of the Body" and "The Orestes Trilogy" are by far the longest, each approximately one hundred manuscript pages, and the three catharsis essays account for roughly another hundred pages; the remaining seven sections total just under another hundred pages. There is reason to believe that much of the manuscript was written basically in the order presented in the table of contents listed above. We know that during the winter and spring of 1951 Burke wrote—and evidently sequentially—sections on "(1) Logic of the Terms; (2) Imitation; (3) Purgation; (4) Pity, Fear, Pride" in addition to an essay on the Orestes trilogy and at least a draft of "The Thinking of the Body." Making the not improbable inference that "Purgation" corresponds closely to "Catharsis (First View)," this means that the core of PDC was well in place by 1952. The section on "Form" was probably written at least in part during this early period, with the remaining sections most likely written during Burke's stay at the Center for Advanced Study at Stanford in 1957–58.

Publication dates of the published sections of PDC, with one notable extreme exception, support this association of chronology and sequence; the publications ascend more or less chronologically from "A 'Dramatistic' View of Imitation" (1952) and "Form and Persecution in the *Oresteia*" (1952)—which draw heavily from the PDC chapters "Imitation (Mimesis)" and, respectively, both "Form" and "The Orestes Trilogy"—through "The Poetic Motive" (1958), "Catharsis—Second View" (1961), and "The Thinking of the Body: Comments on the Imagery of Catharsis in Literature" (1963), which have obvious chapter references to PDC. "On Catharsis, or Resolution" (1959) appropriates heavily from "Pity, Fear, Pride." The early portions of " 'Poetic,' 'Aesthetic,' and 'Artistic' " constitute the major exception to this tendency, appearing in print for the first time in "The Unburned Bridges of Poetics, Or, How to Keep Poetry Pure?" (1964). Although this general correspondence seems accurate enough, there are a couple of further complications.

"The Thinking of the Body" has a uniquely snarled publication history. The initial draft of "The Thinking of the Body" was completed by the time of "Form and Persecution" (1952), and Burke alludes to it therein (378–79); however, no portions of the PDC chapter "The Thinking of the Body" were published until Burke included segments (see SM 75–84) in the 1959 essay, "On Catharsis, or Resolution" (see 354ff). Although Burke had begun work on the "Demonic Trinity" (defecatory, sexual, and urinary analogies to the Holy Trinity) as early as *A Grammar of Motives* (1945, 300–303), the specific texts that Burke analyzes in "The Thinking of the Body" are not there discussed; in "Form and Persecution," however, they are: "as regards 'the thinking of the body,' the purging of the emotions might reveal analogies with the three privy functions of the 'Demonic trinity,'" and in passing he associates pity with the erotic ("A study of the imagery in Wagner's *Ring* helped here"), fear with the diuretic (citing Coleridge), and pride with the anal (378–79). To bolster these associations, Burke continues, "We analyzed 'the thinking of the body' in various writings, not only Aeschylean tragedy and Wagnerian opera, but in *Alice in Wonderland*, Flaubert's *Temptation of St. Anthony*, and other works" (379). This 1952 survey of texts examined corresponds precisely to those treated in both the PDC chapter and the published version of "The Thinking of the Body," leading toward the inference that the text of "The Thinking of the Body" in its PDC version (the longer version, from which the published versions in the *Psychoanalytic Review* and *Language as Symbolic Action* are unquestionably derived) was, at least in an early form, in fact the draft that "wrote itself" in spring of 1951. Additional complications in the publication history of this essay are discussed in the identification of published sections of the PDC manuscript, considered below.

Further confusing the picture is the oddity that in the "final draft" of PDC, Burke includes seemingly original manuscript versions of essays that, by 1957–58, had been revised, albeit sometimes only slightly, and published. "A 'Dramatistic' View of Imitation" (1952), for example, is evidently drawn almost exactly from the PDC manuscript, but with minor adjustments and corrections; yet the PDC chapter "Imitation (Mimesis)" retains mistakes that were corrected in the 1952 publication.

But what, specifically, of PDC is already published, what are we here publishing, and what remains? The very opening paragraph of PDC, preceding even the first section, "'Poetic,' 'Aesthetic,' and 'Artistic,'" is not anywhere else published, at least not directly. However, its substance and indeed many of the same key terms appear as the opening paragraph of "On Catharsis, or Resolution" (1959, 337); that this parallel is to a "later" essay, and not one of the "core" essays, may be read as an indication that the "final" version of PDC was prepared about the same time that "On Catharsis" was written. This would, of course, be consistent with Burke's 1957–58 stay at Stanford.

"'Poetic,' 'Aesthetic,' and 'Artistic'" also has never been published previously, at least not in substantial form. However, portions of it (ms. pp. 2–5) are closely paraphrased, occasionally employing almost identical sentences, in "The Unburned Bridges of Poetics, Or, How to Keep Poetry Pure?" (1964, 391–94). Again, the parallels between the PDC section and a "later" publication suggest that this section may have been written or substantially revised for the final version of PDC, in contrast to some of the "early" essays that appear to have been included in the final manuscript with very few changes from their original versions. The second section of PDC, "Logic of the Terms," has not to our knowledge ever appeared in print; it is published here for the first time. It is worth noting, however, that the table of contents for Burke's unfinished "Symbolic" (see chapter 4) contains chapter titles that correspond to these sections.

"A 'Dramatistic' View of 'Imitation'" (1952) is clearly a slightly revised, truncated version of "Imitation (Mimesis)." Burke begins the published article with three bracketed paragraphs that contextualize the article as part of a larger project: "This essay is an excerpt from a much longer essay concerned with the 'carving out' of a Poetics, and taking Aristotle's treatise as its point of departure" (229). From there, Burke lays out the framework of the dramatistic stress upon action in distinction to the scientistic stress upon knowledge, following which he paraphrases the two opening paragraphs of "Imitation," stressing the entelechial, or cumulative, dimension of Aristotle's conception of "imitation" in distinction to a "statistical" reading of it (229). Beginning on the second page of "Imitation" (ms. p. 15) and also the second page of "A 'Dramatistic' View of 'Imitation'" (230), the texts are virtually identical until their respective closings (there are some rewordings, changes in and/or deletions of footnotes, and short additions/deletions; one of the more significant changes, for instance, is the change of example to differentiate between "typical" and "average" from that of a salesman in PDC to a sailor in the article published in *Accent*). However, in the conclusions, Burke excises from the published version the final seven pages of "Imitation" (ms. pp. 30–37), retaining only a portion of a footnote with which he concluded the section. Instead, after some brief paraphrasing from PDC by way of a summary, he adds two new paragraphs, emphasizing the social, and at least implicitly rhetorical, dimensions of imitation as well as its "entelechial grammar" (241).

Much of the substance of "Catharsis (First View)," the fourth section of PDC, has also been published, although the correspondence between the PDC section and related publication is not so precise as in other cases. Thus, despite close paraphrasing of the beginning of "Catharsis (First View)" (ms. pp. 38–40) in the beginning of "On Catharsis, or Resolution—with a Postscript to the Foregoing" (337, 342) and at occasional later points (ms. pp. 43–44 and 337–38; ms. p. 47 and 352; and ms. p. 49 and 351) substantial portions of this section remain unpublished. They would be essential to a full appreciation of Burke's reading of the Orestes trilogy. In addition, as has been noted briefly above, the opening of the PDC manuscript resonates closely with the opening of "On Catharsis." In the *Kenyon Review,* Burke begins, "This essay is part of a Poetics" (337) and then proceeds in language closely parallel with the opening paragraph of PDC: "I assume that such a project should be developed with Aristotle's *Poetics* in mind. Not that the extant parts of that old text should be taken either as authority or as 'the enemy.' But I consider it an ideal point of departure, or benchmark, a handy spot from which to locate any survey of the field" (337). In the opening of PDC, Burke is a bit milder, desiring to "use Aristotle neither as an authority nor as an authority deposed, but as a remarkably serviceable benchmark for the locating of this survey" (ms. p. 1).

Although the published "On Catharsis" does not correspond precisely with "Catharsis (First View)," it does include large sections of the fifth chapter of PDC, "Pity, Fear, Pride"; additionally, the article is broadly summarized in "Form and Persecution in the *Oresteia*" (1952). In fact, much of "Pity, Fear, Pride" appears virtually unchanged in "On Catharsis," and only the last few pages of the manuscript version are not at least summarized in the article. Additionally, "On Catharsis" contains small portions drawn directly from the PDC's text of "The Thinking of the Body," and it summarizes portions of the early part of that draft essay.

"The Thinking of the Body" presents referential difficulties, in addition to problems discussed earlier, because the PDC version and the subsequent published versions bear the same title; although they are substantially different in many respects, other portions are identical through large sections. Consequently, we will designate them as PDC "Thinking" for the manuscript version and "Thinking" (1963) for the published version (including, unless indicated otherwise, its republication in *Language as Symbolic Action*). To further complicate things, section one of part two of the "Symbolic"—a short, seven-page section —is also titled "The Thinking of the Body" (although the topic itself receives broader treatment in the final forty-nine pages of the manuscript, beginning with a section ironically entitled "Break-Through" and ending, although not concluding, with "In Sum, on Body-Imagery"); however, we do not treat that discussion here.

In fall 1963, Burke published a long essay in *Psychoanalytic Review* entitled "The Thinking of the Body." In an editorial note preceding the essay proper, Burke notes, "The following pages . . . were written in connection with a book I am writing on the subject of Poetics" (25). The published essay does not, however, correspond directly to the PDC chapter by the same name; in fact, as indicated above, portions of the PDC chapter were already by that time published in "On Catharsis, or Resolution." Even excluding those portions, however, there are substantial differences between the manuscript version and the published version. Although, with one major exception, the literary texts that Burke analyzes are the same, the order in which they are examined shifts between versions, and the depth in which they are examined varies. The major exception to this is that in the published version Burke adds several examples of the "Demonic trinity" lurking within his own poetry and fiction, most of it from the 1920s.[8] Burke offers no explanation for this "autobiographical" turn, other than noting that he is able to recall vague, perhaps at the time subconscious, associations while writing the works under scrutiny that tend to confirm his later critical conclusions about them. Using himself (his life, works, and body) as text is not new for Burke; his novel, *Towards a Better Life,* for instance, may be interpreted along those lines, and his 1957 short story "The Anaesthetic Revelation of Herone Liddell," written during the same general time period in which he was still wrestling with "the thinking of the body" issues, certainly has an autobiographical flavor about it.[9] Although there are thus substantial differences between the PDC chapter "The Thinking of the Body" and that which is published in *Psychoanalytic Review,* "The Thinking of the Body" that eventually appears in *Language as Symbolic Action* is virtually identical with the *Psychoanalytic Review* version.

"The Orestes Trilogy," Burke's long, close, creative, and brilliant analysis of the texts of the Orestes trilogy, is in some senses already published, both in the article "Form and Persecution in the *Oresteia*" (1952) and its reprint in *Language as Symbolic Action,* and in some senses not published. "Form and Persecution" contains both the framework of Burke's argument and the asseveration of his conclusions, and it re-presents portions of his textual analysis and lexical legerdemain, but it cannot retain the sheer brilliance and breadth of his extended analysis. The length of the essay (over one hundred pages) precluded its inclusion in this volume; however, should PDC ever be published separately (or, as Rueckert suggests, in combination with the SM manuscript), this essay would surely be its critical centerpiece.

Chapter nine of PDC, " 'Beyond' Catharsis," has never been published previously; nor has chapter eleven, "Platonic Transcendence." They are included in part one of this volume. Chapter ten, "Catharsis

(Second View)," is published with virtually no changes as "Catharsis—
Second View" (1961). With the publication of "Catharsis—Second
View," as noted earlier, the editors footnote the title, "This paper is a
chapter from the forthcoming book by Mr. Burke, *Poetics, Dramatistically Considered*" (107). It is almost a certainty that the text of the article was drawn directly from the text of the manuscript, for not only
are there virtually no differences between the two versions but editorial
notes made on the PDC draft are applied in the *Centennial Review* publication; for example, in the PDC draft, Burke writes of the apostle
Paul's use of the "cathartic principle" even in his building-up of the
church's "ecclesiastical organization": "Yet whatever might be one's
difficulties when it came to troublesome neighbors, these problems
might be lost sight of for one could stress the love of God and since God
could be conceived of as a universal principle personalized, here would
be dogmatic conditions favorable to catharsis" (334). In hand-editing
marks, Burke inserted a period after "of," capitalized "For," added a
semicolon after the first "God," and underlined both "universal" and
"personalized." And it appears precisely this way in the *Centennial Review*: "Yet whatever might be one's difficulties when it came to loving
troublesome neighbors, these problems might be lost sight of. For one
could stress the love of God; and since God could be conceived of as a
universal principle *personalized,* here would be dogmatic conditions favorable to catharsis" (116). The vast majority of changes between the
PDC draft and the essay published in the *Centennial Review* are of this
stylistic and often cosmetic nature; the few exceptions include deletion
of Burke's two section subtitles (and the addition of numerically indicated subdivisions), deletions both of further elaboration promised by
Burke in PDC (for example, use of Nietzsche's *Birth of Tragedy* as "our
way in" to more thorough treatment of universalized love and its corresponding "semi-secularized pattern[s]"; see footnote on ms. pp. 334–
35) and of vague allusions to other critical readings that Burke invokes
to bolster his own reading (for example, reference to Jakob Taubes,
Abendlandische Aeschatologie, ms. p. 347), and addition of the second
paragraph to footnote 4 in the published version (p. 121; see ms. 342).
The text of the addition to this footnote reinforces our belief that the
article was, in effect, borrowed from the text of PDC, for Burke begins the addition to his note concerning Aristotle's six parts of tragedy
in this manner: "However, I feel a bit uneasy about my treatment of
'thought' in this line-up. And I'd like to try again, along these lines . . . "
(121). The final alteration, perhaps from our point of view also the
most telling, is the deletion of the last paragraph of the draft version
from the published article, for in this last paragraph Burke picks up his
discussion of Nietzsche's *Birth of Tragedy* as a means of transition into

the next "chapter" of the nascent book, "Poetics, Dramatistically Considered" (ms. pp. 359–60).

The final chapter of PDC, "The Poetic Motive," has likewise been published without change, as "The Poetic Motive" (1958).

It is quite evident that Burke published early sections of PDC prior to his writing later sections; as was the case with many of his books, the process was not one of writing a self-contained manuscript and then publishing articles from it but rather of writing articles, publishing them along the way, and trying to "add them up" later into a coherent book. A general scheme may have guided the process of article writing, but its entelechial culmination could not have been—and was not—seen prior to its writing. Nowhere is this more clear than in the one significant change from the PDC draft of "Catharsis (Second View)" and the published article "Catharsis—Second View" (1961): In the opening paragraph of the manuscript, after briefly genuflecting toward the implications for a critical understanding of catharsis contained in proper appreciation of "the *individuality* intrinsic to the *centrality* of the nervous system," Burke writes, "So our second view of Catharsis will shift the emphasis, though many of the observations in this second view might as well have been considered in the first, had we then thought of them" (ms. p. 320). In the published version, Burke simply omits "had we then thought of them" (107).

The long-promised book PDC, of course, was never forthcoming, although, as we have seen, significant chunks of it have in fact been published. With the publication of the selections from PDC contained in the current volume, at least parts or versions of all the sections of PDC are now published and, depending upon access to some of the 1950s journals, available. This does not mean the PDC as a whole is completely available: the longer essays that are published only in truncated form, notably the essays on the Orestes trilogy and on "The Thinking of the Body," attain far greater luster in their full and unabridged versions. And again, as we have seen, the entire PDC manuscript may in some sense be "abridged" in SM, although to our knowledge none of SM has been published previously, at least not in the form that the material takes in that manuscript.

Why did Burke never finish the design for PDC? Why did he "start over" with SM? Did the *Motivorum Trilogy*, after expanding in design to a tetralogy, revert to a trilogy? Did Burke abandon his plans for an *Ethics of Motives* entirely, or did it become subsumed back into the design for the unwritten portions of SM? What happened to the "Devices" manuscript? These and other questions still remain, but we believe that both the narrative of the "Symbolic" that emerges from

Burke's personal correspondence and the headnotes and textual references offered in his publications since the early 1950s offer some useful insights. We could speculate on various scenarios for why the *Motivorum* project was never finished—and there are many. They start with theoretical entanglements that never got straightened out, including the functioning of comic catharsis, the problematic status of the "subject" in Burke's theories after *A Grammar* (see Wess), and the relationship both of logology to the project (see Wess 247–48; Rueckert, *Kenneth Burke and the Drama of Human Relations* 336) and the *Motivorum* project to counter-nature concerns. Obstacles also ranged from teaching and lecture-related distractions and writing-related psychogenesis of debilitating physical symptoms, to Burke's professed inability to complete books following Libbie's death (see Jay 360). But let us instead close by emphasizing what Burke in fact did finish, especially during the decade of the 1950s.

The ten years or so following publication of *A Rhetoric of Motives* was one of the most productive periods of Burke's career: he published roughly thirty essays between 1950 and 1960 (see Frank and Frank), one book of poetry, and the second editions, with new essays, of both *Attitudes Toward History* and *Permanence and Change,* and he wrote the essays that would become *The Rhetoric of Religion.* And, of course, the manuscript PDC. Yet, despite Burke's productivity during the decade of the 1950s, with the exception of those articles later collected in *Language as Symbolic Action* (1966) or in Stanley Edgar Hyman's two Burke readers, *Perspectives by Incongruity* (1964) and *Terms for Order* (1964), both now long out of print, Burke's work from the fifties remains largely unknown. William H. Rueckert makes the point:

> Though parts of the "Symbolic" are well known and frequently used, the "Symbolic" as a whole is not, and even such notable critics of Burke as Wayne Booth, Fredric Jameson, and Geoffrey Hartman write about Burke's literary theories as if the "Symbolic" did not exist. In fact, most students of Burke jump over the fifties, going from the *Grammar* and *A Rhetoric of Motives* (1950) right to *The Rhetoric of Religion* (1961) or *Language as Symbolic Action* (1966), ignoring one of the most fertile and productive periods in Burke's remarkable career. Hundreds of pages of truly vintage dramatistic Burke remain largely unread and unused. (*Encounters With Kenneth Burke* 181)

Although most of Burke's work from this productive decade has been published, and hence is available to the dedicated student willing to search out diverse and often obscure and now defunct journals, substantial portions of his work remain unpublished. The selections contained in part one of this volume take a small step toward making more of the previously unpublished work of Kenneth Burke readily accessible to readers.

Notes

1. At the risk of pressing a psychological interpretation too far, it is nonetheless worth considering that Burke's featuring of motives in his work from the early 1940s on may have been in part his own essentially patriotic response to the outbreak of the Second World War. On December 17, 1941, he wrote Matthew Josephson, "For as the damned Japs rained down, I suddenly wanted fervently to get into things somehow. So I wrote to [Archibald] MacLeish, as the person most likely (or least unlikely) to be able to think of some function for me" (BL). No official function was ever forthcoming; instead, Burke began his *Motivorum Trilogy*. MacLeish became director of the Office of Facts and Figures; he did employ Burke's lifelong friend Malcolm Cowley as "chief information analyst" until an early wave of Congressional "red scare" hysteria stirred up by the ill-fated Dies Committee on Un-American Activities forced him to resign in early 1942 amid a mild media frenzy (see Bak 477).

2. Burke is referring probably to his collection of short stories, *The White Oxen and Other Stories* (1924), although possibly just to the story "White Oxen" itself, and certainly to his novel, *Towards a Better Life,* the title of which is a constant source of play for him.

3. On April 10, 1952, Burke tells Cowley that he has immersed himself in a new chapter on "the Negative." "Yet this one," he exudes, "praise God, does not furiously write itself all night, as did the chapter on 'The Thinking of the Body'" (NB).

4. It is from a multilithed copy of PDC that Burke sent to William H. Rueckert in 1959 that our selections in this volume are drawn.

5. Barbara A. Biesecker makes a powerful argument that relative at least to the question of motives proper, *The Rhetoric of Religion* "has come to take its ['A Symbolic of Motives'] place" in the signification of Burke's "trilogy": it "reopens the inquiry into motive by seeking to explain not the condition of possibility for individual human action per se but, rather, the condition of possibility for collective human action." In this sense, she argues that whereas *A Grammar* "proffers a theory of the semiautonomous subject," *The Rhetoric of Religion* can be read as offering "a theory of collective subjectivity or identity that cannot be derived merely by generalizing from the individual" (Biesecker 20, 21–22; see also Rueckert, *Encounters With Kenneth Burke* 181).

6. A brief indication of the questions to be considered in a discussion of comic catharsis is provided as the "conclusion" of the section in PDC on "Platonic Transcendence," that is included in this volume; Rueckert suggests in his chapter for this volume that Burke's 1966 essay on E. M. Forster "is an example of the comic criticism or the criticism of a comic work which Burke . . . said was still missing from his poetics"; Burke makes related intimations about *A*

Passage in the selections from SM published in this volume. The issue of comic catharsis, however, may be central to the *Motivorum* project since it seems to contain the essence of purgation through criticism (and hence suggests the motivational force of criticism as a means of "purifying" warlike motives into something else); in his 1959 "Afterword to the Second Edition" of *Attitudes Toward History,* Burke writes, "however 'tragic' tragedy itself may be, the critical analysis of 'tragic' motives is in essence 'comic.' Much of our material on this subject it still to be published in our projected volume, *A Symbolic of Motives"* (348–49).

7. And the significance of such difficulties looms rather ominously above a critical project of that nature, especially given Burke's explicit insistence that the Oresteia trilogy is a unified tragedy requiring critical treatment as a whole and his frequently—but not always—implicit acknowledgment that the very writing of his poetics is itself a form of catharsis (a critical working through of the tragedic in poetics and hence its "transcendence" in the comedic). In this vein, for instance, Burke writes, "though I favor Meredeth's view that a wholly civilized world is a comic one, I believe that Aristotle was correct in building his *Poetics* about the analysis of tragedy. I reconcile the two positions by further contending that the analysis of tragedy is itself essentially comic" ("On Catharsis, or Resolution" 339). That is, the unity of design of the "ultimate" PDC may, in Burke's mind, have been central to its form; it would be impossible for anyone else to re-create precisely that unity (indeed, his own inability to enact the design, one might suggest in a mode of pure speculation, may have contributed to his reluctance to publish the manuscript).

8. In PDC he does consider his sonnet "Atlantis," but that is the only work of his own that he examines; moreover, in citing the poem in PDC "Thinking," Burke makes no reference to "Atlantis" being published in his 1955 volume of poetry, *Book of Moments,* whereas in the published version of "The Thinking of the Body" Burke does reference his book of poetry (51), lending further textual support for the inference that the PDC "Thinking" was written in the early 1950s and not substantially altered before its inclusion in the 1957/1958 manuscript.

9. In passing, the juxtaposition of Burke's short story with his "body-based" reading of *Alice in Wonderland,* a part of both versions of "The Thinking of the Body," makes clear that his "hero" is no "Alice." And bearing in mind that the "real-life" Alice was Alice Liddell, one may say that, for him, hero né Liddell. Somewhat along these lines, Burke offers this note about his "autobiographical narrative" in his "AFTERWORD: In Retrospective Prospect" to the third edition of *Attitudes Toward History:* "The character's name is pronounced 'Heron Liddell,' an ironically twisted way of saying 'little hero'" (391).

Bibliography

BL = Matthew Josephson Collection, William Carlos Williams Collection; Beinecke Library, Yale University
NB = Malcolm Cowley Collection, Newberry Library, Chicago

Bak, Hans. *Malcolm Cowley: The Formative Years*. Athens: University of Georgia Press, 1993.

Biesecker, Barbara A. *Addressing Postmodernity: Kenneth Burke, Rhetoric, and a Theory of Social Change*. Studies in Rhetoric and Communication Series. Tuscaloosa: University of Alabama Press, 1997.

Burke, Kenneth. *Attitudes Toward History*. 1937. Rev. 3d ed. Berkeley: University of California Press, 1984.

———. "Catharsis—Second View." *Centennial Review of Arts and Sciences* 5 (1961): 107–32.

———. *Counter-Statement*. 1931. Rev. 3d ed. Berkeley: University of California Press, 1968.

———. "Curriculum Criticum." In *Counter-Statement*. Rev. 2d ed. Los Altos, CA: Hermes Publications, 1953. 213–19.

———. "Curriculum Criticum: Addendum." In *Counter-Statement*. Rev. 3d ed. 1968. 220–25.

———. *Dramatism and Development*. Barre, MA: Clark University Press, 1972.

———. "A 'Dramatistic' View of Imitation." *Accent* 12 (Autumn 1952): 229–41.

———. "A Dramatistic View of the Origins of Language." *Quarterly Journal of Speech*, 38 (Oct. 1952): 251–64; continued (Dec. 1952): 446–60; continued 39 (Feb. 1953): 79–92; rpt. in *Language as Symbolic Action*. 419–79.

———. "Form and Persecution in the *Oresteia*." *Sewanee Review* 60 (Summer 1952): 377–96.

———. *A Grammar of Motives*. New York: Prentice-Hall, 1945.

———. *Language As Symbolic Action*. Berkeley: University of California Press, 1966.

———. "On Catharsis, or Resolution—with a Postscript to the Foregoing." *Kenyon Review* 21.3 (Summer 1959): 337–75.

———. "On the First Three Chapters of Genesis." *Daedalus* 88 (Summer 1958): 37–64.

———. "Othello: An Essay to Illustrate a Method." *Hudson Review* 4 (Summer 1951): 165–203.

———. *Permanence and Change*. 1935. Rev. 3d ed. Berkeley: University of California Press, 1984.

———. *The Philosophy of Literary Form*. 1941. Rev. 3d ed. Berkeley: University of California Press, 1973.

———. *A Rhetoric of Motives*. New York: Prentice-Hall, 1950.

———. *The Rhetoric of Religion*. 1961. Berkeley: University of California Press, 1969.

———. "Social and Cosmic Mystery: *A Passage to India*." *Luganu Review* 1 (Summer 1966): 140–55; rpt. in *Language as Symbolic Action*. 223–39.

———. "The Thinking of the Body." *Psychoanalytic Review* 50 (Fall 1953): 25–68; rpt. in *Language as Symbolic Action*. 308–43.

———. "Three Definitions." *Kenyon Review* 13 (Spring 1951): 173–92.

———. "The Unburned Bridges of Poetics, or, How to Keep Poetry Pure?" *Centennial Review of Arts and Sciences* 8 (1964): 391–97.

Frank, Armin Paul, and Mechthild Frank. "A Checklist of the Writings of Kenneth Burke." In Rueckert, *Critical Responses*. 495–521.

Hyman, Stanley Edgar, and Barbara Karmiller, eds. *Perspectives by Incongruity.* By Kenneth Burke. Bloomington: University of Indiana Press, 1964.

———. *Terms for Order.* By Kenneth Burke. Bloomington: University of Indiana Press, 1964.

Jay, Paul. *The Selected Correspondence of Kenneth Burke and Malcolm Cowley, 1915–1981.* New York: Viking, 1988.

Rueckert, William H. *Encounters With Kenneth Burke.* Urbana: University of Illinois Press, 1994.

———. *Kenneth Burke and the Drama of Human Relations.* 2d ed. Berkeley: University of California Press, 1982.

Rueckert, William H., ed. *Critical Responses to Kenneth Burke, 1924–1966.* Minneapolis: University of Minnesota Press, 1969.

Wess, Robert. *Kenneth Burke: Rhetoric, Subjectivity, Postmodernism.* Cambridge: Cambridge University Press, 1996.

2

"Watchful of Hermetics to Be Strong in Hermeneutics": Selections from "Poetics, Dramatistically Considered"

Kenneth Burke

Since we are here to be concerned with poetics, and since Aristotle's *Poetics* is basic to the Western tradition, we shall proceed with special reference to his treatise. We shall use Aristotle neither as an authority nor as an authority deposed, but as a remarkably serviceable benchmark for the locating of this survey. The work is doubly suited to our purposes through being so "Dramatistic" an approach to drama. So we shall keep hovering about it, alternately departing from it and returning to it, as the occasion requires.

"Poetic," "Aesthetic," and "Artistic"

Though there are often better contributions to knowledge in plays, poems, and stories than in works designed for nothing else, and though art may be treated as a kind of knowledge, the direct approach to art is through its nature not as knowledge, but as a species of action (symbolic action). Thus the word "truth" does not appear even once in Aristotle's *Poetics* (which requires merely that a tragedy be "plausible"), though sometimes the word for the universal (the "on-the-whole"—*to katholou*) is translated as "universal truths."

Just as in scholastic philosophy "form" and "act" are interchangeable terms, might we not see, in the form of an art object, the congealed sum total of all the acts that went into its making? In any case, Aristotle gets his definition of tragedy by successively narrowing terms for action, thus: (1) He would deal with a making *(poiesis)*; (2) A making of what?

The making of an imitation *(mimesis)*; (3) An imitating of what? The imitating of an action *(praxis)*; Then follows a definition of the particular kind of action typical of tragedy; also, Aristotle observes that the word "drama" was derived from a word meaning "to do."

But though the approach is in terms of act or form, with the plot viewed as the most important "part" of tragedy, knowledge figures secondarily in two ways. First, there are the processes of "discovery" *(anagnorisis*— "a change from ignorance to knowledge") that help to make a plot effective; and the Dramatistic grammar in general gets to knowledge by a dialectical route whereby a character, having acted, suffers the consequences of his act and thereby learns from his sufferings (with the audience poignantly participating in the disclosures). Second, imitations are said to please because man is by nature more imitative than other animals and because people like to learn things.

News, and even gossip, can be classed as kinds of "learning," and give us a certain intrinsic pleasure in learning that things are as they are (though Aristotle can't resist observing that the philosopher gets much more of such pleasure than the run of men). Likewise, sheer sensation might be said to fall under the head of "learning," insofar as the senses bring us information about our environment, since sensations are in effect like signals once we learn to interpret them. And if the word "poetic" is essentially an action-word, coming from a word meaning "to make" (and being the Greek grammarian's word for the active voice, to match "pathetic" for the passive), the word "aesthetic" comes from a word meaning "to perceive," thus being essentially a knowledge-word. But in view of the fact that "poetic" and "aesthetic" can be used almost interchangeably in many cases, we can see how close the realms of "knowledge" and "action" are at this point—a closeness also suggested in the expressions "knowledge of" and "knowledge how."

"Artistic" points to other possibilities, though "artistic imagination" might be but a synonym for what we have in mind when referring to the "poetic imagination" or the "aesthetic imagination." Embracing such words as "arms" and "articulate," the root of the word "artistic" is apparently related to a Greek word meaning "to join." (Further back, in Sanskrit, there were related roots meaning "to attain" and "to fit.") "Art," in its etymological beginnings, is a skill at joining, whereat we are reminded of Socrates' notion that the dialectician knows how to carve ideas at the joints, while dialectics is rooted in two kinds of terms, those that generalize and those that differentiate (the work of art being always an ingenious interweaving of composition and division).

Where are we, then? We want to uphold the position that the most direct approach to the work of art is by considering it as a species of action, the slant that is etymologically embodied in the word "poetic."

But we had to grant that the word "aesthetic" points rather towards a different (but not necessarily antithetical) stress upon *knowledge*. And we noted that the etymological inklings in the word "artistic" point towards *dialectic,* or *articulation,* with appropriate modes of generalization and specification—and this trend would come to a head in principles of *classification* (as with the order of the terms in a Platonic list of classes arranged like the rungs of a ladder).

In the course of this discussion we came upon the word "imagination," that goes equally well with "poetic," "aesthetic," and "artistic." Etymologically, however, it is probably nearest to "aesthetic." For the material of the imagination is first of all the realm of "images," the stuff of *sense perception* in general. Thus the term had a broader meaning in psychology than it came to have in aesthetic theories, as with Coleridge's distinction between "primary" and "secondary" imagination. For the poetic or "mythic" image, as distinct from the sheerly physical or animal sensations of sight, sound, and the like, is saturated with "idea," involving a purely "spiritual intuition" that takes us from heard melodies to the "unheard" melodies implicit in them or transcending them.

"Ideas," as so conceived, are intensely "active"—whereat the term "imagination" comes to take on connotations of "action" and "passion" (the Dramatistic pair *par excellence,* hence the ones that would belong first of all with "poetic"). Philosophic tinkerings add further impetus to the "poetic" stress by considering the realm of sensation "passive" insofar as the senses "receive" impressions from without, and "active" insofar as the senses "impose" their own modes of interpretation upon the impulses that they record (as when certain vibrations are experienced in terms of light and its various colors, certain ones in terms of heat, certain ones in terms of sound, or taste, etc.).

The Coleridgean view of imagination as an "esemplastic power," a faculty for discerning "multëity in unity" *(il più nell uno)* and for infusing multëity with unity, moves us towards the dialectics of joining ("artistic"). And as a matter of fact, if you look closely at the notion of the senses as modes of interpretation, you see that they are, by the same token, modes of *classification*—since some vibrations are naturally "classified" as sounds, some as sight, some as tastes, some as pleasures, some as pains, some as hot, some as cold, etc.).

When the various strands have thus become interwoven, a pleader for the Dramatistic emphasis (upon poetry as a mode of action) might, if only as a sheer debater's trick, note that poetic production, sensory perception, aesthetic imagination, and artistic composition are all of them species of action ("symbolic action"). But we need not be so absolute, and can settle for less, along these lines:

Aristotle's reference to the appeal of learning as an ingredient in the appeal of poetic imitation does not concern the Dramatistic kind that is beaten into the tragic protagonist by dint of hard knocks and that affords the audience tragic pleasure insofar as the audience sympathetically participates in the protagonist's sufferings with their corresponding insights. Rather, such appeal of learning is akin to what Veblen would have praised, and St. Augustine would have condemned, as "idle curiosity."

We shall consider later how the kind of "learning" that goes with an audience's engrossed participation in the successive disclosures of a plot may be more directly explainable as a sympathetic delight in the perfect unfolding of a form, with its "natural" order of attitudes, somewhat as though we were to call it a matter of "learning" when we watch with delight a motion picture that shows the gradual bursting of a blossom, thereby enabling us as onlookers to unfold with it. We do unquestionably "discover" things, when contemplating such a series of "disclosures"; but there is also the satisfaction of the development as such, of graduated movements in which we "empathically" participate —and this satisfaction can be more accurately explained in terms of action than in terms of knowledge (for reasons that will be considered as we proceed).

It is important to stress the sheerly *empirical* ingredient in Aristotle's analysis of tragedy. Critics who ignore this element incline to two excesses: Sometimes they deny the possibility of any tragedy but the Attic species that Aristotle was observing and reducing to a set of principles; sometimes they consider Aristotle to have been outmoded or disproved by the rise of new tragic species lacking, for instance, the solemnity or magnitude of Attic tragedy. In both cases, a stress upon the empirical element in the *Poetics* helps set things right, as we are then able to take it for granted that his generalizations, or "laws," based on the observing of one species need not strictly apply to other species.

But there can be too much stress upon the empirical nature of Aristotle's observations. And though the six "parts" of tragedy are "inductively" derivable from the systematic observing of particular tragic specimens, we should also note that they are *deductively* derivable from the logic of the Dramatistic terminology itself.

Logic of the Terms

Thus the first and most important part, Fable or Plot *(mythos),* is but a further localizing of the term for action *(praxis).* Whereas *praxis* covers "action" in general, *mythos* is the name for some particular action, this story rather than that. And it in turn is divided into incidents (called *pragmata,* a word for "doings"). An action must be by Agents—hence the need for Characters *(ethe).* Character *(ethos),* being moral, involves the ability to act by making choices (the merely automatic processes of natural movement being neither "moral" nor "immoral," but lying quite outside the ethical realm). Such movements of choice *(proairesis),* while expressing Character, will involve the exercise of Thought *(dianoia).* In a literary form, Thought and the unfolding of disclosures in general will necessarily depend upon Language, or Diction *(lexis).* And since an action can only take place in a scene, there will be Spectacle *(opsis).* Perhaps the sixth part, Melody *(melopoiia),* is not thus derivable *ab intra,* from the sheer "logic of action" as such (though it could be derived from the sheer word for "tragedy" itself, the "goat song," a term incidentally that could also have led to such concerns with curative victimage by scapegoat as are in the idea of tragic *catharsis).*

Subsequent sections in the work proceed to track down the ramifications of each term. Thus: If Plot, then the use of Reversal and Discovery, to make it effective. If Action, then its reciprocal, Passion (hence, the pages of Pathos). If Imitation, then considerations about the plausibility of imitations. If Character, then the recipe for Character. And concern with the mutual relations among terms can be expressed preferentially; thus, in this descending order: "complex" plots embodying Reversal and Discovery, then the tragedy of "suffering" *(pathetike),* or "character" *(ethike),* and of "spectacle" *(opsis).*

The point we are trying to make here might be summed up thus: You best get an insight into the genius of Aristotle's analysis if you note that his terms are not merely a set of shrewd observations connected with one another by "and" (there is plot *and* character *and* thought, etc.). Rather, these terms all share in common Dramatistic logic (if action, *therefore* plot, *therefore* character, *therefore* choice, *therefore* passion, etc.).

Once you agree to look at the *Poetics* thus, not only do you have a generating principle to explain the internal consistency of its terms; you also have the proper approach to a concern with the Dramatistic terminology in general, as extended beyond the realm of "imitations" to the discussion of human behavior in general. Here is a case where empirical observation *(ab extra)* meshes perfectly with a self-consistent logic generated from within.

We should emphasize that the Dramatistic perspective is not merely "analogizing," or metaphorically transferring a term from an area where it literally belongs to an area where it does not literally belong. Men *do* act (their choices being shaped by "thought," or terminology, in contrast with kinds of things that merely "move"). Poetry *is* a kind of action *(symbolic* action, a purgative exercise enjoyed in and for itself).

And the reader, with varying degrees of fidelity, *does* symbolically reen-act the poem by such kinds of inchoate "suffering-with" as are called sym-pathy or em-pathy *(Einfühlung)*.

Here is an ironic state of affairs: Dramatism can play its cards face up, in frankly developing a systematic vocabulary that tracks down the ramifications implicit in the key term "action." Yet often this very frankness is naively taken to be an evidence of "analogizing," and by persons who themselves escape the charge only by exemplifying the same principle, though in so inexact and fragmentary a way that their position is obscured. Suppose, for instance, you took the five basic Dramatistic terms (act, scene, agent, agency, purpose), but gave for each of them a set of scattered substitutes, thus:

For "act"—substitute words like "response," "transaction," "con-duct," "operation," "behavior";

For "scene"—substitute words like "environment," "conditions," "circumstances," "stimulus," "situation";

For "agent"—substitute words like "individual," "person," "ego," "subject";

For "agency"—substitute words like "instrument," "method," "means," "intermediate step," "resources";

For "purpose" substitute words like "ideal," "target," "drive," "impulse," or the one ("value") now so much in favor possibly because it's a dignified synonym for "price."

Or, going a step further, we might talk not of "act" but of some high generality implicit in the idea of an act, such as "novelty," or "freedom," or "creativity." Or we could translate the notion of scenic limitations to some such grander order of terms as "compulsion," "ne-cessity," "inevitability," "destiny," "historical morphology." And so on, with the other members of the Dramatistic Pentad.

Or we could go in the other direction of concealment. Rather than meditating upon any such generalized term as "act," we might linger with a whole thesaurus of words for particular acts, such as "go," "come," "say," "send," "buy," "cure," "kill." And so with all the five—as "agent" might be replaced now by "consumer," now by "entrepre-neur," and now by "citizen," now by "Mr. Aloysius Q. Blackwell, born at such-and-such a date, died at such-and-such a date," etc. Or instead of "scene," we might have particular combinations of when and where, such as "Times Square at three o'clock in the afternoon of July 7, 1897." Historical narrative is usually implicitly Dramatistic in this sense.

The question arises: If we substitute "response" for "act" and "stimulus" for "scene," have we maneuvered ourselves into a position whereby, though Behaviorism is the very antithesis of Dramatism, we must now treat it as but a brand of Dramatism in disguise? Not so.

Rather, we should class Behaviorism as a misshapen *fragment* of Dramatism in disguise. But if you inspect terms for action systematically, in their fullness, as the Dramatistic emphasis not only permits but demands, you promptly see how much is lost by the reduction of motives to Behaviorist terms.

The current search for "models" that will assist in the analysis of human behavior should be viewed in this light. Mathematical models, animal psychology, accounts of learning, decision making, "stochastic processes," and the like are "anti-Dramatistic" only in the sense that their stress upon some particular aspect of the problem deflects attention from the Dramatistic logic as a whole. And we may expect to find the ingredients of Dramatism lurking in every terminology of motives, since a terminology of action and passion is as "natural" to the human species as the dialectic of the one and the many, or the idea of "substance," are "natural" to human speech.

And though at an earlier stage in this project, the author would have been inclined to think of mechanistic models as intrinsically anti-Dramatistic, he would now incline rather to think of them as inescapably "anthropomorphic." Indeed, how could they be otherwise, in embodying so efficiently certain processes of the human mind (or, more specifically, certain resources of man's *terminologies*)? To be sure, our machines burlesque us, as Bergson pointed out when analyzing laughter; they exaggerate some of our foibles while suppressing others, as with all caricatures. But even models that would reduce action to terms of sheer motion cannot avoid the charge of being Dramatistic in a fragmentary way. Dramatism is the inescapable "old Adam" in us, the *lingua Adamica* of human self-reflection.[1]

Even within the realm of symbolic action proper, when we turn from drama to other subject matter, certain *transformations* of the Dramatistic terminology are in order. As we showed in our section on "'Incipient' and 'Delayed' Action" *(Grammar of Motives)*, "attitude" is the key word for treatment of the lyric, the stress being upon the "lyric attitude" rather than upon the "dramatic act." Yet the term "attitude" itself implies a "philosophy of the act," being a term for "incipient action," and thus itself representing an integral aspect of the Dramatistic perspective. (See also, in the appendix of the *Grammar,* the analysis of Keats's "Ode on a Grecian Urn," as indication of the way in which appropriate transformations are made for the application of Dramatistic terms to the lyric.)

Elsewhere in the *Grammar,* when discussing the theory of constitutions, we made other transformations that adapted the Dramatistic terminology to the analysis of legal enactments. And still other transformations were made for the description of philosophic schools considered as modes of action. For reasons of space we omitted a section built around the prefaces of Henry James, whose slogan was "Dramatise it, dramatise it!" as he explicitly and repeatedly used Dramatistic terms in his analysis, yet transformed them to make them a fit for the species of novel with which he was primarily concerned (a species that probably yields best to an approach having *Agent* as its key term). In *A Rhetoric of Motives,* the stress was upon transformations needed insofar as processes of persuasion and identification involve extraliterary situations as well, leading particularly into problems of sociopolitical division and the resultant "hierarchal psychosis."

Aristotle himself does something similar when, near the end of his *Poetics,* he indicates how his terms for the analysis of tragedy can be applied *mutatis mutandis* to the epic, though his treatment of the epic is quite skimpy. Epics like the *Iliad* and the *Odyssey,* by the way, seem best approached in terms of *Purpose,* as the aim of sacking Troy is the central theme about which the manifold incidents of the *Iliad* are organized, and the many episodes of the *Odyssey* are given epic unity by their relation to Ulysses' "nostalgic" purpose, his troubled homecoming the longest way round.

Where, then, are we: Taking Aristotle's treatise as point of departure, we are involved in the business of carving out a Poetics. So far we have tried to get the best of two worlds by indicating how a Dramatistic analysis of drama provides a set of purely empirical observations connectable by "and" while at the same time the logic of the terminology is under the sign of "therefore," with the terms all spun from the genius of a common generating principle (for making explicit the implications of the term "act"). We shall next consider in succession five key terms: "imitation," "catharsis," "pity," "fear," and "pride" (the "tragic flaw").*

Form

In one sense, any poem is "pure" form: For it is the literary actualizing of nonliterary matter (that is, it has transformed extrasymbolic potentialities into an end-product by nature wholly symbolic). This is probably Croce's meaning when he equates poetry, expression, and form. And there is a formal kind of "catharsis" that goes with it: the

---

*These sections are omitted herein, along with "The Thinking of the Body," which followed. The vast majority of those sections are already in publication. Please consult the "Textual Introduction" for specific bibliographic information. We pick up again with Burke's section on form. *Ed.*

satisfaction (even security) that a symbol-using animal feels when reducing extrasymbolic motives to symbolic terms.

Such categorical catharsis is too general for analysis of the tragic
pleasure specifically, or for the pleasure peculiar to any other species of
poetry: hence in his *Aesthetics,* Croce proposed to scrap entirely the
concern with literary species. And, in addition to his just contention
that the theory of literary genders had been fantastically misused by
critics, he had this further logical point on his side: Where one is concerned with the aesthetic realm in general (as distinct from the moral,
scientific, and utilitarian realms in general), the division into specific
kinds of aesthetic expression is superfluous to the nature of the inquiry.
His *Aesthetics* is not a Poetics but a Philosophy of Art, a "statement of
policy" on art. In comparison with Poetics, his theory is as extreme on
one side as sheer *explication de texte* is on the other. Textual analysis
loses generalization in a welter of detail; Croce transcends detail by setting up a set of conceptual balloons.

There is also a sense in which poems can be *comparatively* pure in
form. Thus, Art for Art's Sake is "pure," as contrasted with "propa-
ganda" art (the modern variant of the moralistic or didactic). When
considering Form in this sense, we do well to recall Longinus's *On the
Sublime.* For here many examples are cited from orations that at the
time of their delivery were most urgently propagandistic (designed as
a rhetoric for moving the audience to practical decisions); yet, as the
works have survived the situations for which they were designed, they
can now be appreciated purely for their "poetry." Here we are still
well within the orbit of Croce. For Croce could note how even a work
discredited as "science" might be enjoyed for its "beauty." So with
theological or metaphysical systems no longer believed in literally, or
the modern aesthetic cult of the "myth." Methodologically, we could
say: Longinus shows how even the most rhetorical of forms, the persuasive oration, can be treated in terms of Poetics. It is a good point
to remember when haggling about the relation between Rhetoric and
Poetics.

It is particularly a good point to remember when considering certain contemporary canons that would set up a *contrast* between idea
and image (treating image as Poetic, and idea as Didactic—hence concluding that a "pure" poetry would outlaw idea). Though Longinus
placed a much higher rating upon image and imagination than ancient
critics generally did, his first requirement for the "sublime" (or, as we
would translate it, the "poetically moving") was the presence of "robust ideas." And we believe that he was right.

Admittedly, in a certain species of lyric, ideas can properly be kept thus in the background, implicit rather than explicit. But unless an image has an idea within it as the soul within its body, not even the most hardened Imagist can make use of it, or can even want to. In any case, since ideas are intensely dramatic, their comparative suppression in certain kinds of lyric or lyrical fiction must not be extended to the "aesthetic" generally. Imagist or Symbolist beauty is not the *only* beauty. There can even be a "didactic" beauty.

But today many critics spontaneously treat Poetics and Aesthetics as identical, and spontaneously equate Poetics with image (*in contrast with* idea). Hence even when teaching Aristotle's *Poetics,* or when seeming to agree with it in spirit, they cannot bring themselves to ask just what it means that the *Poetics* refers the reader to the *Rhetoric* for the function of Thought as one of the six parts of tragedy. If the reference didn't so obviously belong, surely by now somebody would have brought forth the bright notion that it had been inserted by a meddlesome scribe too ignorant to understand the text.

It is quite proper for certain schools of poetry to aim at a species of beauty got by as great an overstressing of image and understressing of idea as can be effectively managed. For instance, think how admirably William Carlos Williams does by his slogan, "no ideas but in things," the word "things" here being a "thinglike" synonym for "images." But when a succession of images comprises the whole of a poem, the logic of the progression is reducible to an implied idea. This idea serves as the generating principle which guides the selection and order of the images. And sometimes it is even so necessary to the sense that the poem becomes in effect like a game of charades, where the reader's job is to discover through the images the idea that is being cryptically hinted at. (Midway between image and idea can be a poem in which, from the sheer nature and progression of the images, one infers what kind of situation is implied by them.) Poetry that relies exclusively on images can have the appeal of reticence; but it can become owlish, too: its silence in the light of ideas being at once wide-eyed and blind. Since images readily become quite ambiguous in their implications, poetry of this sort serves particularly well for the coy confessing of minor sexual peccadillos; and thus, surprisingly enough, it can even be put to scientific use, since it helps disclose the sexual "cathexis" in natural objects not usually thought of as possessing such *charisma* (though, as we have indicated in our *Rhetoric of Motives,* often such sexuality must in turn be studied for traces of purely social relationships not reducible to sexual terms). Psychologically, the attempt to write exclusively in such a medium can encourage a kind of meditative evasiveness that can lead to self-deception beyond the conditions of the poem.

But while granting the strategic importance of the image in poetry, we should not allow an imagistic aesthetic canon to usurp the field. Images and imagism are not the same thing; and there are poetic species, such as tragedy, to which ideas are proper. However, we grant that in these species, ideas are not used precisely as in rhetoric, even though critics can legitimately consult a rhetoric when classifying them, and in a classroom witticism Aristotle says that characters in the earlier Greek plays talk like statesmen, in the later ones like rhetoricians.

In sum: Here the *lawfully* Aesthetic approach would be to demand not that ideas, even wholly "didactic" ones, be avoided, but that they be used Aesthetically. Whatever the shortcomings of Pater's *Marius the Epicurean*, it seems right in its way of *using* ideas. Here they serve as an aspect of personality, as a novelistic means of giving a sense of scope and dignity to the plot, and as a device for the dramatizing of contrasts. However, Pater's "aesthetic" emphasis is already one step away from the more "robust" use of ideas, and towards a kind of moodiness that later writers could more "efficiently" establish by imagery. Great playwrights like Aeschylus or Shakespeare are, of course, the complete instances of "robust" ideas used in profusion yet aesthetically. In both cases, though their work is filled with the language of body imagery and personal emotions, it has a constant proverb-like sententiousness that heads in an almost *legalistic* kind of thinking.

Besides the categorical equating of all expression with form, and the calculus whereby some forms can be considered "purer" than others, there is a dialectical shifting of the terms whereby the form at one place can be treated as the matter for a later place. In a five-act play, for instance, insofar as the first act leads to the second, there is a sense in which the first could be called the matter, or potentiality, that is fulfilled, or actualized, in the second. This second act, in turn, could be grouped with the first act as making up the matter that comes to fruition in the third act. Hence, particularly when analyzing plays constructed along classical lines, at each step of the way we always ask ourselves: "What *potential* has been established at this point? How has the author in effect promised what is to be resolved 'in our next'? What has been made so pointedly or poignantly irresolute that it demands resolution later? And what general kind of resolution is indicated?"

We here approach from another point of view a subject we considered earlier when noting how poetic development could be analyzed either as a kind of action or a kind of discovery. If the beginning of a work is viewed as setting up potentialities which are fulfilled at later stages in the work, in this sense the beginning can be thought of as matter that is subsequently actualized. The beginning, we might say, has "the makings" of the ending. And any step along the way can be treated either as an actualization of previous potentialities or as the potential of steps still to be actualized. But in contrast with this shifting dialectic, there may be an at least *apparently* more "positive" approach, as with the terms "Complication" and "Dénouement" (*desis* and *lysis*) discussed in chapter 18 of the *Poetics*. Whereas, dialectically, the "binding" could be said to establish the potentialities that are fulfilled in the "loosing," Aristotle's "positive" terminology can say, once and for all, that the Complication includes everything up to the beginnings of the change in fortune ("peripety"), while the Dénouement includes everything from the beginnings of the change in fortune to the end.

His terms *(desis, lysis, peripeteia)* are a more specific application of his earlier statement that the completely formed must have a beginning, middle, and end. But though his specific application of this formula in effect includes the middle as part of the end, there is no sheer dialectical shifting of his terms: the peripety remains the peripety and none other, whether you decide to call it the beginning of the end or (as you conceivably might) the final stage of the beginning. Dialectically, it would be the point at which the beginning "abolishes itself," or "becomes its other," or "moves into a higher stage," or some such. Positively, though you may differ as to just where the peripety in a given work is, you can define once and for all just what a peripety is.

Note the difference in tactics of analysis that follows from the difference in the tactics of terminology: Once you call the opening stages not "potentials" but "Complication," you are all set to discuss even the introductory lines as a kind of "fulfillment," an actualization having its own particular kind of perfection (that is, "finishedness"). Such a terministic arrangement well suits the entelechial principle, which in turn well suits the principle of hierarchy: for besides looking at beginnings as such, reversals as such, discoveries as such, endings as such, one can go on to ask what is the best kind of beginning, or reversal, or discovery, or ending, what is next best, and so on.[2]

The concern with beginnings as beginnings, peripeties as peripeties, discoveries as discoveries, etc. is far from foolproof. Maybe it has even made more fools than it has cured, at least if we judge by its traditional use in the hands of petty critics who found it of help in their campaigns against great poets. But when it is judged by its own entelechial principle, it is seen to have its perfection. And much is gained by making us conscious that each step in a process can be viewed as requiring its own particular kind of finishedness. Extending such a mode of thought, one might ask oneself: "What would be the perfect kind of ending for the second act of a five-act play?" Or: "What are the characteristic ways in which plays fall short of this development?"

To say as much is to suggest the dangers in such an approach. Above all, it tempts the critic to burden a poem with categorical demands that may be quite alien to the poem's nature. On the credit side there is the fact that such questions sharpen one's awareness of formal perfection when it is attained.

With regard to the theory of form as "the arousing and fulfilling of expectations" (see the chapters "Psychology and Form" and "Lexicon Rhetoricae" in K. Burke's *Counter-Statement*), though the *Poetics* does not specifically analyze form in such terms, there has been a tendency among some critics to treat this notion as essentially Aristotelian. It seems a bit too dialectical to fit wholly with Aristotle's stress upon "parts," each of which can be subjected to a separate analysis; and it can be easily used in ways quite out of line with such analysis—but otherwise the principle is in the *Poetics* implicitly.

To our knowledge, the first *explicit* statement of it is in Wordsworth's preface to the *Lyrical Ballads,* where it is stated somewhat after the analogy of a commercial contract: "I will not take upon me to determine the exact import of the promise which by the act of writing in verse an Author, in the present day, makes to his Reader; but I am certain it will appear to many persons that I have not fulfilled the terms of an engagement thus voluntarily contracted."

Wordsworth here referred to the kind of categorical expectations which the public may bring to poetry even before reading any particular book, so labelled. Insofar as his poetry fell outside the range of stylistic conventions (including subject matter) traditionally deemed "poetic," he knew that it might seem like the violating of a contract with his readers, who were in effect his customers. Literary species arise to the extent that such categorical expectations become established and make demands that interfere with the development of other forms. And "form" itself comes to be conceived of as a kind of empty vessel or mould which gives a shape to whatever "matter" is poured into it. Such an abstract view of form seems all the more acceptable because we can make paradigms illustrating the sheer meters and rhyme scheme of such poetic species as the sonnet or the villanelle.

Terms like "foreshadowing," "suspense," and "surprise" also subsume expectations on the part of the reader, though here the expectations might arise in the process of reading rather than merely being all set in advance. And as regards Aristotle's concern with plausibility, probability, possibility, necessity, and inevitability in the building of a tragedy, obviously such exactions arise in us while we follow the development of a plot, though they also relate to norms (ideas of logical or ethical fitness, and the like) that characterize the expectancy of audiences prior to their reception of any particular drama. The principle of unity implies the fulfilling of expectations, for if a work violated expectations it would not be considered consistent. As regards Aristotle's overall recipe for character (in chapter 15): The first three requirements (that the character be "good," "appropriate," and in some notable way "like" us) involve categorical expectancies, along with ingredients that make the character a fit for the particular play in which it figures. The fourth requirement (that the character be self-consistent, even to the extent of being "consistently inconsistent") will more definitely involve expectations that develop en route.[3]

Art could be said to begin in "self-expression," or simply "expression," spontaneous utterance, as with outcries, oaths, interjections. But such motives are matured by translation into the great complexities of language that owe their development to the use of language as a medium of *communication* (itself rooted in modes of practical cooperation). Most literary critics of this writer's generation began in a period when self-expression was the accepted slogan; but the stress upon communication (art as evocation, medium for affecting an audience) gradually gained prominence, until now "communication" is almost a password in certain circles.

Accordingly, critics might choose to debate the issue in those terms. One group might stress self-expression as the essence of art, others might stress communication, others might compromise by proposing a judicious mixture of the two (such mixtures being conceived in accordance with either the notion that self-expression and communication reenforce each other or the notion that they act as checks upon each other, or that they do a bit of both).

Another possibility would be to turn from a two-term to a three-term dialectic that would view art as starting with self-expression, as developing by tests of communication, and finally as moving *towards the transcending of both self-expression and communication*. This third stage would come about in the following way:

The artist would choose themes that engrossed him personally ("self-expression"). He would develop them by the use of a public medium ("communication"). But in the course of perfecting his work, he encounters possibilities purely internal to the medium; and he may exploit these possibilities "to the end of the line," regardless of either self-expression or communication.

Joyce's later work is an example of this development. Few writers have paid greater attention than he to the public lore (the materials of communication). In particular, his concern with myth involved the exploitation of symbol-systems that were highly communicative and greatly assisted the social processes of cooperation. Yet he did not develop this material purely from the standpoint of its communicability, but rather from the standpoint of its ultimate possibilities (possibilities that could be more efficiently exploited when he deliberately rejected the kinds of expectancy we usually associate with communication). His "efficient" use of myth was the poetic analogue of a museum. It produced the kind of effect, for instance, one gets at the Museum of Natural History in New York City, in the large room displaying a vast assortment of totem poles collected from many different tribes, an exhibit that makes possible an "antiquarian" kind of experience quite unlike the relation between particular Indian tribes and their particular totem poles. In following out such possibilities, got by the jamming of many myths, Joyce would be presumably answering a call (and thus "expressing himself"). Yet the resulting product would be *consummatory* in a way that could not be adequately confined to either of the first two stages, but would have something of both in being beyond both.

This consummation, obtained by exploiting the possibilities of a symbol-system as such, without primary regard for either self-expression or communication, would seem better explainable in terms of self-consistency than in terms of expectation, though the two imply each other. The formal principle of consummatory self-consistency is also of importance when we consider technological developments as the possible manifestation of "aesthetic" motives, rather than as instruments of sheer pragmatic *utility*. In this regard, the various scientific specialists are to be viewed as carrying out the implications of their terminologies, and thereby seeking technological consummation for its own sake, however deceptively their efforts might be justified.

For instance, whether or not it is possible to develop "clean" thermonuclear bombs, some men might well want to go on experimenting with these dismal weapons. For they have brought their calculations to the point where further experimental steps are in order, steps suggested by the present state of their terminologies. And the "principle of consummatory self-consistency" would provide an incentive, or almost a compulsion, to continue in this same direction, quite as an author who had carried a novel to near completion might not be able to rest until he had finished it. Whereas, in some cases, the consummatory principle demands but further purely symbolic manipulations, in other cases unfortunately it is working with materials that can spread great misery and devastation throughout the planet. But though the results vary greatly with different kinds of activity, the principle is the same. Each scientific specialization has its own particular idiom, making for its particular idiocy, in line with its particular possibilities of communication. A clutter of such autonomous formal principles, each aiming at its own kind of perfection, can add up to a condition of considerable disarray— and especially insofar as many of the new powers thus being developed lend themselves readily to destructive purposes, while even their "peaceful" uses are menacing, as with the pollution that goes with the disposal of atomic wastes. Yes, the "aesthetic" of recent technological consummations can become quite ugly.

However, along with these paradoxes whereby the principle of self-consistency can have tragic consequences, there is a route more directly related to tragedy as a form, and based on the theory of form as the arousing and fulfilling of expectations. The steps are as follows:

Whatever happens to a character, the audience must be made to acquiesce in his destiny, whether it be to triumph, or to be yielded up for sacrifice, or to play some villainous or subordinate role. Such acquiescence is not merely inert, after the event; it involves participation through vigorous anticipation. Here figure the tragic playwright's many ways of guiding an audience's expectations (expectations that in turn amount to *demands* placed upon the playwright, who violates them at his peril). Now, such predestinating of roles, each in accordance with its nature, and in accordance with an overall logic relating the parts to one another is, technically, Form. But such a network of expectancies and fulfillments is summed up dramatically in terms like Right, Law, Fate, Justice, Necessity *(Dike, Themis, Moira, Nemesis, Ananke),* terms which are but dramatic equivalents for the principle of expectancy summed up in the term Form.

We might add *Aga* (or *Age*), which means *respect, wonder, reverence, awe*—hence derivatively, *envy, hatred, jealousy,* since the word applies either to men's reverence for the gods or to the gods' jealousy at the sight of a human too powerful or proud. Thus, the verb *agamai* begins by meaning *to regard as high* (that is, to respect) and ends by meaning *to regard as too high* (that is, to envy). *Agan,* of the same root, appears in the classic formula, "nothing to excess" *(meden agan,* the Latin *nil nimium),* hence in the Aristotelian cult of the mean we see the philosophic variant of the basic tragic admonition. Another term, *phthonos,* meaning "malice" or "grudge" (Latin *invidia)* is similarly used, in referring not just to human malice, but to the malice or envy of the gods with relation to men's pretentiousness.

Whatever the social origins of such motives may be, once they are converted into the fullness of tragedy they have become *cosmologized,* whereupon an almost terrifying *thoroughness* of human honesty is demanded of us. For we are now in our very essence *persecuted,* and there can be no comfort until we have disclosed and appropriately transfigured every important motive still unresolved within us. That is, once the irresolutions of the body, of personal relations, and of social relations have been heroically transmogrified by identification with the Great Persecutional Words, which are in turn identified with the vastness of Nature and the mystery of Super-Nature, no pleasantly pluralistic dissipation of outlook is possible. Whatever the diversity of the world, we must become pious in doing homage to some threatening principle of oneness. We cannot deny the persecution; we must admit it: for by the nature of the tragic playwright's cosmologizing, it is integral and everywhere. Under such conditions, form may be felt not just as imposing, but as oppressive, however grandly. For instance:

The author had been working steadily on the Orestes trilogy, throughout the morning, afternoon, and evening of one day. Awakening in the night, he lay in the dark, with somewhat the sense of looking down upon the world as though it were a kind of *relief* map, stretched out beneath him. He could "see," or "feel" its curving, from the coast off to the Great Lakes then down towards the Gulf, and on across the Plains and the Rockies to the Pacific. The reasons for this fantasy were obvious. The half-awakened, half-dreaming sleeper was responding to what Henry Sams has called "the illusion of great physical space and magnitude" in Aeschylus and Job.

But there was another step. To the man lying there in the dark, this notion of the curved world stretching out through the night was somehow frightful, even monstrous. He felt as though he had awakened from a nightmare, and had not yet shaken himself free of it. And this further step seems to have resulted because Aeschylus, in using the ultimate vastness of scene to dignify his tragedy (which was also infused with the spirit of the Great Persecutional Words), had contrived to infuse nature itself with the terrors of tragedy (hence also with the *civic virtues* that gain much in authority if backed by such terrors). All the magic of dominion was operating here, in all its dimensions. By thus making fear universal, Aeschylus had made the universe fearsome. Thus there was fear in the mere thought of all those places lying just where they were. And when fear is thus made radical, an equally radical pity can be the only antidote.

But now we have (at least "in principle") a sufficient range of terms to consider the Poetic tactics of the Oresteia generally, and thus to get a glimpse into the kind of *thoroughness* to which the tragic playwright is necessarily vowed once he sets out to cosmologize his fable in the spirit of the Great Persecutional Words.†

---

†Burke follows this section on form with a long, brilliant, textually virtuoso reading of Aeschylus's trilogy on Orestes, *Agamemnon, Libation-Bearers,* and *Eumenides.* The "substance" of this section is published, though the published version lacks the stunning range of almost line-by-line dramatistic explication offered in the full essay. Please consult the "Textual Introduction" for specific bibliographic information.

In the subsequent section Burke summarizes his argument to this point before he returns again to the topic of "catharsis," but with a difference. *Ed.*

"Beyond" Catharsis

Where, then, are we?

We began by considering the "Dramatistic" logic of the terminology used in the *Poetics*. We next examined the key term, "imitation," and attempted to show the importance of the "entelechy" in Aristotle's use of that term. Since Aristotle's Poetics hinges about his definition for Tragedy, and since he situates the tragic pleasure in "Catharsis" yet has no discussion of this important term, we centered upon that problem specifically. Since he defines Catharsis with relation to Pity and Fear, we looked into these terms, attempting to show that they should be treated not as "simples" but as complex and even contradictory emotions.

We did not mean that the functions named by the two terms are complex and contradictory solely with relation to each other, though they sometimes may be so. Rather we had in mind the possibility that Pity itself might be complex and contradictory, and similarly with Fear. For Pity and Fear are not intrinsically pleasurable, whereas their function in Tragedy is pleasurable. We suggested that both these emotions, as experienced in Tragedy, contain elements of social and moral elevation not intrinsic to the corresponding emotions in nature.

We filled out this statement by adding "Pride" as a third term. For though Aristotle does not discuss Pride specifically, he does stress the importance of the "tragic flaw," and in the Tragedies themselves Pride is the key term for this "flaw." Here we suggested that there can also be a complexity, or contrariety, in Pride. For the disapproval of it (an attitude of "moral indignation") can be a kind of "counter-pride" (or, in theological language, "self-righteousness"). And the thought of a proud man humbled can have vindictive elements, however piously the vengefulness is accounted for.

Having chosen these three terms, and considered them as a kind of trinity, we next asked what might be their "bodily" equivalents, as regards the symbolizing of Catharsis. In answer to this question, we then tried to show their relation to sexual, fecal, and diuretic functions.

"Dramatistically," the "Little Monster" that resulted might be accounted for thus: The author has set himself the problem, "How carve a Poetics out of a Rhetoric?" A study of Purgation, as so conceived, is itself undergoing a kind of purge. The secondary nature of criticism as a medium permits the writer to symbolize such a purgative process by dwelling upon the topic as exemplified in works of art. And since he has divided the realm of motives into civic, personal, and physical, the first or "lowest" step in the "purification of the essay" involves a concern with the bodily analogues of purgation. However, the element to be critically purged (by being made explicit) is not confined to Rhetoric. There is likewise a "hidden imposthume" in Poetics. Hence, the chapter appropriately sought to disclose its presence in poetry.

However, the subject of Catharsis could by no means be reduced to the imagery of bodily behavior. The personal order exists in its own right. (This is the order of the emotions as such, Pity, Fear, Pride, etc., qualitatively experienced as Pity, Fear, Pride, etc.) There is also the civic order as such, an order that comes to a head in such terms as Justice, Right, Necessity; Vengeance, Fate, Ruin; and the intermediate terms to do with moral Pollution and Purification.

Having considered the Personal and Bodily orders, we considered Form in terms of the Civic order. (That is: We had considered the Personal order "before the divide"; and now, "on the other side of the divide," we considered the Civic order.) To this end, we discussed Aristotle's notions of Form. We noted how they might be lumped together by a definition of form as the arousing and fulfilling of expectations, though we questioned whether the definition was wholly Aristotelian in spirit.

The gist of our discussion was this: That form in its grandeur involves a vast structure of proprieties headed in the great abstractions we have called "civic." ("Social" or "moral" or "philosophic" would be equally usable.) And, as regards Greek Tragedy at least, Form as so conceived was found to have a "Persecutional" element, that demanded *tremendous thoroughness* in the symbolizing of purification, or Catharsis.

To illustrate this point, we next considered in some detail the Aeschylus trilogy. And we tried to show how, in the thoroughness of its concerns, it even sought to resolve a "civic" problem of conscience by transforming the nature of conscience itself to fit the civic proprieties.

In the course of analyzing these plays, we found ourselves obliged to argue against a position shared by critics for whom we have great admiration. The position we attacked is very well stated by Elder Olson in his essay, "William Empson, Contemporary Criticism and Poetic Diction" (*Modern Philology,* May 1950). On page 238, he writes:

> Greek epic and drama are mimetic poetry; despite their origin in ritual and myth, they require no reference to these in order to be intelligible and effective. Whatever the mythical origin of an Odysseus, or an Orestes, these are characters simply, and must be interpreted as such; neither they nor their actions and fortunes require allegorical interpretation; whatever symbolic significance they may have possessed as myth they have lost as materials of poetry.

The principle underlying this statement has much to recommend it. It might be summed up thus: Poetry is poetry, religion is religion, biology is biology, physics is physics, etc. Don't confuse the species. Decide which you are dealing with, decide on what principles it operates, and study individual works in term of these principles.

These are excellent critical scruples. And no critic can be firm in his thinking unless he has felt the force of their discipline. But what if a certain kind of poetry gets certain of its effects by allusion (not just superficial allusion, but profound allusion) to certain religious practices that preceded it? Such allusion would not be merely a matter of "origins." It would be an *intrinsic aspect of the poetry itself*. Ironically, the critic who failed to recognize this fact would really be victimized by the very historicism and geneticism which he is trying to avoid. For he would let himself be forced into a directly contrary position. In effect, the assumption would be that, if a religious rite preceded a poetic form, and a poem got a kind of beauty by material and formal analogies that alluded to the religious rite, the critical analysis of such beauty would be not "poetic" but "historical" or "genetic."

The clearest case for the position we are upholding would be Euripides' *Bacchae*. For this drama *specifically imitates* the Dionysian rites. There is not even allusion here: the play, on its face, is the staging of the religious services, interwoven with a set of purely personal relationships and using the "civic" structure of proprieties to suggest a particular "philosophic attitude" towards the gods. (In this respect, Euripides resembles Bernard Shaw, or the Ibsen of *Ghosts* and *Enemy of the People*. He plans a work in accordance with the society's sense of propriety, but he "tendentiously" tries to play such an order against itself, in this case playing the audience's humanitarian sympathies against its respect for the traditions of worship.)

Just as Euripides here specifically imitates the religious rites, there is an important intermediate area in which Tragedy is neither wholly free of religious analogy nor wholly concerned with it, but uses it allusively. And one must certainly distinguish between the poetic use of allusion and the historicist concern with earlier nonpoetic forms or contemporary nonpoetic situations which do not figure at all in the work as such. Allusion is not genetic, it is poetic. Owing to historical change, an allusion may be lost, just as it may be lost on a contemporary owing to insensitiveness or ignorance.

A work may be so great that, even when some of its intrinsic poetic qualities are obscured, enough are left to provide great enjoyment. But if, say, there were in a certain language a syllable that meant "thank you," and had been so translated, there might still be an important *poetic* fact omitted here. For suppose that this word was properly used for "thank you" only in cases where a social superior was addressing a social inferior. Then its presence in some context where it was used in reverse, by a social inferior addressing a social superior, would be a *poetic* fact about it, not just a matter of lexicology, or extrapoetic background and the like. We have tried to disclose something of this sort in allusion as used by Aeschylus. And a statement that allusions to ritual and myth "require no reference to these in order to be intelligible and effective" would be like stating that the translation, "thank you," is in itself sufficient to be "intelligible and effective." The context might be such that enough drama would come through, despite the loss. Yet the recovery of the qualification would not be sheerly "historical." It would recover a moment intrinsic to the poem.

To think otherwise would be like saying that, when a painting has become darkened by the film of centuries, an uncovering of its original colors is mere "historicism." True, the expert who removes the film is not being a painter (quite as the critic is not the poet). But he is making a disclosure intrinsic to the painting. And in this sense, we have tried to show, the use of allusion in Greek tragedy was intrinsic to the form.

Our debt here to such literary anthropologists as George Thomson, in his *Aeschylus and Athens,* is obvious. But the particular point about method we are trying to make may not be. We are trying to show how, in the process of Carving out a Poetics, an approach to Greek tragedy from the standpoint of *terminology* makes for a cut that falls on the bias across the usual way of separating the realms of Poetics and Anthropology. Insofar as the terms used in a work written centuries ago had public connotations not present in the words now generally taken to be their modern equivalents, and insofar as those connotations had important bearing on the appeal of the work to the audience for which it was designed, any *anthropological* lore that can help recapture such lost connotations is making a contribution to the study of the work for purposes of *poetics.* Public connotations are to a *word* what color is to a *painting.*

True, the major stress in Poetics should be upon the internalities of a work, as with the relations of the terms to one another. But just as we cannot properly study the relation of the colors to one another if they have become discolored, so we cannot properly study the relation of terms to one another if a portion of their value was in an allusiveness that is not being taken into account. Anthropologists have helped us to glimpse some of the allusiveness behind the terms used in Greek tragedy. And no "genetic fallacy" is involved if Poetics draws on such findings. If a Christian writer makes a reference to some secular person "dying on the Cross" of his preoccupations, and if some future age read this line without thinking of it as allusive, an important aspect of its quality would be lost. And if some historian or anthropologist or the like happened to discover what previous developments in the history of our culture were allusively implied in this expression, such recovery would be relevant to *Poetics,* regardless of what science outside the orbit of Poetics may have disclosed it.

Aeschylus used at least these ways of giving mythic resonance to civic offenses (that is, the playwright could deal strictly or loosely with allusive terms having connotations of this sort):

grape imagery (rites of Dionysus);

sacrifice of animals (consecrated victims, particularly goat and bull);

marriage (as initiation, the new, the springlike; related to the sacred ritual marriage of bride with animal);

blood as principle of fertilization (bloodletting as rain);

the ritual cleansing;

partaking of sacramental food (eating of sacrificed animals' innards);

sparagmos, mutilation, dismemberment (close to the ritual banquet);

enigma, mystery, the oracular (prophecy to name the essence of motivation), hiding and unveiling. Hence, just as secrecy can have connotation of treachery, so treachery can be given connotations of the ritually secret;

translation generally of the civic into its "divine" counterpart (inasmuch as the "gods" were a duplication of social motives);

and probably "allusive" *forms,* such as the catechistic style of stichomythia.

In sum: Regardless of the fact that such rites preceded tragedy in history, we contend that the concern with such matters is not merely "genetic" but also falls within Poetics; for the analysis of Diction falls within Poetics, and allusion is a resource intrinsic to Diction.

But whether or not the reader agrees with our point about the intrinsic with regard to this particular application of the term, in analyzing Tragic "allusion," our inquiry should have brought us to the point where we can say how a proposition should be framed, to fit *completely* with the norms of Poetics. When dealing with a poem in its totality, however, there is no reason for confining ourselves to observations exclusively Poetic. We may want to consider the "ethical" dimension of a work, for instance: its nature as a manifestation of the author's character. And since "words are imitations," so that poetic and rhetorical diction overlap (see *Rhetoric*, bk. 3, i, 8–9), it is not always necessary that we phrase a proposition in the form most purely adapted to Poetics exclusively. A statement in the spirit of Rhetoric may sometimes be more convenient (we speak of a Lyrics "stylistic effects," for instance), even when we are considering the poem intrinsically.

Rhetorically, we might say of a certain poem: "Note how it is designed, first, to make the reader fear, then to make him weep, and finally, after appropriate transforming of his expectancies, to make him feel exultant and exalted."

Poetically, this statement should be rephrased: "Note how the poem first imitates or symbolizes fear (that is, note how it is the essence of fear); then note how it imitates or symbolizes sorrow (that is, note how its very style and form and imagery weep); and finally, note the series of transformations whereby it finally arrives at the kind of imitating that, within its internal logic, comes to a head in the imitating or symbolizing of exultation and exaltation." Or, more briefly, "Note how the poem fears, sorrows, and exults after its kind."

Here, clearly, both the Rhetorical and the Poetic statements are talking about the same thing. And either might help us sharpen the observations we might have made when perceiving in terms of only one. Yet despite the real overlap of subject matter here, the two styles point in the direction of a real difference in subject matter.

The classical case of the overlap (as we noted in the *Rhetoric*) is Longinus *On the Sublime*. For here he jumbles citations from both Poetry and Oratory, selecting from both kinds of expression the kind of stylistic moments that he considers touchstones of the sublime (or as we suggest, the "moving"). Even though the works of oratory were originally designed for practical purposes, to influence political or juridical decisions, he considers them purely for their beauty of utterance as such (in this respect, their function as oratory having died soon after the time of their delivery, the overlap between oratory and poetry enables him to appreciate them afterwards as poetry).

To analyze a painting in ways that would be the equivalent of rhetoric, we might discuss it in terms of "empathy." We might note how the lines of the painting invite the observer to follow certain movements through imaginative participation in the suggestions which the painter places in front of us. Or, in the equivalent of Poetics, we should simply ask ourselves how the painting itself so moves and develops, with its system of internal mutual adjustments.

In the formula, "through pity and fear, accomplishing the catharsis of such emotions," the verb *(peraino)* merits close attention. In spirit it is one of the *telos* words, being variously translated as: bring to an end, bring about, make an end of, finish, transfix, pierce, reach, penetrate. Also, as used by Aristotle in other contexts, it means: draw a conclusion, conclude, infer.

But etymologically it is related to *peran,* which means: on the other side, across (Latin, *trans*); in the absolute it meant: over, on the opposite side (especially of water), having crossed over. Similarly, *pera* meant: beyond (Latin, *ultra*). And *peras* meant: end, goal.

To be overliteral, then, we might translate the formula: through pity and fear, "beyonding" the catharsis of such emotions. That is, tragedy goes *through* pity and fear to a point beyond them. (Somewhat as Hegel's term *Aufheben* is often translated in French as *dépassement.*)

In the Orestes trilogy, such "beyonding" is easily observable. The murder in the first play leads to that in the second: and the third play deals with the modes of transformation that can be (and/or must be) worked out, once the "prerequisite" steps in the bloodletting have been passed through, whereat the remission of sins can follow.

We do not mean to imply that the whole problem of catharsis can be resolved merely by a trick of translation. But at least we should *begin* in the inspection of a formula by asking what purely linguistic clues it may offer. And so far as the Aeschylus trilogy is concerned, we note how its structure fits well with the connotations of *trans* and *ultra* that surround the Greek participle *perainousa.*

The formula, as thus literally interpreted, is an even better fit with the structure of the *Divine Comedy.* For might not Dante's epic be said to split fear, pity, and "the catharsis of such emotions" into three successive stages? Would not the *Inferno* be primarily under the sign of Fear, the *Purgatorio* under the sign of Pity (the *Miserere* is sung in canto 6 of the *Purgatorio*), while the *Paradiso* would name the state *beyond* these?

There are complications. For in one sense Dante is never wholly beyond the purgatorial state (his climb continuing in the *Paradiso,* too, though moral purgation has now given place to intellectual clarification). So, in a certain sense, he is a pitiable creature, thus wandering among the great. And as regards Hell:

Hell is designed to awaken, not our sympathy, but our horror. No clearer example of this point could be found than that gruesome incident in canto 32, where the poet rips out the hair of Bocca degli Abbati who lies helplessly frozen in the eternal ice. However, we have one problem to take care of here. In canto 5, when Virgil shows Dante the many shades who had died of the sins of love, there are two references to pity. At the first feeling of pity, Dante says he was bewildered. And at the end of the canto, after hearing the story of Paolo and Francesca, he faints with pity. In accordance with Aristotle's formula, we feel pity for those most like ourselves—and the entire work is under the sign of Venus. We have elsewhere observed that, in Dante's falling as if dying, by the ambiguities of such a fall he inchoately yields to the lovers' temptation. But in any case, we note that at this point in hell he threatens to break the very framework of his structure—and such a threat to the form of his work would also be a threat to the tenets of his religion. The very fact that the temptations to pity cause such disturbance in him would roundabout suggest Hell is in essence the place of Fear. In this scheme, Pity would be a "beyonding" of Fear, while contemplation of the divine radiance would be a "beyonding" of both (the transforming of pity into transcendent love, and of fear into transcendent worship).

We must not try to make this symmetry more perfect than it is. Though the Saints in Paradise do not pity the Hellish sufferings of the eternally damned, mere human frailty is necessarily less absolute in its sympathies. So there is a plentiful scattering of words for pity and fear in all three cancticles. Yet the general pattern is clear enough, when contrasted with a different kind of pattern. For instance, in both the *Oresteia* and the *Divine Comedy* there is clearly a tripartite arrangement that allows for the "beyonding" of catharsis, as contrasted with forms in which the process is distinctly *telescoped*. In Sophocles' *Oedipus Rex,* for instance, consider the audience's final weeping at the pitiableness of self-blinded Oedipus, as he stands like a desolate king in a storm, pathetically clutching at his children. This ending is in itself a purging *of* tears *through* tears. We are released, and thereby exalted, in feeling generously *such fears as are in their very essence social-minded.*

Aristotle's entelechial stress upon the *single* play as cathartic instrument leads to the preference for such *simultaneity* as attains at the same moment, the "beyonded," the "beyonding," and the beyond. But we submit that such an "empurposed" structure (where the end is one with the act) should be approached through the analysis of works where the stages are clearly spread out as a spectrum—then we might next look for instances where the colors are merged into a unitary radiance.

Sophocles' *Oedipus at Colonus* is another instance of such simultaneity. Here the "beyonding" is even topically figured, as we are present at Oedipus's final mystic departure for the realm beyond death. Fear attains exalted stature through being transformed into fear of the gods (piety, *sebas*), the playwright also using mechanical thunder to help him overwhelm his audience with the sense of divine wonder. Pity for the dying blind old man is thus both felt and "beyonded," since in his very passage beyond this life he is being made into a mysterious tutelary deity, whose secret grave at Colonus will be like a pact with the gods, protecting Athens against its neighbor, Thebes.

Here, surely, we are at the center of our thesis: Here we see the

moment where tragedy, through pity and fear, *takes us beyond* the catharsis of such emotions (and, in this sense, *fulfills* the catharsis).

We could then spin from this point, as generating principle. For
instance, if we are to feel the beyonding of pity and fear most intensely,
certain kinds of character will be required for the best effect here—and
Aristotle makes his statements general enough to cover a multitude of
individual cases.

Naturally, when we are analyzing individual works, this high level
of generality cannot be maintained. We become involved in "casuistry."
To ask specifically wherein a given character is appropriate, lifelike,
consistent, or "good" is to become concerned with problems not treated
in the *Poetics* as such. With Aristotle, only generalized knowledge was
truly "scientific" knowledge. Hence one must depart from Poetics as a
"science" insofar as one asks in detail, say, about the appropriateness
of a particular character; and if such a discussion is to avoid the superficial, it must carry us into extrapoetic realms, matters to do with history, sociology, psychology, religious doctrine, politics, and the like. In
sum: The *poem contains more than can be discussed in terms of Poetics
alone.*

For instance, if you but try to decide wherein a character is "good"
(chrestos) for tragedy, unless you are to content yourself with a comparatively trivial answer you must consider matters of "vicarage" or
substitution (in brief, the *scapegoat* as a cathartic agency). In *Oedipus
at Colonus*, line 498, Oedipus states the principle when he says that one
soul, if properly disposed, can act in behalf of tens of thousands. But
though the original Dionysian rites unquestionably effected catharsis by
scapegoat, and though the *Poetics* is dealing with the recipe for producing at least an analogous kind of catharsis, the text as it survives never
once discusses the tragic recipe in such terms. However, there is one
passage in the *Rhetoric* (bk. 2, iii) which at least touches upon the
pattern:

> Vengeance previously taken against one person appeases an-
> ger against another, even though it be greater. Wherefore
> Philocrates, when someone asked him why he did not justify
> himself when the people were angry with him, made the ju-
> dicious reply, "Not yet." "When then?" "When I see some-
> one accused of the same offence"; for men grow mild when
> they have exhausted their anger upon another, as happened
> in the case of Ergophilus. For though the Athenians were
> more indignant with him than with Callisthenes, they ac-
> quitted him, because they had condemned Callisthenes to
> death on the previous day.

To ask just what fits a given character for such a sacrificial role in a tragedy (that is, to ask what makes him "good" for service *as a tragic victim*) is to ask questions that are certainly not answered in the extant sections of the *Poetics*. The four general requirements listed in chapter 15 (that the character be good, appropriate, like ourselves, and consistent) do not seem directed to the question of vicarious victimage specifically.

Or, again, even if everyone were to agree that tragedy, as a civic ceremony, seeks by symbolic means to transcend the evils of political faction, some critics might still maintain that such an observation is not germane to Poetics as such. They might allow for general talk of "transcendence," yet resent the more specific question, "the transcending of what?" However, one could still note the places where the given work itself refers to the need of transcending faction, and relates its plot to such concerns (as with the *Oresteia*). And one might next proceed to discuss processes of transcendence in general, the "beyonding" of such a list as Sophocles offers (*Oedipus at Colonus*, line 1233): envy, sedition, strife, murder, war, and the evil of evils, age (all of which are conditions or situations highly appropriate to the emotions of pity and fear).

Above all, we believe, it would be an observation wholly within Poetics to distinguish between the kind of pity and fear that marks a terminus (as with the "beyonding" at the end of *Oedipus Rex* or *Oedipus at Colonus*) and the kind that motivates a further act of vengeance (as the pathos of Agamemnon's murder motivates Orestes' retaliation, or as the murder of Macduff's children arouses the audience's vindictiveness along with their pity). The pity and fear that motivate a vendetta justify an act that must in turn be "beyonded." Or we might distinguish between the terminal kind of pity, and the kind used so often by Shakespeare in act 4 (the "pity act") as a "softening" that makes the violence of act 5 more intense by comparison.[4]

All such procedures, you will note, can be stated either as means of guiding the audience's expectations and responses, or as stages symbolized or imitated in the work itself. That is, they are in the area where Rhetoric and Poetic overlap; for the critic is here talking about the work intrinsically, but is sharpening his perception of its methods by thinking of his response to them. Further, the response itself is "intrinsic," in the sense that there is no specific program of extra-aesthetic action recommended, as with oratorical exhortation.

Poetically, we believe, any use of religious or moral counters should properly be treated simply as a Poetic device. Perhaps a poet cannot effectively portray religious attitudes unless he personally shares in them somehow. But such a relationship would be extrapoetic. The model here would be Aristotle's reference to the use of the "miraculous" *(thaumaston)* as a device for improving a tragic plot (see end of his ch. 9).

As regards our present project, the shift from Poetics proper to Symbolics in general would involve speculations on the relation between the poem as act and the poet as agent; hence here would belong notions about the poet himself as a believer in the religiosity which his work exemplifies. But as regards Poetics in its purity, we should simply note how the poem manipulates *religion* or morals or "fate" and the like as counters. The same would apply to the poetic use of political views.

Or suppose, hypothetically, that you fully agreed with our notions about the relation between the civic and the mythic. That is, the mythic order of terms duplicates the civic order "on a higher level." Hence, "pride" can be considered either as an offense against one's neighbors or as a sacrilege against the gods. Here, clearly, we are concerned with a Poetic resource that has its grounding in linguistic resources generally. In mythology proper, only the "higher" level would need to be considered. As regards the Rhetoric of social relations, we might study the ways in which men can shift from one level to the other, depending on the particular effects aimed at. But the same issue might be discussed, within the special realm of Poetics, simply as a resource for the producing of "beauty" in diction and sentiment by the use of "elevated" ideas and images.

And thus we might note how, by the same token, other kinds of poetry aiming at other kinds of "beauty" or "pleasure," can reverse these same directions, as when the satyr-play burlesques the heroics of the tragic posturing.

As regards the principle of expectancy: Particularly when we are dealing with classical plays, it is good to sharpen our perception of form by asking ourselves how, at the end of each step, some further potential is built up. This "materialistic" question about potentials is especially helpful when one is asking questions about the structure of some individual work, considered in its uniqueness.

But where the continuous series of expectations and fulfillments is "entelechially" divided into Complication, Peripety, and Denouement, one can arrange a hierarchy for each. Each is said to have its own kind of perfection, somewhat as though one were to think of a Complication in and for itself, quite as though a writer were commissioned simply to write the Compleat Complication and nothing else, or the best kind of Peripety-with-Discovery, or the Perfect Ending. Similarly, characters would be considered, not explicitly as "yieldable" and "serviceable" within the terms of the particular tragic catharsis (as "good" for the plot of this particular tragedy), but with reference to the character recipe in general. And this recipe would be spontaneously guided by such tests, since it took them for granted.

However, as we have previously noted, relative superiority of kinds need not apply in a particular case. That is, a character or plot *generically* "inferior" may be *just right* for some unique poetic situation. Thus whereas, considered in itself, the *Eumenides* might be classed as a kind of tragedy inferior to its companion pieces, its stress upon spectacle *(opsis)* seems to fit it perfectly for its place "beyond" these other two.

Aristotle holds that tragedy (not played, but read!) is categorically superior to the epic, just as many later writers have held that the epic is the higher species. We question whether such arguments are fruitful, except when interpreted as symptoms of wholly extrapoetic motives. (We may discover, for instance, that an argument about the relative merits of two artistic species is an indirect reflection of rival social or political trends.)

A more fruitful problem is this: When do we test a work by reference to other works which we include as members of its kind, and when do we invent a new kind in which to class it?

Croce, in his *Aesthetics,* considering the long history of misuse to which the theory of literary genders was put, proposed to throw out such concerns entirely. Whereas poets were striving after beauties and pleasures of one sort, their critics attacked them in the name of Aristotle for departing from models that were striving after beauties and pleasures of another sort. Here the authority of the world's greatest schoolteacher was invoked for stupid ends—and Croce's radical resistance deserves our sympathy.

Yet is not another solution possible? Why not retain the critical concern with literary species, but treat the formulation of species *tentatively,* and as an aid to analysis, rather than in the spirit of the legislator or magistrate? For there is something beautifully "finished" about the definition of a literary species. Maybe it is the literary critic's equivalent of a lyric. Though he may ponder on a form, the heart of his definition may be found only at some flashing moment "when the mood is on." And once such a formula is found, insofar as the critic has really hit upon the critical equivalent of the generating principle which the poet embodied in his poem, his definition can lead to the discovery of new perfections in the work, perfections that are central to its nature.

The critic in this sense is not legislator or magistrate. Rather he is "terascopic." That is, he looks upon the work as a portent—he studies its portentousness. (We got the word, you will recall, from Aeschylus. *Teras* means prodigy, marvel, omen, portent; it is the New Testament word for miracle. Sometimes it even means monster. The *skopos* is, of course, the watcher, the seer. Hence, the "terascopic" critic would be the patient observer of the poetic wonder.)

He would study the range and integrity of a work's relationships. True, to perfect himself in his task ("watchful of hermetics, to be strong in hermeneutics"), he must often pause to criticize his medium. He will thus turn to questions of method, or even of methodology, that may take him far from the poem, sometimes even so far that we may never get back!

But not necessarily. And in any case, criticism generically is not a derivative or secondary activity. It is a primal and natural expression of language and thought. And by allowing it its autonomy, rather than thinking of it as a handmaiden of poetry, we may, as is usually the case with freedom, give it the full opportunities for development that will best serve the ends even of those who otherwise would have subjected it to their special demands. For if it fully matures its instruments of analysis, then when it turns its attention to a writer of integrity, it will be best equipped to show how thorough that integrity is.

Throughout this treatise, we have by program both concerned ourselves with criticism in general and kept returning to particular works. And to complete this chapter, we would return once more, by considering specifically an instance where criticism too often dealt with a new kind in terms of an old kind, whereas it should have formulated a new kind, with laws appropriate to its specific nature.

We refer to the difference between Greek "cathartic" tragedy and the neoclassic tragedy of Corneille. But we believe that by considering still another *literary* species, we can best find the transition between these two species of tragedy.

The intermediate step here would be what we might call Plutarch's "biography of admiration." The formula is ours, after the analogy of Corneille's "theatre of admiration," but throughout Plutarch's *Lives* the term "admiration" recurs at all strategic spots. The theory is most succinctly expressed, perhaps, near the opening of the essay on Pericles. (We quote from the "Dryden" translation, Modern Library Edition, 182–83).

> As that color is more suitable to the eye whose freshness and pleasantness stimulates and strengthens the sight, so a man ought to apply his intellectual perception to such objects as, with the sense of delight, are apt to call it forth, and allure it to its own proper good and advantage.

Such objects we find in the acts of virtue, which also produce in the minds of mere readers about them an emulation and eagerness that may lead them on to imitation.

Virtue, by the bare statement of its actions, can so affect men's minds as to create at once both admiration of the things done and desire to imitate the doers of them.

Similarly, Plutarch speaks of Theseus as "entertaining such admiration for the virtue of Hercules, that in the night his dreams were all of that hero's actions, and in the day a continual emulation stirred him up to perform the like." Or of Coriolanus, "conscious . . . of the admiration of the best and greatest men of Rome." Etc.

To read the biographies of this Romanized Greek is to see how well they mediate between the "good" characters of democratic Athenian tragedy and the courtly cult of *belles actions* in Corneille, with its constant resonant repetition of such words as *royaume, honneur, grandeur, dignité, vertu, justice, gloire, triomphe, conquête, dompter, venger.*[5]

The steps from Greek tragedy through Plutarch to Cornelian tragedy are, briefly, these: In cathartic tragedy, a character to fit such sacrificial roles must be "serious" *(spoudaios)*. But if you write of important public figures in such a spirit, you present them as models to be imitated. Thus imitation becomes equatable with emulation and admiration. Then if later dramatists look to Plutarch for classic figures whose lives were well suited to dramatization, one outcome could well be the "theatre of admiration." Here the theme of honor and glory (with its countertheme, revenge) could rationalize conduct by a secularizing of an attitude, with relations to the monarch taking the foreground claimed by relations to God (though, of course, the entire cluster of sympathetically related terms would include king, God, justice, Providence, reason, authority, honor, virtue, and military prowess, an easily understandable grouping in an art that is an aesthetic equivalent to monarchy and empire). The fatal curse seems to have been replaced by a secular devotion to rule until, looking again, you see that this imperialist devotion is itself a curse.

But our main point is this: The cathartic tragedy required a certain solemnity of posturing, as a means to the end. But, by the Plutarchian route, this solemn gesturing could come to be the end, the "soul" of a later tragedy. Insofar as such a change of aesthetic purpose took place, one really had a species of tragedy different from the Greek. Whereat critics wavered in their application of Aristotle's *Poetics* to the new conditions.

Sometimes they measured the new works by the old models. For instance, they insisted upon unity of place. Yet so great a work as Aeschylus's *Eumenides* begins its action before the temple of Apollo at Delphi and ends in Athens, on the Hill of Ares. Sometimes they sought new principles. Many critics, for instance, doubted the importance of catharsis, or even its presence, in the later tragedies. And they were correct insofar as such tragedy placed the stress upon the *heroics of dignification:* grandiose conduct in the face of danger and suffering was emphasized, and the moral virtues that went with it were identified with the idealizing of monarchy. (We consider elsewhere the ironies whereby, since such tragedy necessarily imitated conflict, the emergent revolutionary motives received expression there, too, though round-about, usually in the guise of feminine sentiment breaking through the controls of masculine reason.)

Here is a case where the issue should have been, explicitly: To what extent should the new tragedy be tested by the rules for the Greek tragedy; and to what extent should it be recognized as a new species, requiring a new definition? Eventually, out of the muddle came the for-mula for the "well-made play," and the new ideals of entertainment were on their way.

Such ideas point eventually towards triviality as a "sound aesthetic demand"; for if the semiannual dramatic festivals of Athens were even-tually to be replaced by the Hollywooden art of an amusement industry that would sell its brand of theatrical wares to the same customers sev-eral times a week, not only should the depths of true catharsis be sac-rificed, but even the heroics of dignification must be used sparsely, ex-cept insofar as the mechanics of zooming and whining and bursting in modern adventure movies and war films can be considered as a childish species of dignification by heroics.

In general, the tragedy of admiration would dignify a cause or an institution by associating it with the grandeurs of suffering and risk. Cathartic functions may figure secondarily, but the "mimetics of hon-oring" is the major stress here. Perhaps such stress "positively" re-stylizes the "mimetics of supplication" that played so great a part in the Athenian tragedy, with its major emphasis upon catharsis.

As for our point about the civic nature of such catharsis, Plutarch makes several mentions of ostracism that are much to our purpose:

> At length the Athenians banished him (Themistocles), mak-ing use of the ostracism to humble his eminence and author-ity as they ordinarily did with all whom they thought too powerful, or, by their greatness, disproportionate to the equality thought requisite in a popular government. For the ostracism was instituted, not so much to punish the of-

fender, as to mitigate and pacify the violence of the envious, who delighted to humble eminent men, and who, by fixing the disgrace upon them, might vent some part of their rancour. (148)

The ostracism . . . was not usually inflicted on the poorer citizens, but on those of great houses, whose station exposed them to envy. (391)

As for the ostracism, every one was liable to it, whom his reputation, birth, or eloquence raised above the common level. (392)

They banished Aristides by the ostracism, giving their jealousy of his reputation the name of fear of tyranny. For ostracism was not the punishment of any criminal act, but was speciously said to be the mere depression and humiliation of excessive greatness and power; and was in fact a gentle relief and mitigation of envious feeling, which was thus allowed to vent itself in inflicting no intolerable injury, only a ten years' banishment. (396)

It was performed, to be short, in this manner. Every one taking an *ostracon,* a sherd, that is, a piece of earthenware, wrote upon it the citizen's name he would have banished, and carried it to a certain part of the market-place surrounded with wooden rails. First, the magistrates numbered all the sherds in gross (for if there were less than six thousand, the ostracism was imperfect); then, laying every name by itself, they pronounced him whose name was written by the larger number banished for ten years, with the enjoyment of his estate. As therefore, they were writing the names on the sherds, it is reported that an illiterate clownish fellow, giving Aristides his sherd, supposing him a common citizen, begged him to write *Aristides* upon it; and he being surprised and asking if Aristides had ever done him any injury, "None at all," he said, "neither know I the man; but I am tired of hearing him everywhere called the Just."

Do we not see here, in ostracism, a solution in one way (pragmatically) for the very condition which tragedy sought to solve in another way (symbolically, by cathartic ritual)?

As for the condition itself Plutarch is equally explicit:

> For, indeed, there was from the beginning a sort of con-
> cealed *split,* or seam, as it might be in a piece of iron, mark-
> ing the different popular and aristocratical tendencies; but
> the open rivalry and contention of these two opponents
> made the gash deep, and severed the city into the two parties
> of the people and the few. (190)

> At length, coming to a final contest with Thucydides which
> of the two should ostracise the other out of the country, and
> having gone through this peril, he (Pericles) threw his an-
> tagonist out, and broke up the confederacy that had been
> organised against him. So that now all schism and division
> being at an end, and the city brought to evenness and unity,
> he got all Athens and all affairs that pertained to the Atheni-
> ans into his own hands. (194)

In his essay on Solon, there is a succession of ideas (102–4) that
bears upon the tragic motivations: First, there is talk of Solon as de-
fender of the oracle at Delphi; this is followed by a discussion of "pollution" involving the "faction of Cylon"; this talk of "purifying and
sanctifying the city, by certain propitiary and expiatory lustrations"
leads into a Chorus-like meditation on the blindness of mankind—and
next proceeds:

> The Athenians, now the Cylonian sedition was over and
> the polluted gone into banishment, fell into their old quar-
> rels about the government, there being as many different
> parties as there were diversities in the country. The Hill
> quarter favored democracy, the Plain, oligarchy, and those
> that lived by the Seaside stood for a mixed sort of govern-
> ment, and so hindered either of the parties from prevailing.
> And the disparity of fortune between the rich and the poor,
> at that time, also reached its height; so that the city seemed
> to be in a truly dangerous condition and no other means for
> freeing it from disturbances and settling it to be possible but
> a despotic power.

Plutarch was clearly thinking of biography in tragic terms. Thus he
describes as a "spectacle worthy of pity and admiration" the occasion
when, owing to the threat of the Persians, Athenian elders and children
were sent away, despite entreaties. And the defeat of the Persians is foreshadowed in the best tragic style, when we read: "Xerxes placed himself
high up, to view his fleet, and how it was set in order," one authority
saying "he sat upon a promontory," and another: "upon those hills

which are called the Horns, where he sat in a chair of gold." Or this, of Pericles who had been embarrassed by a law of his own making:

> The present calamity and distress which Pericles laboured under in his family broke through all objections, and prevailed with the Athenians to pity him, as one whose losses and misfortunes had sufficiently punished his former arrogance and haughtiness. His sufferings deserved, they thought, their pity, and even indignation, and his request was such as became a man to ask and men to grant; they gave him permission to enrol his son in the register of his fraternity, giving him his own name. This son afterward, after having defeated the Peloponnesians at Argenusae, was, with his fellow-generals, put to death by the people.

Though Plutarch is indignant with another historian, whom he accuses of inventing incidents "to incite or move compassion, as if he were writing a tragedy," his own factual scruples are infused with the same spirit.

But the factuality is as scrupulous as he can make it. And he treats the whole era of Solon in terms of social improvements following the harsh laws of Draco, which had so drastically upheld the rights of property. (When Draco was asked why he made death the punishment for most offenses, according to Plutarch he replied: "Small ones deserve that, and I have no greater for the greater crimes." We wonder whether St. Augustine had the form of this epigram in mind when he said that all men in their depravity deserve eternal suffering in Hell, but God in his great mercy saves some.) Something halfway between financial and moral absolution is revealed in reference to the *seisacthea,* a cancelling of debts or "shaking off of burdens" here referred to as "relief," "disencumbrance," and "public sacrifice."

To this same period, fittingly, Plutarch assigns the rise of tragedy, though Solon (like Plato later) is said to have looked upon tragedy with disfavor. The enmity may have derived from the fact that the ruler, like Plato, was offering a rival system of "catharsis." Or tragedy itself in its beginnings may have shown a more rebellious cast. (The benevolent despot Pisistratus, for instance, is known to have closed the theatres—and we dare remember that, though Aristotle attributes the use of iambic metre in tragedy to its greater naturalness, he also tells us that it was first used in invective.)

But by introducing a wholly different species (the Plutarchian biography) as a bridge between two species of tragedy, we have again shifted from Poetics to aspects of symbolic action not directly analyzable in terms of Poetics alone. We permit ourselves these deflections, because our project as a whole concerns not Poetics alone but the analysis of language generally. And we must use whatever opportunities present themselves to point up the interrelationship among the realms.

Also, since we are here attempting to define the nature of Poetics, one convenient method of doing so is by antithesis, by considering the points at which linguistic analysis, to be complete, *requires* us to abandon the strictures of Poetics. Or perhaps we should better say that the abandonment is required, not so much by the desire to be complete as by the desire to be direct. For the extra-Poetic motives are *subsumed* in Poetics. Hence, there is a sense in which they are there, even when unmentioned. For this reason, the practitioner of Poetics, to the exclusion of other disciplines, might feel that he is thoroughness itself, as might a philosopher who writes on a subject so all-inclusive as "being" in general.

But even so fine a poet as Sir Philip Sidney, in an apology for poetry, clearly steps beyond the bounds of Poetics proper, when he writes of

> . . . the high and excellent Tragedy, that openeth the greatest wounds, and showeth forth the Ulcers, that are covered with Tissue: that maketh Kings fear to be Tyrants, and Tyrants manifest their tyrannical humors: that with stirring the effects of admiration and commiseration, teacheth, the uncertainty of this world, and upon how weak foundation gilden roofs are builded.‡

Platonic Transcendence

Though transcendence and "catharsis" may often be used as synonyms, there is also a sense in which a purely dialectical cleansing is better described as "transcendence," while "catharsis" better applies to dramatic cleansing by tears or laughter.

The resources and forms of dialectic have been discussed so often in these *Motivorum* books, we shall here try merely to sum up. Dialectical transcendence involves devices whereby a problematical term can be progressively redefined, until it has become transformed to the point where its problematical meaning has been surpassed, and what first looked *like* A can now be interpreted as non-A. When all the steps of transformation are present, the design is as follows: At the beginning,

---

‡ " 'Beyond' Catharsis" is followed by a lengthy, two-part section on "Catharsis (Second View)." This essay has been published in its entirety. The following essay is the penultimate section of the "Poetics, Dramatistically Considered" manuscript; the final section, "The Poetic Motive," has also been published in its entirety. Please consult the "Textual Introduction" for details. *Ed.*

there is a kind of dispersion, scatteredness, conflict among the terms; then the terms (which begin in the realm of mere opinion, imagery, appearance) are subjected to progressive ideological criticism by the give-and-take of controversy; this is an "Upward Way" moving towards some "higher" principle of unity; once this principle is found, a whole ladder of steps is seen to descend from it; thus, reversing his direction, the dialectician can next take a "Downward Way" that brings *him* back into the realm of dispersal, or diaspora, where he began; but on reentering, he brings with him the unitary principle he has discovered en route, and the hierarchal design he saw implicit in that principle; accordingly, applying the new mode of interpretation to his original problem, he now has the problem "placed" in terms of the transcendent, unitary, hierarchizing principle—and thus, instead of being merely scattered, the problematical element has become "structured," seen as part of a comprehensive context; thus, while it is still there, it is there "with a difference," and that difference makes all the difference.

For instance, in the Socratic erotic, the seeds of mere bodily love are placed in a terministic context whereby we finally become concerned with doctrinal insemination. Or whereas in the *Republic,* the division of labor begins as a problem; by the time we have completed the dialectical operations to which Plato subjects it in his upward climb towards a unitary, hierarchal vision of ideal justice, we find this same problem at once present but transcended (in the notion that each man should do that special work for which he is naturally most fitted).

We might point up the "diplomacy" in such a method by a perhaps somewhat unfair simplification thus: (1) Justice to be justice must be the *universalizing* of a principle, so that it applies equally to all; (2) The division of labor involves a *discriminatory* principle; (3) Plato's dialectic paradoxically *universalizes* this principle of *discrimination* by tying it to the universalistic assertion that everyone should do that for which he is naturally best fit; (4) A problem essentially economic is thus seen transcendently as a problem essentially ethical.

As regards such an idealistic solution in terms of principles, Marxist dialectic tried to interfere with the Platonist Upward Way by starting with the materialistic, or situational assertion that "justice can never rise higher than the material conditions permit." This statement would frustrate the particular kind of Platonist climb that is contrived in the *Republic.* But on the other hand, a materialist dialectic of history allows for its own kind of manipulations whereby the merely "empirical" nature of a given moment is transcended, as that moment becomes placed in a wider context, thus being interpreted as one rung in a ladder of "inevitable" developmental steps that are the Marxist equivalent of a Platonist hierarchy.

Imagery can play a dual role in such a process. At the beginning, there can be the imagery of mere sensory appearances, the realm of opinion and uncriticized perception. Then by ideology (the disciplined critique of ideas), this realm can be transcended. But though the discipline of ideas serves as a way of criticizing the naïveté of mere sensory opinions (the realm of appearances), ideas in turn must be transcended. For after all, they are but a symbol-system, and no symbol-system can be expected to serve as a wholly adequate description of reality. For insofar as reality is nonsymbolic and thus outside the realm of the symbol-systems by which we would describe it, to that extent reality is being described in terms of what it is not. At the point where we have gone from *sensory* images to ideas that transcend the sensory image, we might next go beyond such ideas in turn by introducing a "mythic" image (an image that is interpreted not literally but ironically, since it states the new position by analogy, and analogies must be "discounted"). Such use of "myth" as a step in a dialectic may carry the development across a motivational gulf by providing a new ground of assertion at some crucial point where a further advance is not attainable through strictly logical argument.

The Upward Way is contrived by a process of progressive abstraction and generalization, until the highest order of such development is reached—and this ultimate step will provide the necessary principle of unification, to be used on the way back. The "process of progressive abstraction and generalization" is along lines like this:

(1) beginning with such words for individual physical things as "table," "chair," "desk," we might group all such classes under the heading of "furniture";

(2) grouping furniture with such words as automobiles, plows, ammunition, we might class all these under the heading of "manufactured objects";

(3) manufactured objects in turn could be grouped with the output of mines, farms, lumber companies as "commodities";

(4) commodities could be grouped with animals, elements, people, under the head of "entities" or "beings";

(5) beyond all entities or beings there could be in turn a term for "being" in general.

Ordinarily, such dialectical operations are contrived in but a fragmentary way, the process being further concealed by the use of ideas that were never quite freed of their original linkage with sensory images. Thus the sensory image can play a double role since it also furtively performs the function of a mythic image. A behaviorist terminology treating of human motives in terms of strictly mechanistic processes would be an example of such a fragmentary dialectic. The same would be true of any attempt to make the findings in animal psychology serve as a total statement about human motives. A drastically truncated dialectic is implicit in all such *reductive* terminologies, which could be said to "transcend" a given motivational complexity by translating it into terms that by simplification impute to it an essence.

This ambiguity whereby idea and image merge through never having been formally divided also makes possible the adaptation of dialectic to purely narrative and lyrical developments. Cf. analysis of Keats's "Ode on a Grecian Urn," in K. Burke, *Grammar of Motives,* in which volume there is also a discussion of the *Phaedrus.* And an article "Three Definitions" (*Kenyon Review,* Spring 1951) analyzes along the same lines both Joyce's *Portrait of the Artist as a Young Man* and his story, "The Dead," in *Dubliners.* In all these, there are processes whereby a sheerly sensory image is given the function of a mythic image, as the context endows the sensory image with attributes that transcend its nature as a sheerly empirical object. Thus the image becomes a kind of "revelation," or "epiphany." (By reason of its place in a developing context, the Urn's nature as an empirical object becomes transcended; it takes on the role of a viaticum intermediating time and eternity. The mere image of the Urn as an object would be "sensory"; the vision of this same Urn as viaticum would be "mythic." In the *Portrait,* the bird girl comes to stand for Stephen's new Daedalian vocation. In "The Dead," a reference to snow on one of the character's galoshes and overcoat is finally revealed to have been the enigmatic annunciation of a vision that unites the living and the dead.)

The subject of death may be used as a dignifying device in this form. For instance, as regards the steps in the Platonist dialectic of Castiglione's *Book of the Courtier:*

> Fittingly, the change in the quality of motives is signalized at the start of the last book by a deathy note. Though the talks were supposedly held on four successive nights, as the author prepares to write out the record of the fourth discourse a "bitter thought" causes him to remember "that not long after these reasonings were heard, cruel death bereaved our house of three most rare gentlemen, when in their prosperous age and forwardness of honor they most flourished." The device is perhaps borrowed from Cicero, who uses it similarly to make the final section of his *De Oratore* more solemn. (*RM* 229)

The point is relevant for two reasons. First, there is an analogue of dying (with corresponding rebirth) in the very form of such dialectical operations. The Upward Way progressively divests the world of its particular sensuous immediacy; in this respect, the development towards the abstract and generalized is the technical equivalent of "mortification," though such a dying to one's original scheme of purposes is completed by birth into a new scheme of purposes (whereby everything is, as it were, shined on by the same sun, the unitary principle that was discovered en route, so that entities previously considered disparate can henceforth be seen as partakers of a single substance, through being bathed in a common light). Such systematic "dying" to sensory immediacy is sometimes called the *via negativa,* and is at the bottom of the process in negative theology whereby God becomes defined in terms of negatives: invisible, intangible, incomprehensible, unbounded, etc. But we should always be on the lookout for the compensatory ways whereby such divesting attains a corresponding mode of reinvesting, analogous somewhat to the fact that those who have been spiritualized by their faith are promised the return of their bodies in heaven. Or the analogy would be to the ways whereby, though money transcends the immediate sensuous reality of objects, and thus is in itself a kind of "mortification," it can enable people to buy more of the very objects which, in its "spiritual" nature as sheer symbol-system, it has "transcended."

But besides this "technical" kind of dying (implicit in the dialectical search for a unifying principle that, by reason of its very nature as a unifier lacks the positive particularity of immediate sensory objects), there is another reason for our considering the subject of death here. For Nietzsche's *Birth of Tragedy,* while condemning the Socratic dialectic as the death of tragedy, is nonetheless so tragic in temper that it stresses the mythic image of the "dying Socrates" as emblem of the dialectician's art. And we promptly realize how close the analogy is to the kind of "tragic dignification" the Christian doctrine got, thanks in large measure to the firmness with which the Pauline dialectic interwove it with the "mythic image" of the Crucifixion.

Nietzsche's own dialectic (in his attack upon dialectical modes of purgation!) begins with an application of the one-many alignment. He equates the principle of individuation with Apollo, and equates "Primordial Unity" with a band of revelers intoxicated in the worship of Dionysus. This principle of individuation is also equated with the aristocratic (the sense of propriety, of limits, embodied in such maxims as "know thyself" and "nothing to excess"); and the Chorus is equated with the primitively democratic, hovering on the edge of riot. And

while Greek tragedy is thus viewed as a merger of popular and aristocratic tendencies, there cluster about one or the other of the two poles
several other terms which a different kind of calculus would distribute
differently. For instance, music is equated with the Dionysian side of the
equation, though there was also the music of the Apollonian lyre. And
the visual element is equated with the Apollonian, owing to the strong
visual aspect of dreams, and the fact that the oracle of Apollo at Delphi
specialized in the interpretation of dreams and visions.

We need not here detail the particular ways in which Nietzsche
stacks his cards.[6] But we might note that a dream can be treated either
as a process of individuation (since it does present a specific sequence
of images) or as a kind of "Primordial Unity" that is prior to all con-
sciously differentiated motives. And we might note that, although the
principle of individuation can be embodied in aristocracy, there are also
democratic forms of individuation. In fact, individuation as a *principle*
is not exclusively equatable with any one social class, since it is not exclusively a social principle. Consider, for instance, Aquinas's treatment
of matter in general as the *principium individuationis*. Furthermore,
regarding dialectical processes in general, any expression or articulation may legitimately be considered as embodying a principle of individuation.

In fact, our whole notion of the relation between the "formless"
nature of a "pollution" and the sense of catharsis that can arise when
this *miasma* has been translated into terms of some particular process
from a beginning *through* a middle *to* an end involves a variant of the
Nietzschean dialectic. But we should have to observe that there is as
much "Primordial Unity" behind the Apollonian dream as behind the
Dionysian dance. On the other hand, after having said as much, we
must retrace our steps to the point of granting that scholarship does
seem to provide good backing for his point about Greek tragedy as
the marriage of conflicting social motives. And when he speaks of attempting to find his way through "the labyrinth of the origin of Greek
tragedy," we should only add that not only is the attempt to trace its
origins a labyrinth, but also its place of origin is itself a labyrinth, a
labyrinth of the inarticulate, *as brought into being by the ability to articulate.*

Our qualification in italics is most important here. A labyrinthine
tangle is not a mere jungle. It is a *confusion of paths already formed.*
The calculus we are using implies the assumption that only symbol-
using animals experience the Daedalian motive.

The most important point about Nietzsche's analysis, with reference to our present purposes, concerns his ironic treatment of the development, through Euripides, to the method of Socrates, and thus to

Platonic transcendence as a mode of cure in direct competition with kinds of tragic catharsis most perfectly embodied in Aeschylus and Sophocles. Our objection would be that his attacks upon Euripides and Socrates would seem to make them responsible for the civil situation with which they were coping.

The Nietzschean attack upon Socrates' "optimistic" cult of knowledge must be somewhat discounted. For it tends to conceal from us the essentially Dramatistic nature of the Platonic dialogue, with its stress upon the *personality* of a given doctrine. Also, ironically, Nietzsche's reference to the "dying Socrates" as his slogan for such doctrinal "erotic" (the "love of knowledge") tends to conceal the fact that the principle of victimage is there, though greatly altered, in the method itself. As with the Christian doctrine that was later to incorporate so much of Platonism, the absolute kill was eliminated, except for this one moment of inauguration.

Yet Christianity was to universalize and attenuate the principle in its regimens of "mortification"; and the give-and-take of a Platonic dialogue could be relevantly analyzed as an attenuated variant of the tragic principle ("learning through suffering") since the victimage involved one's methodic "suffering" of one's opponent in order that exposure to such counteraction might thus contribute to the mature revising of one's own position. The Dramatistic design remains strong, even in the next stage (which Nietzsche does not deal with), Aristotle's transforming of the Platonic dialogue into the scholastic catalogue; but here it survives in the sheer terminology (with its stress upon "action," "passion," and "purpose") rather than in the use of a method that itself imitates an "ordeal." (However, even a modicum of discovery through victimage could be said to survive in the systematic review and criticism of other doctrines with which Aristotle frequently begins the exposition of his own.)

We have already tried to indicate how the Platonist method lends itself to a kind of lyrical transcendence (including similar effects in "lyrical" novels). Such transcendence doesn't often arouse the "bodily" response that goes with group attendance at a tragedy designed to establish a sense of unity so radical as to seem "primordial." But there are also more contemplative modes of purgation. Indeed, the contemplative attitude in itself is a mode of purgation. And Aristotle showed his leanings in that direction when indicating that he preferred the written text of a tragedy to attendance at actual performances.

Though contemplative poetry, read in privacy, would rarely have the intense effect of tragedy witnessed by a uniformly responsive audience at a great public festival, today poets and novelists employ various antiquarian devices for imparting a "mythic" dimension to their works.

Judged sheerly as showmanship, this is apparently a substitute for the sense of the "marvelous" which the tragic playwright got, according to Aristotle, by suggesting the intervention of fate or the divine in the unfolding of the plot. Joyce is perhaps the writer who exploited such resources most thoroughly to give his story a "cosmic" dimension.

Also, by cutting ideas to a minimum and playing up images, the craftsman can suggest that in his story or poem there's "more than meets the eye." Or, when ideas are prominent, certain images can be made enigmatic if the explanation is left insufficient with regard to these particular moments. Another device is the merging of terms which are themselves midway between ideas and images, as were night, death, mother, poetry, a crossing, and a vision of the future all to be treated as somehow synonymous (along Whitmanite lines).

We may not be able, at this time, to complete our remarks on Comedy. But here is, roughly, the sort of things to be treated:

First, by using as a model the three comedies of Aristophanes on peace, we shall be able to dwell on the pleasing antics of peace.

We want to consider the relation between wholly cathartic laughter and derision.

We want to ask in particular about the role of "body-thinking" in Aristophanic comedy.

We want to inquire further about laughter, tears, and appetite, as regards the materials of poetic form.

Notes

1. To call such models "fragmentary" is not by any means to call them "wrong." For many purposes a narrower calculus may be precisely what is needed.

2. Somebody could do a picturesque job cataloguing the beginnings of our typical motion-picture plots. One, for instance: The police whistle in the darkness, the sound of running feet, the siren of the prowl car; finally, the shape hiding in the shadows. Or another: View of office building; camera climbs up side of building, pauses at one window on high floor; next we advance through outer offices, past clerks variously busy; door opens to inner office, where there is a troubled consultation of executives sitting around a big table. Or another: Camera approaching bridge over small stream; assorted sounds of domestic fowls; from other direction, herd of sheep being driven slowly towards bridge. Another: Bus pulls up at out-of-the-way bus stop; out steps girl noticeably incongruous with the surroundings; she hesitates, enters nearby beanery and approaches counterman, or perhaps goes to pay phone, while being eyed by local loafers dully curious. Or: Last-minute packing in preparation for a trip. Or: Students pouring out of building; apparently bell has just rung; camera finally settles on our hero, in some indicative situation—either very popular or very

lonesome. Or the types of beginnings that seem to have to fight their way through a conglomeration of fragmentary vistas, blaring music, credit lines on cast and staff, everything so urgently cluttered that one gets the feel of being rushed, crowded, and trampled into admiration even before he knows what the admiration is to be about. Or the misty sea scenes, while narrative voice of unseen speaker begins solemnly reminiscing, whereupon cut back to some years previously, and thus early there emerges a rebeginning; it is quite innocuous looking, in contrast with the previous solemnity; perhaps there are children playing. Etc.

Such a study could make a serviceable companion piece to George Polti's ingenious book on the Thirty-Six Dramatic Situations. And it might have the double value of making us more clearly aware of both platitudes and form; for such beginnings do indeed have the formal quality of being very definitely beginnings. And as considered from the standpoint of the relation between potentiality and actualization, the thought of beginnings qua beginnings is particularly engrossing. For the very idea of a beginning is quite paradoxical. Whereas the steps that follow the beginning can be said to actualize the potentialities of the beginning, the beginning can only be the actualization of its own potentialities; yet these potentialities include the ways in which the beginning *implicitly* contains what is to follow.

At this point, another problem enters: In his attempt to show how, in a well-formed work of art, the beginning implicitly contains what follows, the critic must also note wherein each step along the way is a *new* act, too. Prophesying after the event, the critic can treat *innovation* as though it were simply a kind of *deduction;* but innovation does not merely *obey* the proprieties of form, it also *creates* them. Every successive step in a work of art is, in a tiny way, like a political revolution in which the revolutionaries become conservative by setting up the laws that will prove them law-abiding. If the innovations succeed in convincing the critic, he can proceed to show that they are not departures, but "logically deducible" from the work's premises. If they don't succeed in convincing the critic, they are like revolutionaries who failed to make their position orthodox—and to that extent, the work is felt to "lack form." A work of art is logically deducible not in the sense that it *follows* a logic, but in the sense that it *makes* one. But though it *discovers* a consistency, once a consistency has been discovered that very nature as a consistency makes the relations among its parts "inevitable." So the critic, in his search for the work's consistency, must not be overzealous in showing how the beginning contains all that follows from it. Otherwise, his demonstration would be like showing that yesterday's traffic accident was implicitly foretold in the first three chapters of Genesis. The beginning sets up conditions that can be progressively narrowed down as the work proceeds. But though a category such as "cities of the United States" allows us next to pick some one city rather than another, there is a sense in which this choice is a "new act"—and so on down, as when we next pick one street in that city, then one house on that street, etc.

The process of poetic selection is complicated by the fact that many motives figure in the progressive narrowing (or enlarging!) from the beginning to its complete unfolding. And a manifold of motives calls more imperiously for a "pinpointing," quite as an earthquake shock is located by a comparison of the records from seismographs variously located. But even if an incident is "foreshadowed," when it comes it is a novelty, a bundle of particulars not contained in the signs that "foretold" it. In this sense, each step in a work of art is a new thing, not "deducible" from its beginnings. And you could as justly analyze it as an *addition* to the steps that preceded it.

3. Compare these four highly generalized traits listed in the *Poetics* with the more particularized character recipes in the *Rhetoric*—and then, going a step further, consider how, when any one play is being discussed, our terms for the description of character would have to be more specific even than the recipes in the *Rhetoric* or the *Ethics*. The notable paradox here is in the fact that, though the study of the characters in a particular play eventually involves combinations that are unique, the formal recipes for tragic character are the most highly generalized of all. The same is true as regards the idea of "fitness" *(decorum, to prepon)* in classical theory. Each moment of a literary work must have its peculiar way of being "fit." Poems being unique, Poetics is forever trying to *universalize the unique*. However, its task but makes more apparent an embarrassment that applies to all language.

4. Some instances of the way in which Shakespeare uses pity in his fourth acts are discussed in our "Othello: An Essay to Illustrate a Method," *Hudson Review* (Summer 1951).

5. In connection with some work that a former Bennington student, Miss Shaila Rubin, did on Corneille's *Cinna* under the present writer's guidance ("A Study of Corneille's *Cinna,*" Bennington College Senior Thesis, 1955), it was found that the Cornelian terminology lent itself well to four categories, tentatively called the Imperial Order, the Natural Order, the Universal Order, and the Counter-Order.

Since the play explicitly concerns a political conspiracy (a plan to assassinate the emperor of Rome), the sheer nature of the subject matter seemed to offer sufficient justification for beginning with the imperial order and treating the others as derivatives from this. The other three are "implied" in the terms for the Imperial Order, inasmuch as every kind of government must be grounded in nature, and nature can in turn be thought of as grounded in a realm beyond nature, while by definition the motives that are counter to an Imperial Order necessarily take form with regard to the order they are opposing (and thus, however roundabout, both the Imperial Order and its direct Counter-Order are part of the same motivational complex).

As regards the Imperial Order: Here would be such words as *empire, état, puissance, souverain, maître*. Various related terms may be spun from this source. Thus, if the empire is upheld by loyalty, loyalty in turn is motivated by the value of dignity, which is identified with empire and is treated as the moral reward of loyalty. Loyalty also implies duty—and accordingly there is a cluster of terms: *devoir, servir, soumission, esclave, sacrifice, supplice, forfaits, mort* (the ideas of "death" becoming strongly tinged with more general ideas of such mortification as might go with submission). Service leads into such correlatives as *honneur, gloire, vertu*. And honor in turn serves as rational ground for an act of *vengeance*, which becomes interwoven with connotations of moral indignation.

From the standpoint of Poetics and in accordance with our previous remark about the use of religion as a *poetical device* regardless of the poet's actual beliefs, the Universal Order would be treated as a means of adding scope and dignity to the tragedy in general, and to the Imperial Order in particular. Here would belong: *univers, ciel, destin, sort, la volonté des dieux,* which merges with *l'amour de patrie.* In its relation to love and mercy *(clémence)* this Order provides the ultimate source of the play's subtitle: *La Clémence d'Auguste. Générosité* perhaps stands at the meeting point between the Imperial and Universal Orders.

The threats of disorder, or Counter-Order, give rise to an attitude which views the Order as *tyrannie,* such words as *liberté* and *affranchir* being conceived in this spirit. Here would figure such acts and attitudes as *ingratitude, conjuration, trahison. Vengeance* may be either criminal or emancipatory, depending upon the position from which it is viewed (and much of Corneille's effectiveness derives from his skill at constructing a plot whereby these positions abruptly shift).

Words for the Natural Order, such as *sang, coeur, noir, mains, tempêtes, larmes* are as a rule used so closely in connection with the social order, the reader will find few works in which the sociopolitical connotations implicit in our ideas of natural objects are so clearly revealed.

The terministic approach which was here proposed in connection with Corneille was worked out more fully in our essay "The First Three Chapters of Genesis."

6. Lessing's principle that each art must be evaluated in terms of its particular resources as a medium becomes transformed into the notion that different arts represent correspondingly different *psychological motivations.* Such can be the case, in the psychic economy of an individual person, for whom eye and ear might take on contrasting connotations. But for other persons, the psychological alignment might be quite different, with much in the "ear" category which a different mentality would class in the "eye" category.

3

"Glimpses into a Labyrinth of Interwoven Motives": Selections from "A Symbolic of Motives"

Kenneth Burke

Imitation (Mimesis)

Individuation and Amplification

A philosopher might write, say, about, "The Conflict Between Love and Duty." But whenever a drama is written around this topic, the treatment must be in terms of some particular situation or situations, with characters having particular personality traits, and so on. Such considerations open into a world of novelistic information as endless as the range and variety of description in merchandising catalogues, plus all the terminology of moral, social, political, religious, psychological placement that makes up the lore of human relations (the gluttony for details typical of writers like Balzac and Zola).

As against this almost limitless lore of materials and impressions, for sheerly heuristic purposes let us imagine an overly strict game of this sort: If the story concerns a certain agent who is about to perform a certain act in a certain scene, the agent must be described only by such traits as pertain to the act, in equipping the agent for the act, or in causing the reader to feel that this act is wholly proper to the agent. (Included here will be any details that portentously foreshadow the act.) Similarly, the scene in which the act is to take place should be described only in terms of details needed for the act—and similarly, the description of the instrument needed for the act will be confined to absolutely necessary details.

Thus, if the act is typical of both a man and a woman (for instance, writing a letter) then the sex of the agent will not be specified. If the act is to be, say the buying of new shoes, the observation that the agent's present shoes are worn out would be relevant; but it would be excessive to say in exactly what respects they are worn out. If the act is to involve a theft, one might foreshadow it by noting that the agent looks furtive; but one could specify that the agent has a furtive *glance* only if a glance is to figure specifically in the performing of the theft. If the act is to involve murder by drowning, the description of the scene should specify water; but one shouldn't say whether the water is fresh or salt, cold or warm, clear or muddy, unless this distinction made a difference. (For instance, if the murder was to imply also a dishonoring of the victim, a reference to muddy water might be in order.) Or if the murder is to be accomplished by gunfire, one should not specify the calibre of the gun unless this detail serves either to account for the slaying or to provide evidence for the detection of the murderer. Finally (and perhaps here's the one limitation in which a writer could most easily concur), the purpose of the act should be kept to its minimum. For instance, in specifying that the aim of the act was to rob a bank, it might be excessive to specify why the robber wanted the money.

Though writers would find such rules intolerable, there are kinds of narrative in which economy of this sort comes close to full realization, such as: anecdotes that build up to a punch line; case histories cited to illustrate some point in a scientific exposition; Aesop's fables; parables, histories, "acts" of Biblical cast. By comparison, the vaunted economy of writers like Hemingway or De Maupassant looks quite garrulous. Dramatic dialogue omits much; but as soon as it is to be staged, the actors must fill in with a whole catalogue of histrionic routines (for instance, the highly novelistic kind of accessories prescribed by the school of Stanislavsky).

There are many compelling reasons for such particularization, beginning with the fact that imagery naturally makes for individuation. The most obvious need for "excessive" thoroughness of description is confronted in historical novels, or any works designed to establish the "reality" of a background removed in time or place from that "natural" to the reader. Thus, the "perfect" paradigm for a story by Walter Scott would be: chapter 1, description of general conditions in some past era of Scottish history; chapter 2, description of a forest in that era; chapter 3, description of the costumes, weapons, bundles, and relationships of a band of men making its way through that forest. (Surely, *Ivanhoe* begins thus "in principle.") Often, and with much less justification, stories that begin by a leap *in medias res* end by giving us as much detail, though in a more scrambled fashion. A clutter of personal and scenic specifications is scattered about, presumably for "atmosphere" —

and who is to say when a story has details enough to give it "atmosphere"? The reader's observation is enlisted much as if he were a detective inspecting the scene of a crime and admonished to take note of everything because he could not yet be sure which items, if any, would turn out to be the significant ones.

In any case, it is obvious that a story built around one particular background of motives should not be written in exactly the same fashion for readers who are as familiar with these motives at first hand as for readers to whom such a background is "news." What could be more "realistic" than a primitive jungle? Yet it can be "romantic" in its literary appeal to the imagination of an inveterate city dweller, who need never confront its reality. People who have experienced such a background at first hand are more like "specialists" in this field; the others are more like "amateurs"—and many observations needed for the amateurs would seem garrulous to the specialists.

In his later works, James Joyce found an ingenious solution for this problem. He wrote for the most exacting of specialists, demanding of them an equipment which in very many instances they could not possess. Under tests so strenuous, his readers were in an aesthetic position analogous to the moral condition which Luther attributed to all mankind; namely, they could not possibly "keep the commandments" (that is, they would necessarily miss the relevance of many statements). Whereupon there rose up another group of specialists, the dedicated band of Joycean exegetes, critical Jesuits, who devoted themselves to the task of making Joyce's difficulties viable to amateurs. Other writers often rely on such critical goodwill somewhat.

Many different principles of propriety may be embodied in such "revelations." Besides the general criterion of "atmosphere" (which comes close to being a catchall, and can thin out like the higher areas of the earth's atmosphere itself) there is the almost equally extensive range of "foreshadowings." If, for instance, as regards the opening sentence of Ernest Hemingway's *For Whom the Bell Tolls*, one were to bear down on the first detail ("He lay flat on the brown-pine-needled floor of the forest," etc.) and were to ask, "Why 'flat'?" etc., the answer is in the last sentence of the book: "He could feel his heart beating against the pine needle floor of the forest." The opening posture is repeated, but with a notable difference that sums up the plot of the novel.

Or near the opening of Virginia Woolf's *Mrs. Dalloway*, we read:

> What a lark! What a plunge! For so had it always seemed to
> her, when, with a little squeak of the hinges, which she
> could hear now, she had burst open the French windows and
> plunged at Bourton into the open air. How fresh, how calm,

stiller than this of course, the air was in the early morning;
like the flap of a wave; the kiss of a wave; chill and sharp
and yet (for a girl of eighteen as she then was) solemn, feeling as she did, standing there at the open window, that
something awful was about to happen; looking at the flowers . . . etc.

Suppose that we bore down on those words "plunge" and "plunged."
Surely, we'd find the answer, worked out piecemeal, in other parts of
the text, thus: page 44, "as felt often as she stood hesitating one moment on the threshold of her drawing-room, an exquisite suspense, such
as might stay a diver before plunging while the sea darkens and bright-
ens beneath him, and the waves" etc.; page 54, " . . . as if to catch the
falling drop, Clarissa (crossing to the dressing-table) plunged into the
very heart of the moment"; page 55, "Her evening dresses hung in
the cup-board. Clarissa, plunging her hand into the softness, gently detached the green dress"; page 270, " . . . kiss and caress the snouts
of adorable chows; and then all tingling and streaming, plunge and
swim"; and then, on page 281, just a few pages from the end of the
book, there is the revealing reference to Septimus, the psychogenically
impotent suicide with whom Clarissa identified herself, and who had
leapt to his death by deliberately falling on rusty spikes, "But this young
man who had killed himself—had he plunged holding his treasure?"

Judged terministically, the question of propriety here would involve
us in other details, notably flowers, waves (which would lead in turn to
moths), and the many references to crossing (Septimus, on page 127, is
called "a border case"), all eventually tying in with the unresolved issue
of homosexual and heterosexual love that repeatedly recurs in Mrs.
Woolf's fiction (the love of woman for woman attaining its ultimate formulation thus, on page 47: "Then, for that moment, she had seen an
illumination; a match burning in a crocus; an inner meaning almost
expressed," a formula that, besides tying in with the flower theme, also
gives special significance to a favorite word, "moment").

Considerations of this sort lead eventually into enigmas that would
take us still farther afield. For instance, it is a simple phonetic fact that
the heroine's name is made of the same consonantal elements (c-l-r-s) as
compose the epithets applied to her father: "querulous" (62), "careless-
ness" (118), though the order is slightly scrambled. Of Peter Walsh, the
suitor whom she had refused to marry, it is said, on page 53: "Always when she thought of him she thought of their quarrels for some
reason"—and there's the c-r-l-s set again. We find part of the combination (the c-r-l) in the reference to Clarissa's daughter as "queer-looking"
(84). The whole four sounds are present, with an m added, in reference

to Peter Walsh on page 60; "the *same queer look.*" If we are allowed to stretch across a semicolon, we find all four consonants in the combination applied to Septimus, page 38: "the man *looking queer; so* that. . . . " They figure again when, Septimus having asked his wife to try on another woman's hat, she says, page 219: "But I must *look so queer!*" But Septimus himself only gets three-fourths of the ingredients, page.. 126: "To look at, he might have been a *clerk,*" though a bit above that, there was a reference to him and his wife in connection with "*queer-looking* armchairs." And when Clarissa's highly honored but not sexually gratified husband is moving towards his act of buying flowers for her, is not the problematic theme enigmatically present (171) in the description: "The speed of the morning traffic slackened, and single carts rattled *carelessly* down half-empty streets"? Or, turning things around, might we not also say that Clarissa's cult of visual sensation is in its way "queer-looking" (or that "Clarissa" and "queer look" are, in an enigmatic way, interchangeable terms)?

As regards terministic "enigmas" of this sort, much of a work's internal consistency is lost on the reader, and does not ordinarily reveal itself except through the kind of postmortem anatomizing that the printed word makes possible. As most of such effects are lost in translation from one language to another, so they readily become lost even within a given language, to the extent that each writer has his own idiom that everyone else must speak with an accent. And there is the further fact that an author usually has no need to inquire into such relationships. In selecting names, epithets, backgrounds, etc. for his characters, all he need ask is whether they "sound right" or "feel right" to him. And if he is sensitive and exacting enough, his choices will naturally embody principles of internal consistency that need not explicitly concern anyone, unless one happens to be interested (as critics are or should be) in tracking down any and all principles of internal consistency. For be they deliberate or not, *they are there;* and the critic should, above all, be concerned with what is there.

Both the selection and order of details can be guided by theoretical considerations, as is so often the case in *The Divine Comedy,* which is remarkable for its welding of the schematic and the intuitive. By the "schematic," I have in mind his use of scene-act ratios in such a way that the sinners get in hell the quality of scene corresponding to the quality of their sinful acts on earth. By "intuitive," I have in mind the particulars in terms of which he works out such ratios. For instance, in canto 18 the flatterers are depicted as "dipped in excrement" *(attuffata in uno stereco);* and in canto 8, the circle of the wrathful and sullen who were likened to swine dipped in swill, the same verb figures: *attuffare in questa broda.*

Beyond the use of imagery to illustrate ideas, there is the use of
imagery in lieu of ideas (as per William Carlos Williams's formula, "no
ideas but in things," which is to say, in images). And there is, of course,
the puzzled pilgrimage through the world of particulars. If one begins
with this, only in glimpses one finds out what some particular object
happens to "stand for." (Thus, one could offer a lewd explanation for
Williams's much mentioned red wet wheelbarrow glistening among the
white hens. A doughty, handy vehicle that! Or are we crowding things
here? For the poem refers, more generally, to chickens.) Reversing the
direction, one gropes towards some such overall frame as Dante started
from. With Thales, one holds in effect that the world is "full or gods"
(another way of saying what Goethe had his Chorus Mysticus say at
the end of *Faust: Alles Vergängliche/Ist nur ein Gleichnis,* or what Bau-
delaire said in his sonnet *Correspondances* about the *confuses paroles*
of Nature's temple, and how *L'homme y passe à travers des forêts de
symboles).* In brief, insofar as man is likely to be himself by "anthropo-
morphizing" everything despite his efforts to the contrary, anything he
observes is likely to have the form of himself as observer. But the modes
of such duplication are usually concealed (possibly in part because the
meanings are shifty, hence lack the uniformity that would be needed
before we could work out a whole reality of expectations with regard
to them). Freud indicates certain sexual ambiguities that can be concealed in such particulars. In my *Rhetoric,* I tried to indicate how social
"spirits" could be contained in them as in "soul boxes." (Indeed, we
can also catch glimpses of such "spirits" in the quasi-natural realm of
Freudian sexuality, as I there tried to indicate.)

The hypothetical rule on which we began this section, the test of
economy whereby no specification would be mentioned unless it figured
in the action, may help us force ourselves to discover how many kinds
of propriety there may be in incidental forms of this sort. I indicated a
great many more in my discussion of incidental form (in the *Lexicon
Rhetoricae* section of *Counter-Statement).* And we could probably include here all the figures in the old rhetoric books, such as Quintilian's.
Usually quite rational tests of order would be involved, even where
more diaphanous motives also figure. See, for instance, in Virginia
Woolf's diary for September 7, 1924. After a reference to present par-
ticiples, which she finds "very useful on my last lap of *Mrs. D.,*" she
continues: "There I am now—at last at the party, which is to begin in
the kitchen, and climb slowly upstairs."

Often such tests of order are not noticed by the reader. This one,
for instance, is not likely to be. As a matter of fact, the movement begins: "Lucy came running full tilt downstairs" (250). On page 252,
though, "There, they were going upstairs," the party is still being seen

from the standpoint of the servants. On pages 260, 266, 271, there are references to guests mounting the stairs as seen through Clarissa's eyes. But on page 265, the Prime Minister had come and already was leaving: Clarissa "saw the Prime Minister go down the stairs." And in the back of her mind there is the theme of the other descent (279–81), Septimus's plunge: "Always her body went through it first, when she was told, suddenly, of an accident; her dress flamed, her body burnt. He had thrown himself from a window. Up had flashed the ground; through him, blundering, bruising, went the rusty spikes." And the thought of his death (involving thoughts on death in general as "defiance," and "attempt to communicate," an "embrace," there is an associational shift to a remembrance of herself, before marriage, "in white," descending the stairs, and going to meet the girl she loved—whereat we note that the reference to crossing figures also, page 51: "going downstairs, and feeling as she crossed the hall 'if it were now to die 'twere now to be most happy' ").

All told, though the account of the party, which is used in *Mrs. Dalloway* as the grand finale, is conceived quite schematically in terms of ascent, the scheme leads into reciprocal notions of descent, and the two shade off into a tangle of motives both social and sexual (social climbing and the sexual fall, while the fall, in turn, involves homosexual attitudes towards heterosexual deflowering, a psychic accountancy that was ambiguously foreshadowed in the book's opening sentence: "Mrs. Dalloway said she would buy the flowers herself"). In this sense, even if we had specifically noted the descriptive design of the progress from the kitchen via the "climb slowly upstairs," such conscious perception of the writer's design *as stated in her diary* would not by any means have exhausted the "logic" of the movement. Yet there would be a certain gain in noting this design for its own sake (at least, if one happens to like that sort of thing, as does this correspondent).[1]

Primarily, however, we are here concerned with the fact that the entelechial principle in imitation tends to dissolve into what the old rhetorics called "amplification": modes of restatement that are sometimes justified only on the pedestrian grounds that a mulling over a certain kind of details may be needed merely to sustain the attention upon a topic over a stretch of time long enough for the point to "sink in." And as we have shown, "amplification" in turn may sometimes dissolve into possibilities of duplication whereby the use of "imitation," in even the most realistic of books, is found to impinge upon an enigmatic dimension. For insofar as the symbol-using animal approaches "reality" in terms of symbols, and insofar as "the received is in the receiver according to the nature of the receiver," then in the last analysis, the forms of poetic imitation will be found to reflect the logic of the symbol-systems in terms of which the imitation is conceived. We may disagree as to what kind of "likeness" *(Gleichnis, correspondance)* will ultimately be found intrinsic to the forms of symbolicity. For the present, we need but affirm the *principle* whereby "imitation," in the realistic sense of the term, dissolves into a logological equivalent of the "transcendental" (in the technical sense that the word "plunge," as analyzed with reference to its use in *Mrs. Dalloway*, can be said to "transcend" its sheerly dictionary meaning, giving glimpses into a labyrinth of interwoven motives).

The Language of "Thisness"

General and Particular

There are several places we might use as our text for this chapter. For instance, we might start with an old scholastic battle. Whereas Thomas Aquinas had treated matter as a "principle of individuation," Duns Scotus proposed to get around this problem by *beginning with* the concept of an individual "thisness," *(haecceitas)*. The amount of reasoning involved in the controversy is prodigious. Scotus was on the road that led into nominalism, though he himself was decidedly not a nominalist. But you can get there the quick way via Edmund Wilson's title for some early plays of his: *This Room & This Gin & These Sandwiches*. (The formula is from a sentiment expressed by a flighty character in one of the plays).

Or we might recall how greatly considerations of this sort exercised Goethe, doubtless in keeping with the fantastic genius of that German prefix *ur-* (roughly, "fore-" or "pre-") which has never ceased to entrance me. As used in German, from this one syllable alone there could be bred a whole line of great Idealistic metaphysicians. For, to transcend the workaday world, all you need do is take any word, however unpretentious, and put an *ur-* in front of it—whereupon, lo! you're in the realm of the basically primeval; nay more: you confront ready possibilities of shifts between temporal priority and logical priority (shifts between metaphysics and myth) such as I discuss at some length in my book on *The Rhetoric of Religion)*.

Thus, as soon as Goethe began studying plants, he plunged into speculations on the *Urplanze*. Or when he wrote on "polarity" as a fundamental principle of nature, it became *Urpolarität*. In optics, he talked of an *Urphänomen*, which would be found not just in an original *(anfänglich)* contrast, but in one that was *uranfänglich*. He sought for the prototype *(Urbild)*. He wrote an *Urfaust* that preceded the first and second parts we now usually study. He saw in Proteus the principle of the primal *(ursprünglich)* identity of all differences. And he used many other words in the same spirit. For instance, he talked of unoriginal virtue, to match original ("hereditary") sin *(Erbtugend Erbsünde)*. He considered granite the *Grundveste unserer Erde* (the "basic foundation of our earth," *Veste des Himmels* being the firmament). And he held that there is a "world spirit" speaking to the "human spirit" *(Weltgeist, Menachengeist)*. And in the second part of *Faust*, the realm of "The Mothers" (a theme that would seem to have had an affinity with Paracelsus's notion of *matrices rerum*), was a mythically personalized principle of ultimate human motivation, obviously related to the often-quoted last two lines of the work's conclusion: *"Das Ewig-Weibliche/ Zieht uns hinan."*

Yet at the same time, he always insisted that such firsts were to be found not *behind* the phenomena, but were themselves the ultimates. And though he sometimes called them "ideas," they presumably differed from the Platonic archetypes in that they were to be found in the concrete materials of experience.

Or, for a third text, we might consider the opening pages of Hegel's volume on the *Phenomenology of Spirit*. First asking about the "This," then dividing it into the "Here" and "Now," he next dwells on the metaphysical paradoxes that can be spun from the fact that if, at nighttime, I write down, "It is now night," when I look at the sentence in the daytime the *is* will be found to have contained an *is not*. The Universal This must be joined with a concrete sensory This, to be immediately a this, here and now. Etc.

For the metaphysical ranging that is possible here, the reader is referred to Hegel. For our purposes, we can be content merely to confront the simpler *linguistic* situation, namely, that anything can grammatically meet the tests of a "this," simply by being the subject of a sentence. In its *immediacy,* as an entity here and now, each existing thing has its own unique and concrete thisness—yet the *word* "this" can be applied to any and all such particulars. In brief, without regard to the "metaphysics" of the case, there is a linguistic situation common to all subjects of a sentence whereby they can be referred to by the use of the demonstrative "this," though there can be vagueness as to just what is being classed under the general head of the "pointed to." (For instance, is one pointing west, or to a house due west, or to a door in the house, or to a keyhole in the door, or to the key, etc?) Contexts, either verbal or situational, can help make the demonstrative "this" more precise— but in itself, as a means of classification, its "thisness" makes it assume rather the nature of an "allness.")

Thus, when considering the language of poetry, we must always keep reminding ourselves that the so-called concrete terms especially sought by poets are in essence quite *generic*. We must keep remembering that words like "fish," "star," "rain," "run," "see," "bright," "sweet," etc. are terms for classes or categories of things, operations, and qualities (an admonition to which Bertrand Russell's analysis of language makes us particularly sensible).

"Concrete" Words Are Abbreviations for Situations

In ways that were considered somewhat in my *Permanence and Change* (for instance, "Examination of a Case Described by Rivers," Hermes edition, 136–42) and that will be discussed more fully later in this text, such words are really abbreviations for the kinds of *situation* in which they can appear. In this respect, they are like words for family relationships (mother, father, brother, sister, etc.) that one learns first of all in connection with a specific *personal* situation. Thus, for instance, "Mother" would originally mean something like "one particular person in one particular set of circumstances in which there are various needs and discomforts with regard to which this person acts with regard to me."

I am not very proud of this translation, for even in its vagueness it is overexact. In particular, the formula may suggest too sharp a distinction between "self" and "not-self." As Hegel's analysis makes clear, awareness of a *situational* complex is a necessary condition of self-awareness. But at least the quoted combination serves to indicate the point I would bring out; namely, that the word for a family relative is first of all a personal "this" rather than a "universal," generic term for a certain family relationship common to many; yet, at the same time, its "thisness" is really *situational,* applying not just to some isolable "thing," but to one distinctive aspect common to many different sets of circumstances (for instance, one notable ingredient common to various hunger situations, sleep situations, fear situations, etc., quite as the undefined "self" is also common to these several situations).

If we think of the human body as a physical participant in the nonsymbolic situations of sheer material motion, and if we think of symbolic action as the logological counterpart of "mind" or "spirit," then the Thomist view of "matter" as the *principium individuationis* is found to be quite relevant for our purposes. A certain kind of individuality is implicit in the sheer physical "centrality of the nervous system" whereby the food that this particular body consumes or the pains that this particular body suffers are exclusively "mine." But the word "mine" belongs to language as a *collective* medium of expression. Like "this," for all its apparent particularity of reference, it is a universal, and applicable under appropriate conditions to *everybody.* Hence, though analysis of the terminologies perfected by individual poets clearly discloses respects in which each such idiom is unique (as with our references to some uses of the word "plunge" in a book by Virginia Woolf), the communicative nature of symbol-systems also reenforces a kind of awareness that transcends individuality. (Indeed, when a younger child first learns the word "mine" by hearing it spoken by his older brother, Joseph, he may not understand the word as having anything to do with personal possession, a distinction or property he has not yet grasped; rather, he may take it to have such a situational meaning as: "the sort of toys Joseph will not allow me to play with when he is around.")

In sum, we'd probably come closest to the roots of all poetic terminology by thinking of all primary words after the analogy of proper names, names that also *implied ingredients of the situations in which the bearers of these proper names happened to participate.* (Possibly we catch a glimpse of such motives behind the fact that, whereas the Franciscans had much to do with the development of nominalism, St. Francis himself spoke of "Brother Sun," "Sister Water," "Brother Ass, the body," etc. Poverty, in such a view, would be a kind of *ur*-motive conceived in terms of personality, as Lady Poverty, ultimately present at all crucial moments, like Goethe's "Mothers," a sort of personalized absolute, representing a quasi-Adamite kind of spiritual nudism.) And the poet's search for essence would involve a temptation towards "regression" in the sense that, if the poet would meditate profoundly enough, say, on the word "dog," he must eventually come to the sources of its meaning as an ingredient in moody situations of his own childhood. (Here is the point at which the mythic "temporizing of essence," the search for definition in terms of some *ur*-condition, overlaps upon a realm of motives touched upon by Freud in his search for the "primal scene," though we shall later find cause to consider how the "primal" and the "entelechial" can become confused, in a quasi-eschatological merging of "first" and "last" things.)[2]

The importance of this stress upon the *situational* aspect of any term for the *individual* becomes obvious when we consider any one character in a drama or novel. Conceivably, you might do a special "portrait" of this one figure. Yet could you do so in any but a most superficial manner, unless you discussed that character's relations to the *dramatis personae* in general? Though the titular role of Hamlet has given us a "universal" (whereby we can observe that "So-and-so is the Hamlet type"), could anyone talk adequately about that character in Shakespeare's play without telling us about his relations to his father, his mother, his uncle, Ophelia, Polonius, etc? Indeed, could *any* character be what he is, except insofar as he is an *ingredient in the situations* in which he acts or attitudinizes? We are but contending that this

Dramatistic truism should be remembered when we speculate on matters to do with the essence of an individual's thisness.

In sum, the problem splits two ways: First, there is the fact that words for even the most personal of entities are "shorthand" for the situational backgrounds in which such individual persons or things or topics participate either actually or "in principle"; and second, there is the fact that the ultimate public identity of a word (its "lexical" value) resides in its usability as a "universal." Such "usability" allows for either particular personal application of the word "Caesar" to the assassinated Julius Caesar or for the extension of the word to designate imperial types of rulers in general, along with variants like *Czar* and *Kaiser*. And even when applied specifically to one historic individual, it is found to possess the rudiments of a higher classification in the sense that under this same head would be included relations to Brutus that are quite different from relations to Antony or Pompey, etc. (Another way of putting this would be: Caesar is not the "same person" in relation to Brutus as to Calphurnia, etc. since his nature as a representative ingredient of a "Caesar-Calpurnia-*et-al.* situation" is not identical with his nature as a representative ingredient of a "Caesar-Brutus-*et-al.* situation").

"Universalizing" a Plot

But we have not yet introduced all the elements needed for this chapter. We should certainly include, for instance, the observations in chapter 17 of the *Poetics,* where Aristotle shows how to outline a plot. From the standpoint of our present concerns, the important thing to note about such outlines, besides their brevity, is their use of *generalized* terms. For instance, his sample outline of Euripides' *Iphigeneia in Tauris* makes no mention of Iphigeneia or Orestes by proper name. She is "a certain maiden who had been offered in sacrifice," etc., and he is referred to as "the brother of the priestess," etc. Similarly, the *Odyssey* is said to be about "a certain man who has been abroad many years." Penelope and Telemachus are designated thus: "Back home . . . his wife's suitors are plotting to kill his son." And the episodes detailing the dangers and hardships of Ulysses' voyages are treated thus summarily: "After grievous sufferings, he reaches home."

Perhaps we should note in an aside, for possible relevance to contemporary concerns with patterns of "myth," that despite their brevity both outlines mention how the character was *saved*. (The Greek noun and verb here used are from the same root the New Testament word for Christ as Savior.) Yet in the extant version of the *Poetics* there is no specific concern, along the lines of contemporary anthropology, with Greek tragedy as a partial secularization of religious rites. But I should hasten to qualify that statement. Aristotle makes it perfectly clear that Attic tragedy was derived from such rites. But naturally, his great stress upon the entelechial principle of consummation directs attention to the artistic fulfillment of such trends rather than to their incunabula. The important consideration is what they had become rather than what they had been. And in any case, the discussion of such matters would fit best with the observations on "catharsis" that were presumably in the lost portion of the treatise.

Unless we are willing to make much of a little, contemporary Aristotelian purists can feel quite justified in rejecting the concerns of modern literary anthropologists. But, in line with what we previously said with regard to Croce's notion of historical "palimpsests," we should always consider these methodologically discomforting possibilities: A subject may be omitted from discussion either because it never crossed the writer's mind or because he took it for granted.

Generalized Outline of *Mrs. Dalloway*

If it were not imperative to hurry on, we might pause here, to experiment at length with "Aristotelian" summaries of modern works. Whatever one may say against them from the "belletristic" point of view (and I must admit that they are not usually very entertaining), it is a sound pedagogical fact that, in thus asking ourselves just what are the rudiments of a given plot, we are forced to face a text directly. And as regards contemporary writings, the task of thus deciding on an outline often helps make clear notable divergencies between literary species. For instance, since we happen already to have used Virginia Woolf's novel, *Mrs. Dalloway*, as an example, we might round things out by giving a tentative generalized outline of that novel:

A *woman* in her early fifties, in a metropolis on a sunny morning of late spring, is being sensitive to the moods and impressions of the present moment, while recalling her past (particularly the bloom of her youth), and planning for the immediate future (a party she is to give on the evening of the same day). Several of the persons whom she had known previously (particularly one woman and one man who had been close friends of hers but whom she had not seen for many years) come variously into contact with her, or people her thoughts. There is also an enigmatic figure, a neurotic man of thirty, whom she does not know or come into direct contact with, but with whose suicide, which takes place that same day, she strongly identifies. The story culminates in an account of the party, including episodes when, alone with herself and her reveries, she meditates on her odd sense of oneness with the suicide and with an old woman whom she does not know but whom she watches preparing to retire in an opposite apartment.

This is about 60 words longer than Aristotle's outline for the story of Iphigeneia, and more than 125 words longer than his outline for the *Odyssey*. As he points out, the episodes are what makes epics longer than dramas—and we already noted how he telescoped them into a few words.

Obviously, some of the details I have introduced could be omitted. But if we did omit them, would we have an adequate outline for this particular kind of story? In fact, I think that there would be good grounds for adding several further clauses, such as: (1) The advance of the day is noted by the striking of a public clock (it's especially hard not to say "Big Ben"; or, since the rules of the game would outlaw any such local name, I feel a bit frustrated in omitting some such specification as: "It is the clock of a former palace now used as a place of assembly for the empire's parliament," since the "imperial" nature of this woman's sensitivity seems to me a major aspect of the plot);[3] (2) We get thoughts on others through her, on her through others, on themselves through themselves (for the novel maintains a kind of high-class gossip that is an essential aspect of a "story" such as this); (3) Other important persons whose attitudes and relationships to her are variously revealed are her husband, her daughter, and her daughter's governess (for all these roles seem necessary ingredients of the narrative itself); (4) A reference to the fact that the Prime Minister is to be at the party seems less pressing, but it would help critically to point up the "imperial" attitudes which are so important an aspect of this one-day argosy, in which "All was for the party" (56); (5) The account of the party might profitably be qualified by words like "as seen through her eyes," though perhaps this aspect of the story's successive disclosures is sufficiently indicated already; (6) I do emphatically feel that we still need a summarizing observation of this sort: The exposition is peppered with references to flowers, serving as images for the enigmatic figuring of motives.

To be sure, once we begin looking at the problem in this way, we may want to add similar clauses to the outline of a classical work. But they seem more urgently needed for novels such as this. In particular, I find it necessary to introduce this theme of flowers, since they manage, at one remove, to represent so well the two important motifs of sexuality and social hierarchy (including the respects in which human relations can thus be appealingly signified in terms of objects that are repositories of "the beautiful"). At the very least, they'd have to be there like the "fine print" in a contract that is designed to take care of more eventualities than are at first apparent.*

Problem of Literary Genera

The "generalizing of thisness" also figures in another way. When the West rediscovered Aristotle's *Poetics,* apparently his treatment of comedy, tragedy, epic, etc. as literary genera each having its own set of principles proved almost as unsettling and unmanageable as the new advances in the physical sciences threaten to be in our age. And after several centuries of excesses, Croce attempted in his *Aesthetics* to overthrow this approach to works of art for good and all.

But was he not caught in a linguistic problem that is by sheer definition unresolvable? How can one talk about anything without telling us something about "what *kind* of" thing it is? If we say what a person did, are we not, by the same token, inevitably saying what *kind* of act he performed? Or if we say how he looked, are we not inevitably saying what *kind* of appearance he had, etc? The classificatory nature of terminology forces such duplication upon us.

However, in defining a work as a particular *kind* of literature, we might add specifications to such an extent that only this one work met all the conditions. That is, in stating what kind of literature some particular work is, one can employ so many specifications that the work, like a Thomistic angel, must be viewed *sui generis,* classed as the only member of its kind. Much later in this book, we shall return to the problem. For the time being we might note one extremely important respect in which Aristotle's definition of Greek tragedy (in chapter 6 of the *Poetics*) obviously does *not* fit all the conditions of the Greek theatre he was discussing. For he never even so much as mentions (at least in the extant portions of his treatise) the difference between an organic trilogy such as Aeschylus's *Oresteia* and trilogies made by the combining of three unrelated plays. In fact, he does not deal with the trilogy as a dramatic form. I bring up the point as a way of indicating how one might define Attic tragedy itself in a way whereby it split into two different "kinds." And, of course, by adding further specifications, one could so define Sophoclean tragedy that it would be classed as a kind different from Euripidean tragedy, etc.

---

*We are omitting two brief sections offered as further illustrations of the technique of generalized outlining: "Similar Outline of *A Passage to India*" and "Outline of *Coriolanus.*" For Burke's published examinations of those texts, see *Language as Symbolic Action,* "*Coriolanus* and the Delights of Faction" (81–97), and "Social and Cosmic Mystery: *A Passage to India*" (223–39). *Ed.*

We are here confronting another variant of Duns Scotus's dispute with Thomas Aquinas. In effect, along Scotist lines, specifications in "fine print" could be so added that Greek tragedy became subdivided into "Aeschylicity," "Sophoclicity," "Euripidicity," etc. And, as we shall later note, in the direction of Croce though certainly not in his spirit, further specifications could be added so that every individual work could be viewed as setting up and obeying its own peculiar body of laws. (Or have we here come upon an aesthetic variant of Kantian ethics, with the conscience-laden tricks whereby "freedom" becomes voluntary subjection to one's own self-legislation?)†

"Poetic Effect" as a Critical Postulate

We are now just about ready for our next phase, the discussion of "catharsis" itself, after one last observation as regards a work's thisness and kind. Our speculation has to do with the question of purpose. There is a German usage which could serve us well here. The idiomatic way of saying in German "What sort of thing is it?" would be *"Was fur ein Ding ist es?"* (that is, "what *for* a thing is it?"). You can say what something *is* by saying what it's *for*. Hence the great usefulness of "teleological" language as an aid to definition. Definition in terms of purpose is so "natural," I have heard a child ask, not "What caused that hill?" or "What is the meaning of that hill?" but "What is that hill for?" And in any case, implicit in the idea of an act is the idea of purpose—hence the question "What for?" is bound to hover about the edges of any symbolic act that is viewed as a poetic form.

Thus, inquiries into the general nature of a work's peculiar thisness will also be found to involve the question which the last clause in our definition of *A Passage to India* (as a literary form considered *sui generis*) is an attempt to answer.‡ I am more interested in arguing for this clause "in principle" than in arguing for it on the grounds that my particular answer is the best (particularly since I am not sure that it is the best). But I am trying to bring out the fact that, whenever we do define an artistic species, we should always ask ourselves what is the equivalent of the question that Aristotle asked himself as a conclusion

---

†We omit here a short section, "Definition of *A Passage to India* as a Literary Genus." *Ed.*

‡The clause to which Burke refers reads, "The story is told from a novelistic point of view that transcends the perspective of any one character, and that is designed to evoke in the reader a mood of ironically sympathetic contemplation. . . . The final clause is an attempt to answer the question: In this novel, what is the equivalent of 'catharsis' in Aristotle's definition of tragedy?" *Ed.*

to his definition of tragedy. That is, in literary forms different from tragedy, what (if any) is the equivalent of the role that his definition of tragedy assigns to "catharsis"? Is there an equivalent? (In comedy, for instance.) If so, to what extent is it similar, to what extent is it transformed? Or, if there is no equivalent, why not, or by what should it be replaced?

As regards the Forster novel, I incline to believe that it evoked in me "a mood of ironically sympathetic contemplation." So I work on the tentative assumption that the book's developments might best be studied by proceeding as if it had been explicitly designed to produce such an effect (whether or not the author so deliberately intended it). If some other critic is convinced that the book can be more effectively analyzed by imputing to it a different effect, he is free to propose *his* definition of it as a particular "kind" of novel, in accordance with the particular kind of effect (as though deliberately intended) he would impute to it. Such an imputing of a formal motive in no way involves "inside information" about the actual intentions of the author, as explicitly stated by him (in case he happened to state his intentions and there happens to be a trustworthy record of his statement). It involves a purely methodological consideration; namely, the critic's contention that the book can best be analyzed from the standpoint of such an effect, a contention which he could properly substantiate only by offering a thorough analysis of its "gender" as so defined.

The question about the nature of the work (what it is "for") has nothing to do with personal gossip about the author. To make our point by being as extreme as possible, imagine a hypothetical case in which the author of the work gave one account of the effect he aimed at, whereas the critic might still feel moved to demonstrate, if he could, that the nature of the work could be better accounted for if some other effect were postulated as its culminating poetic effect. This is not a matter of the critic arrogantly claiming that he "knows more" about the author's purposes than the author did himself. It is simply a matter of the critic's saying that he can account for the work better by using a different postulate. In such a case, the "refutation" would not be the author's word to the contrary, but a competing systematic account that, by using a different postulate, seemed to offer a better analysis. Such an account could, of course, be proposed by the original author himself, but in that case, he would write rather as a rival critic than as an author. He might have the advantage of being an "insider," but his demonstration would be as though "from without."

Obviously, to say as much is also to say that my own few remarks on *A Passage to India* can claim the value not of a demonstration but only of an illustration. The problem of such criticism will be taken up again later, in connection with Poe's essay, "The Philosophy of Composition." The subject is merely introduced here, to indicate the direction in which we are ultimately headed, and which might be obscured by the roundabout route we must take. Since we are using Aristotle's *Poetics* as our point of departure, this roundabout route will begin with speculations on catharsis, the particular culminating effect he attributes to the kind of poetry with which he is primarily concerned.

Notes

1. Thus, in an early story of mine, "The Excursion," there is this sequence: "I passed a barber shop, a grocery store, a little Italian girl, a chicken coop, a road-house, an abandoned quarry, a field of nervous wheat." I had read of a poem, I think by Mallarmé, that listed the objects in a room, in the order of their appearance to the poet, lying awake and observing the rheostatic development from night to dawn. I here tried something analogous, in details intended to mark off the stages of a walk from a suburb into the country. In another story, "Prince Llan," there was an attempt to establish a similar incidental form, thus:

> Logos Verbum the Word—universal brew bubbling and collapsing —then this wad of runny iron and rock settles into a steady elliptic jog—cools, crusts, that objects wriggle in the slime, and box-like things bump against the trees—heroic march of that one tender seed through groanings and agues of the earth, through steaming fevers, through chills slid down from the poles, hunger, fire, pestilence, war, despair, anguish of the conscience, lo! this clean-blooded man, this unscrofulous unsyphilitic neat-skinned gentleman, this ingenious isolated item, Prince Llan.

Since this was to mark the beginning of the story, I wanted to begin with a beginning that on its face had the quality of a beginning. So I started with an impressionistic "telescoping" of universal evolution (a scheme that might be a substitute for the resources of "mythic simplification" we discussed already). The stories (one of which originally appeared in *The Dial* and the other in *Broom*) are reprinted in an early O. P. volume, *White Oxen and Other Stories*.

2. That is, the logically prior can be expressed in terms of the temporally primeval; logical fulfillment can be expressed in terms of ultimate futurity; and either of such "perfections" (either sheer beginning or complete culmination) can come to stand for the other, as with the affinity between the *cognito matutina* of Edens and the *cognito vespertina* of Second Jerusalems.

3. Aristotle's outline of the *Odyssey* mentions Poseidon, but in his world such a usage would probably be equivalent to a modern outline's saying: "He prayed to God." Yet the reference to Poseidon does strain the rules.

4

Kenneth Burke's "Symbolic of Motives" and "Poetics, Dramatistically Considered"

William H. Rueckert

The occasion for this essay was the discovery in Burke's house in Andover of an unfinished manuscript entitled "Symbolic of Motives."[1] No one is quite sure when Burke began writing this manuscript or when and why he abandoned it after 269 pages, but since it closely resembles *A Rhetoric of Motives* in its form, as indicated by the table of contents, we can assume that he began it as soon as he finished *A Rhetoric of Motives* and then encountered problems in the "Thinking of the Body" section where it ends and put it aside until he could rethink that section and what he really wanted to do in his "Symbolic of Motives." At first, it seemed as if this manuscript was an earlier version of the unpublished "Poetics, Dramatistically Considered" (PDC) which we know Burke finished in 1957/1958 and which has been available for study since that time to anyone who had or could obtain a copy. But a study of the two manuscripts makes it quite clear that by the time he came to write PDC, he had rethought what he covered in "Symbolic of Motives" (SM) and refocused PDC almost exclusively on the Aristotle drama-tragedy-catharsis cluster and had resolved whatever problems caused him to abandon that manuscript early in the fifties (see appendix A, "Discussion of Williams's 'Textual Introduction'"). The sudden appearance of SM two years after Burke's death got me rethinking the whole question of Burke's original plans for the "Symbolic of Motives" and his refusal to publish in book form the work he had completed on his dramatistic poetics. So I went back over everything from *A Rhetoric of Motives,* through all of the essays identified as being part of the original

"Symbolic of Motives," through the SM, the long essay on the negative, the long essay "Linguistic Solution to Problems of Education," the manuscript PDC, and on to the many literary critical essays Burke wrote in the early sixties and included in *Language as Symbolic Action* (see appendix B, "A Reader's Guide to Burke's Dramatistic Poetics"). My conclusions about Burke's dramatistic poetics are presented below.

The argument of this essay is that Burke's "Symbolic of Motives," his often mentioned and discussed but never published book, which was to have been Burke's dramatistic poetics to go with his grammar and rhetoric, is, for all intents and purposes, a finished, completed work that could now be assembled, probably in two volumes, under the double titles of this essay. A review of the available documents from *A Rhetoric of Motives* through *Language as Symbolic Action,* including the two unpublished manuscripts of the title, make it quite clear that Burke achieved everything he set out to accomplish in his dramatistic poetics; he left us a complete version of his mature thoughts on literature and literary criticism even though, for reasons that will probably remain mysterious, he chose, most uncharacteristically, not to publish the results as a book or a pair of books. With a few exceptions, everything that was to be part of the dramatistic poetics has now been published somewhere or is soon to be published: in fact, by 1957 or 1958, all the main documents had been written. What literary criticism Burke wrote after that date, most of it collected in *Language as Symbolic Action,* consisted of applications of one part or another of his dramatistic poetics, the main outlines of which were mostly completed by 1955 even before he wrote the long, still unpublished "Poetics, Dramatistically Considered," which was a major revision and expansion of the original "Symbolic of Motives" manuscript.

A brief review of Burke's career and development during the fifties will help place what follows in its proper Burkean context. It is 1950. Burke has just finished *A Rhetoric of Motives,* the book that was to provide him with two of the most basic concepts that were to figure in his dramatistic poetics: the two-part theory of rhetoric (identification and persuasion) developed in parts 1 and 2 of *A Rhetoric of Motives,* and the theory of hierarchy and the hierarchic psychosis developed and illustrated in part 3 of *A Rhetoric of Motives.* Part 3 of *A Rhetoric of Motives,* the long "Order" section, is where Burke introduces not only hierarchy and the hierarchic psychosis, but socioanagogic criticism and the order-victimage-secret-kill sequence that will become the sociopolitical basis of all of his subsequent writing. It is impossible to overemphasize the importance of *A Rhetoric of Motives,* part 3, in Burke's development, just as it is impossible to ignore the place and function of rhetoric in Burke's work from *Counter-Statement* on.

As soon as—maybe even sooner than—Burke finished *A Rhetoric of Motives,* he began writing a manuscript actually entitled "Symbolic of Motives." He abandoned this manuscript after 269 pages for reasons not known to us, though later comments seem to suggest that he encountered problems in the thinking of the body chapter that took him far into uncharted territory. Though he was later to publish parts of the manuscript as essays, he never returned to it as such. Instead in 1957/1958 he began and completed a manuscript entitled "Poetics, Dramatistically Considered." This long manuscript covered much of the same ground as SM, but in more detail and with many additions. Both of these manuscripts are concerned with developing a dramatistic poetics derived from Aristotle's *Poetics,* and both deal at length with imitation, drama, tragedy, form, and especially catharsis.

Between 1950 and 1955 Burke wrote and published all of the individual essays that were meant to be part of the original "Symbolic of Motives." With four exceptions (see appendix B-5) these essays are all listed in an endnote to a 1955 essay entitled "Linguistic Approach to Problems of Education," an essay that is also centrally concerned with how and why Burke analyzes literary texts using his socioanagogic approach. Most of these individual essays concentrate either on a single text or on a single author, and most are demonstration essays that illustrate some part of Burke's dramatistic poetics or some part of his dramatistic methodology—especially what he calls indexing.

So far, then, we have four major sources for what went into his dramatistic poetics: part 3 of *A Rhetoric of Motives,* SM, the individual essays written and published between 1950 and 1955, and the long essay "Linguistic Approach to Problems of Education." But there is more. In the early fifties, probably when or while he was writing SM and many of the individual essays, Burke began his long four-part essay on the negative, "A Dramatistic View of the Origins of Language." Once the negative as a unique linguistic resource was introduced in these essays, it became an essential part of all Burke's thinking. The negative figured in a prominent way in his dramatistic poetics—especially in his thinking about tragedy and catharsis, which is the central concern of PDC—and in such essays as his analysis of Goethe's *Faust, Part I.* He also added it to his socioanagogic mode of analysis, as is most evident in all that he says about the analysis of literary texts in "Linguistic Approach to Problems of Education."

The only new book Burke published during the fifties was his first book of poems, *Book of Moments;* however, as I have tried to indicate, the fifties were very productive years for Burke, and he could easily have published at least two other significant books by collecting the 1950–55 essays written for the "Symbolic" and by publishing PDC as

is, since it is clearly a finished coherent text that does exactly what its
title says it will do: work out a dramatistic poetics based on Aristotle's
Poetics. By 1958, PDC was finished and Burke was at work on *The
Rhetoric of Religion*. We need to remind ourselves that the long analysis
of St. Augustine's *Confessions* in *The Rhetoric of Religion* derives in
part from Burke's dramatistic poetics: in fact, the analysis of St. Augustine's *Confessions* is the longest analysis of a single literary text anywhere in Burke and could well have been part of his poetics. The same
could not be said for the Genesis essay, which is also text centered, but
is concerned with quite different matters than verbal action, the main
focus of the St. Augustine essay. Furthermore, all of the analyses of literary texts in *Language as Symbolic Action,* which were written in the
early sixties, are applications of the dramatistic poetics Burke worked
out in the fifties. As was almost always Burke's practice, each is devoted
to a single text and is single-minded in what it attempts to do with that
text. But more on this later. Finally, we need to remember that Burke
was hardly idle during any part of the fifties; Hermes republished all of
his earlier critical works as well as *Book of Moments,* and two paper-
back editions of *Philosophy of Literary Form* were also published.

Why Burke did not finish off the "Symbolic" and get it published
is still not clear; maybe that is not the right way to put it. He did finish
it off in PDC, and he did have most of it published in one form or another: he just never put it together in a way that suited him. We will
never know what order he wanted the essays to be in, though he has
indicated that he probably would have put the "Ethan Brand" essay first
because it demonstrates how he began to work up a text for later analysis. He might also have been stopped by the sheer volume of what he
had written: 269 pages of SM, 391 pages of PDC, plus more than 300
pages of essays already published, which if put together would have
made for a book longer than either *A Grammar of Motives* or *Language
as Symbolic Action.*

In going over all of this material one discovers two, maybe even
three, separate but related works dealing with Burke's dramatistic poetics and a number of recurrent, even obsessive concerns that are common to all of them. One of these works is the dramatistic theory of
drama, tragedy, and catharsis derived from and based in Aristotle and
worked out in great detail in PDC and partially worked out in the earlier SM. This includes a dramatistic theory of imitation, form, tragedy,
catharsis (both civic and bodily), and the catharsis of catharsis, or some
form of transcendence beyond the work itself caused by the form of the
work itself. There are a number of model analyses that go with and
illustrate this part of Burke's dramatistic poetics: the long, original
analysis of the *Oresteia* that is included in PDC, and was published in

a shortened form in the *Sewanee Review* (1952) and later in *Language as Symbolic Action;* the analysis of Othello in "Othello: An Essay to Illustrate a Method"; all of the Shakespeare essays collected in *Language as Symbolic Action;* and, finally, the *King Lear* analysis in *"King Lear:* Its Form and Psychosis." All of these essays have in common Burke's theory of imitation—that is, that tragedies imitate a tragic tension or psychosis and effect a partial catharsis of this tension by means of the dramatic presentation; all also have in common the treatment of the characters as rhetorical constructs who embody some part of the tension and who work together to affect some form of relief from the sociopolitical (hierarchic) tension or psychosis plaguing the audience. In calling these tensions psychoses, Burke is using Freud's distinction between a curable neurosis and an incurable but treatable psychosis. It is highly questionable whether tragedies still perform this function for a modern-day audience in the same way that Aristotle thought they did for Athenians, though it seems obvious that films and TV, which Burke almost never discusses, most certainly do. At best, live drama in any form has a limited audience, which often makes Burke's text-based analyses of tragedies seem very remote and esoteric for modern-day readers and/or audiences. However, transferred to films or TV, Burke's theory of drama-tragedy-catharsis might very well become a powerful and resourceful "tool" for analyzing and understanding the cathartic function—that is, the cultural function—of films and TV dramas; and it is still a powerful tool for the abstract—purely literary—consideration of a play as a printed text, a verbal action, which is the way Burke analyzed all of the plays he dealt with in detail. So far as I know, Burke never once analyzed the actual production of a play but always worked from the printed text and hypothesized a performance of it, imagining how an audience might respond to it as a powerful and effective rhetorical construct.

The second part of Burke's dramatistic poetics is much closer to the original conception of the "Symbolic of Motives" as Burke described it in *A Rhetoric of Motives* when he was still thinking in terms of his original grammar, rhetoric, poetics, and ethics tetralogy. This conception harkens back to the theory of symbolic action Burke developed in *Philosophy of Literary Form* and applied there to Coleridge and, later, so brilliantly, to Keats's "Ode on a Grecian Urn." (See appendix B-1 for what Burke says about the differences between his grammar, rhetoric, and symbolic early on in *A Rhetoric of Motives.*)

The individual essays Burke began writing and publishing in the early fifties and up through 1955 are almost all concerned with this part of the dramatistic poetics: that is, they focus on individual texts or authors, and they either develop or apply Burke's theory of indexing, which is used to set up a text so that Burke can go on to some form of socioanagogic analysis. The first, and purest, of these essays for the "Symbolic" are the Roethke and Nemerov analyses, both of which analyze groups of poems by a single author but without the paraphernalia that was soon to become part of every analysis done for the "Symbolic." One of the earliest and still one of the most characteristic of these is the "Ethan Brand" essay that begins with the indexing of terms —that is, close terminological analysis to determine what goes with what (identifications), what versus what (agons), what follows what (progressions), and what becomes what (transformations). This preliminary work also includes pun analysis, or joycing, which is one of Burke's most irritating procedures and most unconvincing because its object is usually to reveal the hidden scatological content of a given work in terms of the demonic trinity of urinary, sexual, and fecal motives. Burke's commitment to joycing is indicated by the fact that he did it in Greek, Latin, English, French, and German. Midway through "Ethan Brand: A Preparatory Investigation," Burke switches to his socioanagogic mode of analysis, which is essentially Burke's way to discover the sociopolitical content of the work and the different ways in which literary works reflect and try to deal with the hierarchic psychosis and all that goes with it. "All that goes with it" is, to say the least, considerable, and always involves in some way the negative (the cause of the psychosis) and the order-secret-kill-victimization sequence (one of the most destructive consequences of it).

This is not the place to rehearse or rehash the drama of human relations according to Burke; my point is that every literary analysis he does arrives at some point by some analytic route at a consideration of some part of this drama, which he says is lurking everywhere. Burke's literary criticism is powerfully admonitory, and it is Freudian in the sense that he believes in the power of knowledge that results from the careful analysis of a great text; he believes that if we are warned we might be protected—or at least more self-aware than we were before we read his analysis—as well as better able to do our own kind of analysis on other texts. A lot of Burke's literary criticism, especially his indexing and joycing, is head work, microanalysis for special interests, in which he is trying to work out some theoretical proposition about cathartic completeness. This is exemplified in the "Thinking of the Body" essay in *Language as Symbolic Action,* which was originally written for PDC, or in the analysis of Joyce's *Portrait* in "Fact, Inference, and Proof in the Analysis of Literary Symbolism," where he is trying to "prove" his theory about labyrinthine internal consistency and symbolism by means of pun analysis in which even the most remote phonetic similarity suggests some sort of symbolic linkage or identification. Another example of this sort of analysis can be found in the *Faust I* essay reprinted in *Language as Symbolic Action* and originally written as the second part of "The Language of Poetry, 'Dramatistically' Considered" (1955). That analysis is probably the most masterful example of indexing and joycing that we have from Burke, as well as one of the most complete examples of socioanagogic criticism; it also provides one of the most coherent explanations (part 8 of the *Language as Symbolic Action* version, 155–62) of why he does what he does in his literary criticism. It is a perfect example of what he finds in a literary text and what he thinks he needs to warn us about. It is also a fine example of the care with which Burke chose the few texts he would analyze in detail so as to make sure they would serve his theoretical, methodological, and ideological purposes.

The purpose of this essay is not to explicate or evaluate Burke's dramatistic poetics, but to identify, describe, and characterize the documents (essays and manuscripts) in which he worked out his dramatistic poetics between 1950 and 1958. A complete account of his poetics also has to go ahead to the mid-sixties and *Language as Symbolic Action* because all of the literary essays collected in *Language as Symbolic Action* are applications of one part or another of the dramatistic poetics rather than applications of logology (see appendix B-7). The "Kubla Khan" essay, for example, is an extended application of indexing, using Coleridge as a whole to establish the significance or symbolism of the key terms; and the main purpose of the essay is to refute John Livingston Lowe's thesis that everything in the poem had an external source. Burke's argument, one of the central precepts of his dramatistic poetics, is that all or most of the essential evidence needed for the analysis of a poem is intrinsic to the poem and/or the poet. The Emerson essay is primarily devoted to making an essential distinction between catharsis and transcendence, a distinction that is essential to Burke's theory of tragedy and catharsis as he develops them in PDC and the Othello essay. The three Shakespeare essays are all further applications of Burke's theory of tragedy, which is developed at length in PDC and the Othello essay. The Forster essay is an example of the comic criticism or the criticism of a comic work that Burke, in a footnote to PDC, said was still missing from his poetics. Finally, though it is hard to say just what Burke was about in the Djuna Barnes essay, where all the quotations are missing, it seems to be yet another example of his attempt to extend the range of his dramatistic poetics by analyzing another work of prose fiction, especially one like *Nightwood* that is so concerned with the negative. The *Faust II* essay is another working-out of one of Burke's essential dramatistic ideas about poetry: poetry works through images, but all of the images are also symbolic and one can work through the images to the ideas behind the images. In his Whitman essay, Burke reverses this process by laying out Whitman's policy as he explained it in "Democratic Vistas" and then showing how it was expressed in the images of "When Lilacs Last in the Dooryard Bloomed." Burke's ventures in literary criticism came to an end in *Language as Symbolic Action* (1966), and though he may have written more, he never published any more after that date. His dramatistic poetics was finished and all of his energy was devoted to logology and working out his final position.

Indexing and joycing were major features of all of Burke's literary criticism during this period. He was working with a universal definition of a text as an organically interrelated structure of terms with a beginning, middle, and end, and a universal methodology for exploring the personality of a given text. Indexing is most completely discussed and applied in "Fact, Inference, and Proof in the Analysis of Literary Symbolism," and the whole concept of the "personality" of a text is discussed in "The Language of Poetry, 'Dramatistically' Considered." I'll take up this second essay first because it introduces a concept not found elsewhere in Burke in the same form, which was an essential part of his dramatistic poetics (see appendix B-5). In the first part of this essay, as published in the *Chicago Review* (1954–55), Burke makes the following distinctions. He says that to the traditional three "offices" of the poet and orator (all discourse, really)—to teach, to please, and to move or persuade—we need to add a fourth if we are to do justice to the range and complexity of poetry. This fourth office, he says, is to portray, and portraiture is a three-headed proposition because Burke uses it to discuss (1) the unique personality of a given text as an organically interrelated structure of terms with a beginning, middle, and end; (2) the personality of the text as a revelation of the personality of the agent who enacted it; and (3) the agent, scene, and act relationship as a revelation of the personality of the sociopolitical scene (the social hierarchy and the hierarchic psychoses that are always part of it). All of these (the symbolic action, the agent, the hierarchic scene) are made possible by language and infused with it. The poem is a verbal action; the agent is defined by the ability to use a particular language; the sociopolitical scene and all that is part of it (the laws, the bureaucracy, the social classes, the political structures, the technology, the hierarchic psychosis) are also made possible by and embedded in language. Even nature has been infused with symbolic ingredients.

To put all of this in another way, Burke's tripartite theory of portraiture makes it possible for him to begin an empirical analysis of a text in terms of what it literally is: a verbal or linguistic action, the end result of which is a certain structure of organically related *terms* in a set order. Burke has often argued that a poem (novel, play, book) is nothing but words. Characters in a Shakespeare play are literally nothing but words, names, with a rhetorical role to play. This structure of terms can be exhaustively analyzed using the four equations methodology (indexing). In moving from the personality of the text to the personality of the agent whose symbolic action it is, the pentad and ratios are brought into the analysis in order to establish and study the unique ingredients of personality (psychic and physical) that are necessarily reflected in the words, the terms of the text. Words contain other words, Burke says, and words bring a lot of foreign substances into a poem with them, all of which indicate both the choices the agent made when creating the poem as well as the historical accidentals always present in any language. The analysis that takes Burke deeper and deeper into the terminological inwardness of a poem also provides him with a way back out of the poem as soon as he begins to consider a poem as the verbal symbolic action of an agent in a scene. The resources of language are there for the critic to make use of, and in Burke's case, this offers a formidable arsenal of analytic tools. A classic example of how Burke proceeds can be found in the Keats essay, or, for that matter, in the *Faust I* analysis that is the second part of this essay. Burke can begin with the verbal, symbolic action, as he does in, say, the "Ethan Brand" essay, move to a consideration of the personality of the agent whose symbolic action it is, and finally, move to a consideration, by use of the pentad, to the nature of the sociopolitical scene that is embodied in the text and then to the interactive relationship that necessarily exists between the agent and the scene. Burke has argued since *A Rhetoric of Motives* that the sociopolitical scene is dominated (always) by various permutations of order (hierarchy) and by the ever-present hierarchic psychosis. At this point, Burke is into his socioanagogic mode of analysis in which all symbolism, especially sexual symbolism, is analyzed in terms of its overt or covert sociopolitical content. Again, the analysis of Goethe's *Faust I* is a classic example of what Burke can do with a text as he moves from personality to personality, filling out the pentadic ratios as he goes and locking the text into his own conception of the drama of human relations.

Why Burke did not include part 1 of "The Language of Poetry, 'Dramatistically' Considered" in *Language as Symbolic Action* is something of a mystery to me. It is probably his most comprehensive discussion of what "poetry" is and how it works among all of the essays he wrote in the early to mid-fifties to be part of the "Symbolic of Motives." What he says in part 1 supports the analysis of *Faust I* in part 2.

Quite a lot is lost in the *Faust I* analysis by not having the theoretical support of part 1 and its carefully worked-out theory of the three personalities of a text.

Burke's most inclusive discussion of indexing and joycing and their relationship to socioanagogic criticism can be found in his essay "Fact, Inference, and Proof in the Analysis of Literary Symbolism." Joyce's *Portrait of the Artist as a Young Man* is used as the model text; Burke mines it for examples but makes no attempt to work out a comprehensive analysis. His primary interests in this essential essay are in terminological analysis, labyrinthine internal coherence, and joycing, or pun analysis. Joycing is a technique for teasing an often unlikely meaning out of a term by fiddling with its consonants and vowels. This technique has been around in Burke for quite a while: the joycing of "Beauty is Truth, Truth Beauty" to "Body is Turd, Turd Body" is one of the earliest examples. Burke has also joyced his own titles by arguing that "towards," a word that he uses in four different titles, always contains "turds." (Words contain other words, he said often.) Similarities constitute identities; even remote phonetic similarities do this. Much of Burke's joycing is to scatological ends since he obviously believed that authors do a lot of their writing to transcend the fecal motive. He also believed that all texts are enigmas filled with hidden and deviated motives that pun analysis and socioanagogic analysis should make explicit. Much of this essay is devoted to pun analysis, which is not so difficult in the work of such masterful punsters as Joyce and Dickens. It is sort of surprising that Burke did not use *Finnegans Wake* for this essay, which is an example of punning pushed to the most extreme limits of language. Punning is related to the second major emphasis in this essay, which has to do with the labyrinthine internal coherence of poetic works. Such coherence is basically a function of repetitive form and Burke's notion of what "radiations" are and how they work. Other terms Burke uses for "radiations from" are "range of" and "spin from." "The First Three Chapters of Genesis" in *The Rhetoric of Religion* is probably the best example we have of how this kind of Burke logic works. All three techniques are ways of getting more out of a text than seems to be there and of establishing interrelationships one would never have suspected existed; Burke really seemed to believe that poetic texts were models of a perfect (maybe more perfect) world in which everything is related to everything else in some way to create an overall unity of being that is certainly lacking in the nonpoetic everyday world we all live in.

Finally, there is indexing. It derives its name from the fact that you first make an index of the key terms in a text and then as you go back through the text you fill out the entries in the index. Each filled-out entry is going to give you a cluster of wide-ranging identifications based on purely internal, empirically verifiable evidence. As the title of this essay indicates, indexing is a technique for isolating the salient *terminological* facts in a text, *inferring* a symbolic meaning for the facts assembled under any term or related term in the index. Then, after further analysis of at least the terminological identifications, agons, progressions, and transformations in the text, and after having accumulated a huge amount of empirical evidence, you are able to offer *proof* for your reading of the signs. Other texts by the same author may be used, but basically Burke believes that great texts are self-defining and contain and prove their own meaning because of the nature of language and their labyrinthine internal consistency. They are their own symbol-system, if only one can figure out how to get at it. The best examples of indexing in Burke are in the "Fact, Inference, and Proof" essay, where Joyce's *Portrait* is used; in the *Faust I* analysis, which is included in *Language as Symbolic Action* but dates from 1954/55, and in the "Ethan Brand" and Roethke essays.

A final comment on the PDC and SM manuscripts. (See appendix A, "References to the 'Symbolic of Motives' and/or 'Poetics, Dramatistically Considered,'" and appendixes B-3 and B-6.) With a couple of exceptions (part of section 8, "The Orestes Trilogy," and section 9, "Beyond Catharsis"), the bulk of PDC has been published and could be assembled from these published texts. Also, most of the SM manuscript has been absorbed into PDC, though the material has been revised and rearranged in the process and portions of the manuscript (part 1, section 6) have been omitted and remain unpublished to this day. One can reconstruct most of SM and PDC by studying the two tables of contents and the published record in the Franks' bibliography in *Critical Responses* and Richard Thames's additions to it in *The Legacy of Kenneth Burke*. The "Symbolic of Motives" manuscript is a kind of curiosity. It has material in it that does not appear anywhere else (like comments on Virginia Woolf's *Mrs. Dalloway*); it was obviously abandoned and left unfinished; there seems to be no way to accurately date it; there are numerous references to the fact that Burke was reading from a revised text, having carved out pieces of it to turn them into talks; it is missing part 3, which is referred to many times in the text but never characterized; it seems like a work that was forming, not formed, in Burke's mind. It lacks the long analysis of the Orestes trilogy though there is a reference to it, and it does not have the exclusive focus on tragedy and catharsis found in PDC. It is, however, of interest to Burke scholars because it helps to clarify the whole issue of what the "Symbolic of Motives" is and what happened to the original conception of it.

PDC is what happened to this original conception. Burke's dramatistic poetics, originally to go with his grammar and rhetoric and still-to-be-written ethics, was split into two, probably three parts. The Aristotle imitation-drama-tragedy-catharsis part is developed at length and with coherence in PDC. What Burke started to do in the "Symbolic of Motives" manuscript—which was to develop a general literary theory and methodology, not just a theory of tragic drama—he did in the essays written and published between 1950 and 1955. Toward the end of this intensely creative period, while still working on his general dramatistic poetics, Burke came up with indexing, joycing, and the three personalities theory, which were all applicable to any literary text. At some point in the mid-fifties, Burke must have decided to take what he could out of the original "Symbolic of Motives" manuscript and use it in a single coherent manuscript written under the sign of catharsis. Over three hundred pages of this manuscript are devoted to catharsis in its various forms (sections 4–10), especially tragic catharsis. One hundred and three pages are devoted to the "Thinking of the Body," or to the evidence of bodily catharsis that Burke insists must be part of any cathartic experience if it is to be complete. Most of the examples in this long section (6) have nothing to do with tragedy and are drawn from Wagner's "Ring," Flaubert's *Temptation,* Lewis Carroll's Alice books, Mallarmé's poetry, and Burke's own poetry and fiction. These one hundred pages are certainly among the most tedious in Burke as he struggles to find ways to document the presence of urinary, sexual, and fecal motives (the demonic trinity) in every work he discusses. Burke's long-standing commitment to mind/body dualism is largely responsible for his making this theorizing about the thinking of the body part of his poetics. You can have body without mind, as when a person is brain-dead or born with no brain, but you cannot have mind without body; and, Burke insists, you cannot have a psychic catharsis of pity, fear, and pride (the tragic triad), without their bodily equivalents, sex (pity, love), urine (fear), feces (pride)—Freud's cloacal trio and Burke's demonic trinity. As Burke keeps reminding us, the privy parts are not only in close proximity to each other, but they are usually hidden and covered and are often interchangeable. The same might be said for Burke's pages on the thinking of the body. There really isn't a problem with this angle if you are writing about *Gulliver's Travels* or Djuna Barnes's *Nightwood;* but there is a problem when he insists that Shakespeare's *The Phoenix and the Turtle* is secretly "excrementitious"—a statement that is completely baffling when you take it back to the text. We could argue that this was the persistence of adolescent motives in Burke and they made him turd-brained and pee-headed while he was working this theory out in the fifties. He begins this analysis in the SM where there are forty-six pages devoted to it and continues in PDC where there are a hundred plus pages devoted to it.

Well, almost enough on this topic. We don't have to agree with the emphasis Burke places on the thinking of the body, and we clearly do not have to agree with Burke that no catharsis is complete until and unless the three kinds of bodily images have been expressed, however roundabout. Burke has really "hoisted himself with his own petard" here in his obsessive determination to prove his own theory true. It is obviously true in some cases; it is Burke's insistence on completeness and thoroughness (it is always true and we have only to find the necessary evidence) that causes the problem. This same kind of problem (the to-the-end-of-the-line thinking) exists elsewhere in Burke, especially in his logological analyses of texts. Like it or not, this mind-body thinking theory is an essential part of Burke's dramatistic poetics. He was clearly deeply committed to it and, with some revisions and deletions, included it in *Language as Symbolic Action,* along with an essay on his many "urination" dreams in which the body gives the mind a signal that must be acted on even as one sleeps. Many of us have had these mind-body dreams, especially those in which one is desperately seeking a place to urinate. No one can really deny the fact of or the need for bodily catharsis (purgation) by means of which the body purifies itself in getting rid of its waste materials and satisfies its hormonal, sexual, and romantic needs through sexual acts of some kind. The problem is in the way Burke has hooked up the psychic cathartic processes with the bodily ones, insisting on an exact correspondence between pity, fear, and pride and the bodily equivalents (sexual, urinary, fecal, along with the orifices or appendages for each). Burke has always treated literary texts as purgative-redemptive, as cathartic miracles. The addition of the thinking of the body theory, which was begun at the end of SM and then abandoned to be taken up again and completed by the time PDC was completed, adds a whole new dimension to thinking about catharsis and, hence, to his thinking about literature and criticism.

This is probably a good place to leave—to bid farewell to—Burke's dramatistic poetics, a massive work that is the culmination of Burke's long involvement with literature and literary criticism as well as the culmination of dramatism. I'm not sure any of us has done justice to this work in all of its variety and complexity. Literary critics seem to have abandoned Burke and been replaced by people in speech communication and rhetoric, who are not much interested in Burke's literary criticism or his dramatistic poetics. Burke, of course, was his own worst enemy in these matters because he never agreed to bring it all together and have it published in one, maybe two books when its time had come and he was through with it. Two of the main documents have remained unpublished, in hard-to-acquire manuscripts. The essays remain scattered in various journals and collections and are hard to sort out without some help from the two manuscripts and the various notes Burke attached to some of his essays about the "Symbolic of Motives." Two of the most important essays, *"Othello"* and "Fact, Inference, and Proof" were "buried" in the Burke reader Stanley Edgar Hyman did for Indiana University Press—which is now out of print.

The status of reading and books has become problematic, thanks to TV and computers. Literary criticism has also gone sort of crazy with everybody wanting to get a piece of the action, using literature for purposes even Burke would have been shocked at, pursuing any line of approach that suits them regardless of the actual nature of the text. Can anyone still believe in the seriousness of literature and literary criticism the way Kenneth Burke did? Or pay the loving attention to individual texts the way Burke did to St. Augustine's *Confessions* or Goethe's *Faust I*? (Yes: see Helen Vendler on Shakespeare's sonnets. But she is a rarity.) Move on, move on, the man says. But I say, move back, move back, and give Burke the literary critic his due. One way to do this is to enter his dramatistic literary criticism by way of his novel, *Towards a Better Life,* and his *Collected Poems.* This way you will find out just how much he loved words and what they could do for him (and others).

Note

1. Burke purchased a farm outside of Andover, New Jersey, in 1921. He initially lived on the farm during the summer months only, but by the early 1930s he and his second wife, Libbie Batterham, lived on the farm year-round, although in a different house from the one in which Burke lived with his first wife and their children. Burke died in his home outside of Andover on November 19, 1993.

Appendix A: Discussion of Williams's "Textual Introduction"

David Williams and I wrote our essays more or less simultaneously without either of us knowing exactly what the other was doing. We were both working with two unpublished texts by Burke: "Poetics, Dramatistically Considered," which had been around since 1957, when Burke wrote it, and "A Symbolic of Motives," which was discovered among Burke's papers after his death. Both manuscripts were part of Burke's long attempt to write a version of his dramatistic poetics that suited him. Large portions of both manuscripts had been published as separate essays, but for some reason, Burke never put the many essays he wrote between 1950 and 1956 together to form a book or books. Burke kept fussing with this material well into the seventies, when he finally abandoned all attempts to put together a volume called "A Symbolic of Motives"—or, as he punningly referred to it, "Sinballix of Motives."

I did not read David's essay until mine was long finished. I had an advantage over David because though we both had complete versions of "Poetics, Dramatistically Considered," I had the only "complete" version of the "Symbolic of Motives" manuscript itself, an incomplete manuscript that ends abruptly in the middle of a chapter called "The Thinking of the Body" some 250 pages into the manuscript. Until I read David's essay, I was convinced that this was an early version of "Symbolic of Motives," which we know Burke began writing as soon as he finished *A Rhetoric of Motives*. Much about this manuscript encouraged such a view, especially its form, which was close to the form Burke used in both *A Grammar of Motives* and *A Rhetoric of Motives*, with its many short, titled sections and three-part overall divisions. However, reading David's essay convinced me, as he argued, that the "Symbolic of Motives" manuscript in my possession was in fact a much later attempt on Burke's part to revise the original manuscript. Residues of the original certainly still remain in the "Symbolic of Motives" manuscript but, as David points out, Burke, in a letter to Cowley (and, as I was to discover, in letters to me that I had forgotten), indicates that he has gone back to work revising the "Symbolic of Motives." Parts of the "Symbolic of Motives" manuscript are clearly the result of this later and, as it turned out, final revision of the original material, a revision Burke made after completing "Poetics, Dramatistically Considered" in 1957, and probably after putting *Language as Symbolic Action* together in the mid-sixties.

It is only on the question of the date of "Symbolic of Motives" manuscript that David and I had any serious disagreement. Other points of disagreement are what might be called speculative ones—

about whether "Poetics, Dramatistically Considered" is "finished" and "complete"; about why Burke could never get the "Symbolic of Motives" finished to suit him; why he did not publish "Poetics, Dramatistically Considered" as is. David's conclusions about the date of the "Symbolic of Motives" manuscript seem more or less definitive to me now and have the effect of making that manuscript yet another chapter in Burke's long attempts to finish the third volume of his *Motives* books. In a sense, as I have argued, he did finish that project, he just never wanted to put it in final form by publishing it as a two-volume book.

Finally, my correspondence with Burke begins in August 1959 and lasts until 1984. His first letter to me is mostly about the "Symbolic of Motives" and whether he should take what he had already written and try to put it together as a single volume or do two volumes. Off and on for the next nineteen years, Burke fusses and fiddles with the "Symbolic of Motives" or "Poetics, Dramatistically Considered," vowing over and over again to finish it by such and such a date. Finally, in November 1978 he signs off on the project and abandons it for good. It is perfectly clear in the letters from the early sixties that Burke is revising his original manuscript and that his conception of this project has gradually shifted from the original version of the "Symbolic" as described in *A Rhetoric of Motives* to the whole project as his dramatistic poetics. He says at one point (in June 1963) that "Poetics, Dramatistically Considered" is a first draft of his "poetics," not of his "Symbolic of Motives" or, as he was to refer to it after 1962, his "Sinballix."

References to the "Symbolic of Motives" and/or "Poetics, Dramatistically Considered" in Burke's letters to me

1. August 8, 1959.

2. December 9, 1961. Refers to his revision of the "Poetics" material and vows to finish by the end of the year.

3. June 18, 1962. First reference to "Sinballix." Plans to finish up with Poe material.

4. December 31, 1962. Trying to finish up the last, final, ultimate work on the poetics.

5. January 29, 1963. Refers to the revisions of the poetics and the ways in which the body thinking chapter had been reduced in the manuscript but written up separately as a long monograph.

6. May 24, 1963. How he will end the poetics with a chapter resembling the final chapter of *Towards a Better Life*.

7. June 18, 1963. Same as the above letter. Swears to finish poetics in the fall. Described "Poetics, Dramatistically Considered" as a "first" draft of the poetics.

8. August 16, 1963. Refers to revising poetics.

9. March 16, 1964 and January 25, 1966. Refers to "Symbolic of Motives."

10. November 22, 1969. At Yaddo after the death of Libbie, Burke's wife. Still writing about finishing up his poetics enterprise.

11. July 27, 1977.

12. October 5, 1977.

13. January 13, 1978.

14. January 24, 1978.

15. May 11, 1978.

16. June 9, 1978. (Letters 11–16 refer to "Symbolic of Motives," "Poetics, Dramatistically Considered," and "Sinballix.")

17. October 24, 1978. Signs off project for good.

18. January 28, 1982. At the end, Burke writes that Bob Zachary at the University of California Press and I should select the essays that would go into the "Symbolic." He has given up on the project after forty years.

Appendix B: A Reader's Guide to Burke's Dramatistic Poetics

What follows are some of the essential documents for the study of Kenneth
Burke's dramatistic poetics. These are divided into eight categories, followed by
a brief conclusion.

1. The early description of the "Symbolic of Motives" in A Rhetoric
of Motives (Berkeley: University of California Press, 1969)
>   The *Grammar* was at peace insofar as it contemplated the
>   paradoxes common to all men, the universal resources of
>   verbal placement. The "Symbolic" should be at peace, in
>   that the individual substances, or entities, or constituted acts
>   are there considered in their uniqueness, hence outside the
>   realm of conflict. For individual universes, as such, do not
>   compete. Each merely *is,* being its own self-sufficient realm
>   of discourse. And the "Symbolic" thus considers each thing
>   as a set of interrelated terms all conspiring to round out
>   their identity as participants in a common substance of mean-
>   ing. An individual does in actuality compete with other in-
>   dividuals. But within the rules of Symbolic, the individual
>   is treated merely as a self-subsistent unit proclaiming its pe-
>   culiar nature. It is "at peace," in that its terms *cooperate*
>   in modifying one another. But insofar as the individual is
>   involved in conflict with other individuals or groups, the
>   study of this same individual would fall under the head of
>   *Rhetoric.* Or considered rhetorically, the victim of a neurotic
>   conflict is torn by parliamentary wrangling; he is heckled
>   like Hitler within. (Hitler is said to have confronted a con-
>   stant wrangle in his private deliberations, after having im-
>   posed upon his people a flat choice between conformity and
>   silence.) Rhetorically, the neurotic's every attempt to legis-
>   late for his own conduct is disorganized by rival factions
>   within his own dissociated self. Yet, considered Symboli-
>   cally, the same victim is technically "at peace," in the sense
>   that his identity is like a unified, mutually adjusted set of
>   terms. For even antagonistic terms, confronting each other
>   as parry and thrust, can be said to "cooperate" in the build-
>   ing of an over-all form.
>   The *Rhetoric* must lead us through the Scramble, the
>   Wrangle of the Market Place, the flurries and flare-ups of the
>   Human Barnyard, the Give and Take, the wavering line of
>   pressure and counterpressure, the Logomachy, the onus of
>   ownership, the Wars of Nerves, the War. It too has its peace-
>   ful moments: at times its endless competition can add up to

the transcending of itself. In ways of its own, it can move from the factional to the universal. But its ideal culminations are more often beset by strife as the condition of their organized expression, or material embodiment. Their very universality becomes transformed into a partisan weapon. For one need not scrutinize the concept of "identification" very sharply to see, implied in it at every turn, its ironic counterpart: division. Rhetoric is concerned with the state of Babel after the Fall. Its contribution to a "sociology of knowledge" must often carry us far into the lugubrious regions of malice and lie. (*RM* 22–23)

Carried into unique cases, such concern with identifications leads to the sheer "identities" of Symbolic. That is, we are in pure Symbolic when we concentrate upon one particular integrated structure of motives. But we are clearly in the region of rhetoric when considering the identifications whereby a specialized activity makes one a participant in some social or economic class. (*RM* 27–28)

2. Some major contributions of A Rhetoric of Motives *to the dramatistic poetics*

A Rhetoric of Motives is filled with references to and analyses of literary texts. Over and over again, the two main components of Burke's rhetoric, identification and persuasion, are used in these analyses and comments. Both are essential parts of his poetics, as is the notion that all poems are essentially rhetorical constructs addressed back to the writer and outward to the reader or audience.

A Rhetoric of Motives, part 3: Order. It is in part 3 of *A Rhetoric of Motives* that Burke introduces three of the most important components of his dramatistic poetics: his concept of hierarchy and the hierarchic psychosis, socioanagogic criticism, and victimage.

3. "Symbolic of Motives" manuscript: 269 pages and table of contents
    Part One
    I. The Poetic Motive
        Symbolism an "Unmotivated Motive"
        Deflections from the Poetic Motive
        Special Role of the Negative
        Intrinsic Delights of Symbol-Using
            1. "Expression" as such
            2. The hortatory of language
            3. Intrinsic also to language is its nature as naming
            4. To the intrinsic delight in symbols as expression
        Compulsive Aspects of Symbolism

II. Nature of the Project
   The Project as a Whole
   "Dramatistic" and "Scientistic"
   Plan of This Particular Book
III. Preparatory Etymology
   Specific and General Nature of Terms
   Poetic, Aesthetic, Artistic
   Beauty and War
   Imagination
   Classification and Propriety
   In Sum
   The Sublime
IV. Aristotle's Dramatistic Terminology of Drama
   Literal and Analogical Terms
   "Poetics" Viewed Deductively
   Concealed and Fragmentary Dramatism
   Dramatistic Transformations
V. Imitation (Mimesis)
   "Imitation" Usually Conceived Too Scientistically
   Definitions of "Entelechy"
   Entelechy and Myth
   Imitation of Tensions
   Verisimilitude
   Imitation, Copy, Record
   Perfection
   Individuation and Amplification
VI. The Language of "Thisness"
   General and Particular
   "Concrete" Words Are Abbreviations for Situations
   "Universalizing" a Plot
   Generalized Outline of *Mrs. Dalloway*
   Similar Outline of *A Passage to India*
   Outline of *Coriolanus*
   Problem of Literary Genera
   A Definition of *A Passage to India* as a Literary Genus
   "Poetic Affect" as a Critical Postulate
VII. Recapitulation
VIII. Catharsis (Civic Aspect)
   Catharsis, Religious and Secular
   "Entelechial" View of Tragedy
   Euripides' *Trojan Women*
   How Civic Catharsis Might Operate
   For Personalizing of Conflict *(Antigone, Oresteia, Medea)*

4. The negative, as it worked out in "A Dramatistic View of the Origins of Speech," 1952–53
Once Burke developed the idea of the negative, it figured in almost everything he wrote and was certainly central to all the work he did on his poetics after this essay was written and published.

5. The essays written as part of the original conception of "A Symbolic of Motives"
These essays are listed in a long endnote to Burke's essay "Linguistic Approach to Problems of Education." All of the essays were written between 1950 and 1955 and would certainly have been part of any collection Burke made called *A Symbolic of Motives*. I have added four additional essays to this list, as well as "Linguistic Approach to Prob-

lems of Education" (1955), which is in fact an essential document for the study of Burke's dramatistic poetics. Of the additional essays, "The Language of Poetry, 'Dramatistically' Considered" is especially important because it is in part 1 of this essay that Burke works out his three personalities theory of the text. The endnote to "Linguistic Approach to Problems of Education" (in *Modern Philosophies and Education,* ed. Nelson B. Henry. [Chicago: National Society for the Study of Education, distributed by University of Chicago Press, 1955], vol. 54, pt. 1, 259–302) lists the essays written as part of Burke's original conception of the "Symbolic":

> A work now in preparation, *A Symbolic of Motives,* will deal with poetics and the technique of "indexing" literary works. Meanwhile, among articles by the present author already published on this subject are: "The Vegetal Radicalism of Theodore Roethke" (*The Sewanee Review,* Winter 1950); "Three Definitions" (*Kenyon Review,* Spring 1951); "*Othello:* An Essay to Illustrate a Method" (*Hudson Review,* Summer 1951); "Form and Persecution in the *Oresteia*" (*The Sewanee Review,* Summer 1952); "Imitation" (*Accent,* Autumn 1952); "Comments on Eighteen Poems by Howard Nemerov" (*The Sewanee Review,* Winter 1952); "Ethan Brand: A Preparatory Investigation" (*Hopkins Review,* Winter 1952); "Mysticism as a Solution to the Poet's Dilemma," in collaboration with Stanley Romaine Hopper, *Spiritual Problems in Contemporary Literature* (edited by Stanley Romaine Hopper, published by Institute for Religious and Social Studies, distributed by Harper & Bros., 1952); "Fact, Inference, and Proof in the Analysis of Literary Symbolism" (paper presented at Thirteenth Conference on Science, Philosophy, and Religion, and published in a volume distributed by Harper & Bros., 1954).

To this list, I need to add:

"Thanatopsis for Critics: A Brief Thesaurus of Deaths and Dyings." *Essays in Criticism* 2 (Oct. 1952): 369–375.

"Freedom and Authority in the Realm of the Poetic Imagination." In *Freedom and Authority in Our Time.* Ed. Lyman Bryson et al. New York: Harper and Brothers, 1953. 365–375.

"The Language of Poetry, 'Dramatistically' Considered." *Chicago Review* 8 (Fall 1954): 88–102; continued 9 (Spring 1955): 40–72.

"Policy Made Personal: Whitman's Verse and Prose-Salient Traits." In *Leaves of Grass One Hundred Years After.* Ed. Milton Hindus. Stanford, CA: Stanford University Press, 1955. 74–108.

6. *"Poetics, Dramatistically Considered," manuscript, 1957–58, 391 pages*
I give only the table of contents here, which can be studied in conjunction with the table of contents of SM. Unlike the "Symbolic of Motives" manuscript, which only showed up two years after Burke's death, the PDC manuscript has been around since shortly after Burke finished it. I have had a copy of this manuscript since 1960, when Burke sent it to me, but it is only recently that I have taken the trouble to find out what was really in it. Much of it has been published as essays so that one has to wonder why Burke did not send it off to the University of California Press to be published as a whole. It is certainly a finished work.

1. "Poetic," "Aesthetic," and "Artistic"
2. Logic of the Terms
3. Imitation (Mimesis)
4. Catharsis (First View)
5. Pity, Fear, Pride
6. The Thinking of the Body
7. Form
8. The Orestes Trilogy
9. Beyond Catharsis
10. Catharsis (Second View)
    Vagaries of Love and Pity
    Fragmentation
11. Platonic Transcendence
12. The Poetic Motive

Still to come, Burke says in a note, are a section on comic catharsis, further references to individual works, footnotes indicating other developments, and an appendix reprinting various related essays. See my text, *Kenneth Burke and the Drama of Human Relations,* 2d ed. (Berkeley: University of California Press, 1982) 290–91.

7. *The literary and critical essays from* Language as Symbolic Action (1966)
All of part 2, plus "Poetics in Particular, Language in General" and "*Coriolanus*—And the Delights of Faction," plus "Rhetoric and Poetics," "Myth, Poetry, and Philosophy," and "Formalist Criticism" from

part 3. The bulk of *Language as Symbolic Action* is about literature and Burke's poetics; it represents work Burke did from 1950 to 1966, almost all of which is related in some way to his dramatistic poetics (which includes the "Symbolic of Motives" as originally conceived and later revised to become PDC.)

The literary essays from *Language as Symbolic Action* are as follows:

"The Vegetal Radicalism of Theodore Roethke." 1950

"Form and Persecution in the *Oresteia*." 1952

"Goethe's *Faust, Part I*." 1954/55

"*Faust II*—The Ideas Behind the Imagery." 1965

The three Shakespeare essays on *Coriolanus, Antony and Cleopatra,* and *Timon of Athens.* 1963–66

"I, Eye, Ay" on Emerson's *Nature.*" 1966

"*Kubla Khan*, Proto-Surrealist Poem." 1966

"Social and Cosmic Mystery: *A Passage to India.*" 1966

"Version, Con-, Per-, and In- (Thoughts on Djuna Barnes's novel *Nightwood*)." 1966

"The Thinking of the Body: Comments on the Imagery of Catharsis in Literature." Published in 1963 but written in the early and mid-fifties.

I suppose one could include here the tribute to William Carlos Williams, an essay paired with the tribute to e. e. cummings that appears in *Collected Poems;* and the long essay, "Formalist Criticism: Its Principles and Limits."

All of these essays had appeared in print before they were included in *Language as Symbolic Action*. A final Shakespeare essay on Lear, which is clearly part of this tragedy group, appeared shortly after *Language as Symbolic Action* was published: "King Lear: Its Form and Psychosis," *Shenandoah* 21 (Fall 1968): 3–18. Some of these essays underwent a lot of revision so that if you want to read the original version you have to either go to PDC or the first place of publication. For the long version of the *Oresteia* essay, you have to go to PDC; the same is true of "The Thinking of the Body" essay. The *Faust I* analysis has been taken out of its original context in "The Language of Poetry, 'Dramatistically' Considered" and so lacks its theoretical framework. The other essays are pretty much as Burke originally wrote them for publication, though he was a great reviser anytime he had a chance to go back to one of his essays or talks.

There are other essays in *Language as Symbolic Action* that deal with literature and literary criticism: for example, "Poetics in Particular, Language in General," "Rhetoric and Poetics," and "Myth, Poetry, and Philosophy." Sixteen of the twenty-four essays in the collection are about literature and literary criticism. The rest are about dramatism and logology, but mostly dramatism. Most of the logology essays came later, between 1968 and 1984, and were written after Libbie Burke died in 1969. Except for the *King Lear* essay, Burke did not write any more literary criticism after 1966 but turned to other matters.

Anyone who tries to deal seriously with Burke's dramatistic poetics is going to have to have *Language as Symbolic Action* near at hand, as well as access to the two manuscripts discussed here, and copies of the original "Symbolic" essays for items that did not make it into *Language as Symbolic Action*. Burke's dramatistic poetics is distinct from the larger theory of symbolic action that gives this book its title, even though they tend to merge into each other in Burke's definition of a text as any verbal structure of organically interrelated terms with a beginning, middle, and end. This definition applies equally well to a fourteen-line sonnet or a five-hundred-page book, as does Burke's methodology of indexing. The current trend in Burke studies is to treat everything the same and concentrate on the overall vision, and the place of rhetoric in it. Burke is treated as a pioneer of the New Rhetoric and as an important social critic. His beginnings seem to have been lost sight of, though Jack Selzer's book, *Kenneth Burke in Greenwich Village,* goes a long way toward reclaiming them. The fact that the different parts of Burke's dramatistic poetics are scattered about in numerous essays, in hundreds of pages of uncollected and/or unpublished manuscripts and in many essays in *Language as Symbolic Action* does not encourage one to argue for a final, coherent, dramatistic theory of literature and literary criticism. But both do exist. Maybe Burke did not want to be systematized any more than that. He left three, maybe four potential books behind that he could easily have assembled during his later years. He certainly was not silent after 1966. He was never better known, more in demand, never more famous and recognized than he was during the twenty years after *Language as Symbolic Action* was published. But Burke was very difficult to work with and wanted his own way in all matters. He even wanted to revise some of my essays on him to "get them straight." Rumor has it that he would not collect his late poems because he did not want to argue with the editors at the

University of California Press about what would be included. I offered to do a collection of the late essays—*On Human Nature*—for him, as well as a collection of the original "Symbolic" essays. After many years of asking, he agreed, but I thought better of both projects realizing that every choice would produce a terrific hassle that only Burke could win. I well remember Burke's explosion when a copy editor at the University of California Press made changes in his "Afterwords" to *Permanence and Change* and *Attitudes Toward History*.

I don't know if Burke would agree with my conclusions here: he once sent me a list of what should go in the "Symbolic of Motives" that consisted of material written over a twenty-seven year period (1950–77/78). It was a hopeless list, really, and was the main reason I abandoned the project—until now. The preponderance of literary material in *Language as Symbolic Action* should probably encourage us, now, to reevaluate this collection after thirty-two years. Such a reassessment would surely reveal that *Language as Symbolic Action* is the final work in the dramatistic project Burke began in *A Grammar of Motives*. Dramatism comes to its culmination in Burke's dramatistic poetics and theory of language as symbolic action—the two dominant concerns of *Language as Symbolic Action*. When he moved on, it was not back to dramatism, but forward, from *The Rhetoric of Religion*, where logology was first formulated, to more studies in logology.

Part Two

Criticism, Symbolicity, and Tropology

5

A Rhetoric of Form: The Early Burke and Reader-Response Criticism

Greig Henderson

The early work of Kenneth Burke anticipates and exemplifies many of the significant trends in contemporary literary theory and criticism. In this chapter I want to consider Burke's contributions to reader-response criticism, mainly by focusing on *Counter-Statement* (1931), a collection of essays often misleadingly labeled aestheticist or symbolist. This is not to say that these labels are entirely inaccurate—Burke himself admits that the progression in his criticism is from self-expression to communication to consummation (tracking down the implications of a nomenclature). It is to say, however, that a collection whose showpiece is "Lexicon Rhetoricae" more obviously invites the label "rhetorical." Rhetoric, moreover, is hardly incongruent with reader response, for theory that grounds itself in the latter is self-evidently audience-oriented even if it phenomenologizes or psychologizes the language of traditional rhetoric. If such theory is stripped of its technical vocabulary, one gets a picture of the reading process that is remarkably akin to the early Burke's. "Psychology and Form," "Lexicon Rhetoricae," and "Applications of Terminology," I shall argue, together compose a version of reader-response criticism, though in isolating them one must remember that such an audience-oriented form of criticism is only one dimension of dramatism and logology.

In later works, Burke gravitates toward a text-oriented form of criticism, preferring the language of internal consistency to that of audience expectancy. As he notes in a 1953 addendum to *Counter-Statement,* one of the purposes of *The Philosophy of Literary Form* (1941) was "to sketch a technique for the analysis of a work in its nature as a structure of interrelated terms. Whereas the stress in *Counter-Statement* had been rhetorical (form as the arousing and fulfilling of an audience's expectations), the stress now was upon the work in its internality" (217). Yet even in "Poetics, Dramatistically Considered" (1958), the most resolutely Aristotelian of all of his works, Burke concedes that consistency and expectancy are two ways of talking about the same thing. "Every *development*" in the unfolding of a work, he writes, "can be adequately described as a *revealment* [to the audience] (which is to say: every successive stage in an *act* can be treated as the unveiling of a new *insight* that was prepared for by the foregoing stages)" (36). Therefore, "all such procedures . . . can be stated either as means of guiding the audience's expectations and responses, or as stages symbolized or imitated in the work itself" (301). In spite of his various attempts to keep poetics and rhetoric separate, Burke is at his best when he conflates them, and his pervasive concern with Aristotle, from *A Grammar of Motives* (1945) through "Poetics, Dramatistically Considered" (1958), has more of an impact on his way of talking than on the topic of conversation.[1]

The relationship between psychology and form is at the core of *Counter-Statement*. In illustrating this relationship, Burke insists that the one must be defined in terms of the other. The psychology in question, however,

> is not the psychology of the *hero*, but the psychology of the *audience*. And by that distinction, form would be the psychology of the audience. Or, seen from another angle, form is the creation of an appetite in the mind of the auditor, and the adequate satisfying of that appetite. This satisfaction—so complicated is the human mechanism—at times involves a temporary set of frustrations, but in the end these frustrations prove to be simply a more involved kind of satisfaction, and furthermore serve to make the satisfaction of fulfillment more intense. (31)

This focus on how an auditor's appetites are created, satisfied, frustrated, and fulfilled is at the core of reader-response criticism, a mode of analysis that systematically examines the aspects of a text that arouse, shape, and guide a reader's response. According to this kind of criticism, a reader is as much a producer as a consumer of meanings. Because a reader's expectations may be fulfilled or violated, satisfied or frustrated, sustained or modified; and because reading is a temporal process involving memory, perception, and anticipation; the charting of reader response is extremely difficult and perpetually subject to construction, deconstruction, and reconstruction.

Reader-response criticism, of course, does not denote any specific theory. It can range from the phenomenological theories of Roman Ingarden and Wolfgang Iser—both of whom argue that although the reader fills in the gaps, the author's intentional acts inscribed in the text impose restrictions and conditions—to the relativistic analyses of Stanley Fish—who argues that the interpretive strategy of the reader creates the text, there being no text except that which a reader or an interpretive community of readers creates. Although these theories foreground the relationship between the text and reader, they differ markedly in the weight they assign to each. For the sake of simplicity, I shall divide the field into three categories: text-active, biactive, and reader-active.[2]

At one end of the spectrum are text-active theories. Their proponents assume that there is a single right reading implied and realized by the text itself; that extratextual and extraliterary factors can be defined, identified, and avoided; and that the ideal reader is a *tabula rasa* receptive to the impingements of the text but devoid of any responses that are not caused or conditioned by its verbal structure. Such theories tend to be formalist in orientation, but some versions of reader-response criticism fall within their purview. Georges Poulet, for example, notes that the reader must think the thought of another. According to him, the work is a verbalization of authorial subjectivity, and the reader must strive to attain consciousness of the consciousness of another. In an ideal scenario, there is a dynamic interfusion of the animating subjective principle of the author, its verbal embodiment in the formal perfection of the text, and its incorporation into the receptive subjectivity of the reader. The reader, therefore, submits to the authoritative subjectivity of another. The resultant self-contained world of intersubjectivity suggests that the difference between Poulet's phenomenology and New Critical formalism is not as pronounced as it might initially seem. Both assume communicative efficacy; both disregard all extrinsic or contextual factors such as society, history, or ideology; and both posit a model of uncontaminated transmission such that there is no static between transmitter and receiver. Both, in other words, assume the self-sufficiency of the text; the difference between them is mainly terminological.

At the other end of the spectrum are reader-active theories. Stanley Fish, for example, combines audacious relativism—the interpretive strategy of the reader creates the text—with conservative professionalism—readers belong to interpretive communities, a fact that explains why modes of interpretation become normalized and why communication between interpreters is possible. The defensible claim that no priority can be ascribed to either the formal pattern of the text or the in-

terpretive strategy of a reader gets confused with a claim that is as un-
verifiable as it is irrefutable: namely, that interpretation creates authorial intention and its formal realization, that different strategies
make different texts.

Because they fail to ask why certain modes of interpretation attain
hegemony at certain historical moments, both text-active and reader-
active theories are equally insensitive to the ideological and historical
nature of the horizons of expectation that constitute the work, the
reader, and the interpretive community to which he or she belongs.

Less exciting because less extreme, but also less susceptible to *re-
ductio ad absurdum,* are biactive theories, theories that see the text
and reader as acting together; the text sets limits and the reader re-
sponds to it within those limits and within the limits of his or her own
subjectivity, ideology, psychological makeup, literary competence, and
so forth. Whether the text or the reader has priority is an unanswerable
question, and the greatest wisdom, perhaps, is to learn to unask the
question. Wolfgang Iser, for example, insists on the inherently ambiguous nature of the transaction between the formal structure of a text, a
structure that inevitably has its narrative gaps and places of indeterminacy, and the constructive or deconstructive imagination of a reader, an
imagination that concretizes and realizes the unwritten parts of a text.
The early Burke, I shall argue, anticipates much of what is postulated
in Iser's landmark study, *The Implied Reader.* Although Iser offers a
better account of how the reader's process of anticipation and retrospection builds consistencies in the face of alien associations, Burke
offers a better account of the role of categorical expectancies and ideological assumptions—the generic and cultural foreknowledge we possess prior to the reading experience, what Roland Barthes calls the *déjà
lu.* Burke also has a more workable and comprehensive notion of form
in its progressive, repetitive, conventional, and incidental aspects. That
is, Burke is more attuned to what hermeneutical critics call the horizon
of expectations, a set of culturally and historically conditioned assumptions and conventions implicit in either the verbal meaning of a text or
the interpretive strategy of a reader. Like Hans-Georg Gadamer and
Martin Heidegger, Burke recognizes the historicity and temporality of
interpretation, meaning always being codetermined, the reader's horizon of expectation attempting to fuse with the author's. Perfect fusion,
of course, is impossible, and an inescapable relativity and indeterminacy are thereby introduced into the notion of interpretation. As Burke
reflects in *Counter-Statement:*

> Any reader surrounds each word and each act in a work
> of art with a *unique* set of his own previous experiences

(and therefore a unique set of imponderable emotional reactions), communication existing in the "margin of overlap" between the writer's experience and the reader's. And while it is dialectically true that two people of totally different experiences must totally fail to communicate, it is also true that there are no such two people, the "margin of overlap" always being considerable (due, if to nothing else, to the fact that man's biologic functions are uniform). Absolute communication between ages is impossible in the same way that absolute communication between contemporaries is impossible. And conversely, as we communicate approximately though "imprisoned within the walls of our personality," so we communicate approximately though imprisoned within the walls of our age. (78–79)

Also acknowledging that communication is approximate rather than absolute, Iser builds his reader-oriented theory on the notion of narrative gaps, places of indeterminacy that the reader, actively engaged in the gradually unfolding process of assimilating and incorporating the various aspects and levels of a text, must concretize, making the implicit explicit, the potential actual. The text, however, imposes some constraints; the reader cannot make it mean whatever he or she likes. According to Iser, the text provides "a network of response-inviting structures" (34), prompting the reader to respond to it in certain ways. But although the text has this skeleton of determinate meanings, it is the reader who fleshes out its concrete body by filling in the gaps and realizing the unwritten implications. Thus the reader is both active and passive, constructive and receptive. The actual reader undergoes a dynamic process of memory, perception, and anticipation, whereas the implied reader is controlled by this skeleton of determination, this network of response-inviting structures. That is, the implied reader "embodies all those predispositions necessary for the literary work to exercise its effect—predispositions laid down, not by empirical outside reality, but by the text itself" (34). The implied reader is thus a hypothetical construct of norms, values, ideas, attitudes, emotions, beliefs, and expectations that can be derived or extrapolated from the work or may even be said to inhere in the work.[3] Iser wants both reader response and textual determination. Such a view of the act of reading is overtly biactive. "The convergence of text and reader brings the literary work into existence, and this convergence can never be precisely pinpointed, but must always remain virtual, as it is not to be identified either with the reality of the text or with the individual disposition of the reader" (275).

Positing such a convergence, of course, openly begs the question of assigning priority to either text or reader, but however unafraid of Wolfgang Iser Stanley Fish may be, Iser's recognition of the essentially ambiguous transaction between the reality of the text and the individual disposition of the reader seems eminently preferable to the text-active or reader-active alternatives. As Burke suggests in *Language as Symbolic Action,* terminologies "direct the attention." "Even if any given terminology is a *reflection* of reality, by its very nature as a terminology it must be a *selection* of reality; and to this extent it must function also as a *deflection* of reality" (45). A way of seeing, as Burke is fond of pointing out, is also a way of *not* seeing. To maintain, as Fish does, that interpretive terminologies shape and affect perception but that the verbal structure of the text does not is to be at once sensitive to formative nature of terminologies and insensitive to the dialectical nature of the transaction between reader and text. Reader and text intersect; where precisely we cannot say.

In describing this "interaction between text and reader" (276), Iser notes that the reader's "process of anticipation and retrospection itself does not by any means develop in a smooth flow" (279). "The reader's communication with the text is a dynamic process of self-correction" (67), and "throughout the reading process . . . there is a continual interplay between modified expectations and transformed memories" (111). Blockage is thereby unavoidable because all stories contain omissions, and "it is only through inevitable omissions that a story gains its dynamism" (280). For Iser, the reading process is necessarily selective, and the potential text is infinitely richer than any of its actual realizations.

> For this reason, expectations are scarcely ever fulfilled in truly literary texts. If they were, then such texts would be confined to the individualization of a given expectation, and one would inevitably ask what such an intention was supposed to achieve. Strangely enough, we feel that any confirmative effect—such as we implicitly demand of expository texts . . . is a defect in a literary text. For the more a text individualizes or confirms an expectation it has initially aroused, the more aware we become of its didactic purpose, so that at best we can only accept or reject the thesis forced upon us. (278)

If the text confirms our expectations too predictably, the result is "the boredom which inevitably arises when everything is laid out cut and dried before us" (275). If it violates our expectations too radically, the result is "overstrain" (275).

Burke makes an analogous point but gives it a different twist. For him, the criterion of rereadability is paramount. Works that depend on the psychology of information—such as formulaic detective novels that inexorably move forward until the identity of the murderer is revealed—are not as rereadable as works that depend on the psychology of form. "The hypertrophy of the psychology of information," Burke contends, "is accompanied by a corresponding atrophy of the psychology of form" (CS 33).

> One reason why music can stand repetition so much more sturdily than correspondingly good prose is that music, of all the arts, is by its nature least suited to the psychology of information, and has remained closer to the psychology of form. Here form cannot atrophy. Every dissonant chord cries for its solution, and whether the musician resolves or refuses to resolve this dissonance into the chord which the body cries for, he is dealing with human appetites. Correspondingly good prose, however, more prone to the temptations of pure information, cannot so much bear repetition since the aesthetic value of information is lost once that information is imparted. If one returns to such a work again it is purely because, in the chaos of modern life, he has been able to forget it. With a desire, on the other hand, its recovery is as agreeable as its discovery. . . . We cannot take a recurrent pleasure in the new (in information) but we can in the natural (in form). (CS 34–35)

A plot-driven formulaic work "too often has for its value the mere fact that we do not know its outcome," whereas a work that "deals minutely in frustrations and fulfillments of desire . . . more often gives us the curves of emotion which . . . can bear repetition without loss. . . . Suspense is the least complex kind of anticipation, as surprise is the least complex kind of fulfillment" (CS 36). "The methods of maintaining interest which are most natural to the psychology of information . . . are surprise and suspense. The method most natural to the psychology of form is eloquence . . . formal excellence" (CS 37). With eloquence and formal excellence, "elements of surprise and suspense are subtilized, carried down into the writing of a line or a sentence, until in all its smallest details the work bristles with disclosures, contrasts, restatements with a difference, ellipses, images, aphorism, volume, sound-values, in short all that complex wealth of minutiae which in their line-for-line aspect we call style and in their broader outline we call form" (*CS* 37–38).

Burke's sense of the fourfold nature of form, of the interrelation and conflict of forms, along with his recognition of the role of categorical expectancies and ideological assumptions, as I shall later make clear, offers us a richer picture of the levels on which reading operates than Iser's. Iser, however, offers us a richer picture of gestalt formation and consistency building.

To "the process of anticipation and retrospection," Iser maintains, "we must add the process of grouping together all the different aspects of a text to form the consistency that the reader will always be in search of. While expectations may be continually modified, and the images continually expanded, the reader will still strive, even if unconsciously, to fit everything together into a consistent pattern" (283). Consistency, of course, is a quintessentially formalist and organicist assumption, but even the poststructuralist reader, who refuses to totalize or impose closure on the disseminating text, consistently searches out its inconsistencies. Moreover, Iser is well aware that there are *consistencies;* the gestalt, for him, is not the one true meaning of the text. Reading does not comprise "an uninterrupted building of illusions" (284). "The polysemantic nature of the text and the illusion-making of the reader are opposed factors. If the illusion were complete, the polysemantic nature would vanish; if the polysemantic nature were all-powerful, the illusion would be destroyed" (285). There is no doubt that many contemporary readers prefer to destroy the illusion, and his own protestations notwithstanding, there is nothing in Iser's theory to prohibit *inconsistency-building*—the diligent discovery of an endless play of signification. But even those traditional readers who strive to find a consistent pattern in the text uncover perforce "other impulses which cannot be immediately integrated or will even resist final integration" (285). For "configurative meaning is always accompanied by 'alien associations' that do not fit in with the illusions formed" (286). Even expectations that have already been fulfilled in a prior reading are subject to change, for foreground and background may now switch places. What were places of indeterminacy in a first reading may no longer be so in a second, and this is the major weakness of Iser's account. Since places of indeterminacy may differ from reader to reader and from reading to reading, not to mention from historical period to historical period, there is no way of predicting precisely where they will occur.

The places of indeterminacy, then, wherever they occur, necessitate that we fill in the gaps and at the same time give rise to alien associations. The consistent pattern our interpretation strives to construct or deconstruct is perpetually stymied by these alien associations and threatened by the presence of other possibilities. There is thus an oscillation between the building and breaking of illusions, an interplay between deduction and induction, between a projected sense of the whole and a disconcerting awareness of the obstinate and recalcitrant nature of the parts. Enclosed in a hermeneutic circle, we engage in a process of trial and error, of inference and guesswork, of construction, deconstruction, and reconstruction.

> This process is steered by two main structural components in the text: first, a repertoire of familiar literary patterns and recurrent literary themes, together with allusions to familiar social and historical contexts; second, techniques or strategies used to set the familiar against the unfamiliar. Elements of the repertoire are continually backgrounded and foregrounded with a resultant strategic overmagnification, trivialization, or even annihilation of the allusion. This defamiliarization of what the reader thought he recognized is bound to create a tension that will intensify his expectations as well as his distrust of those expectations. (288)

Annihilation, defamiliarization, tension—from these to undecidability is no large leap, for the clash between consistencies and alien associations may be seen to produce an unavoidable impasse or aporia. The deconstructive abyss is thereby glimpsed.

Although Iser refers to a repertoire of familiar literary patterns and recurrent literary themes, together with allusions to familiar social and historical contexts, he has little to say about them specifically and almost nothing to say about how categorical expectancies and ideological assumptions are implicit in both the text's and the reader's horizon of expectations or about how these expectancies and assumptions affect both the production and consumption of meaning. The deficiency of Iser's theory becomes apparent at the moment of application. How does one identify places of indeterminacy in more than a subjective way? Are they historically or individually determined? What guarantee is there that a reader will be familiar with the repertoire of material selected from literary traditions and social systems? The moment these questions are asked is the moment the concept of the implied reader begins to dissolve, at least insofar as the implied reader is supposed to embody "predispositions laid down, not by empirical outside reality, but by the text itself" (Iser 34). The implied reader turns out be a competent or informed reader, a member of a particular interpretive community. As Susan Suleiman points out in her introduction to *The Reader in the Text,* "the reading subject [that emerges from Iser's account] is not a specific, historically situated individual but a transhistorical mind whose activities are, at least formally, everywhere the same" (25).

In *Doing What Comes Naturally,* Stanley Fish, as one might expect, ups the ante and challenges absolutely "the brute-fact status of the text" (75). For him, even at the most rudimentary level, the very grammar, syntax, and semantics of a text are created by the reader. "Gaps," there-fore, "are not built into the text, but appear (or do not appear) as a consequence of particular interpretive strategies . . . there is no distinc-tion between what the text gives and the reader supplies; he supplies *everything*" (77). As I suggested earlier, Fish's position is as irrefutable as it is indefensible. If all facts are interpretations, then rhetorical per-suasion takes the place of logical demonstration, the latter being a spe-cies of argumentation that ultimately depends on a correspondence theory of truth whereby propositions match or do not match the facts of experience—facts that, for Fish, do not exist apart from their con-ventional acceptance by some interpretive community. Nevertheless, if interpretation is the only game in town, and if criteria of coherence sup-plant those of correspondence, then Fish's position can only be de-fended on the grounds that it is more persuasive than Iser's. In such a game, of course, the only permissible move is to rejoin that Fish's posi-tion is not as persuasive as Iser's and to try to convince others that the admittedly telling objections to some of Iser's ideas do not justify aban-doning the biactive model and embracing the reader-active one. That places of indeterminacy may be either personal or historical or both, and that the repertoire will vary according to the literary and historical competence of the reader, do not provide compelling reasons for plac-ing everything in the reader.

Burke's account of the reading process has the advantage of being overtly rhetorical and thereby avoids being saddled with the spurious scientificity of phenomenological description.[4] "If rhetoric is but 'the use of language in such a way as to produce a desired impression upon the hearer or reader,'" he writes, "then 'effective literature' could be nothing else but rhetoric" (CS 120). And if form is the psychology of the audience, then what is required is a practical vocabulary for describ-ing the various aspects of form. Burke openly admits that such a vo-cabulary is nothing but a terministic screen, an interpretive strategy. "Lexicon Rhetoricae," he writes, is simply a "machine for criticism . . . a set of 'pivotal' or 'key' terms for discussing the processes of liter-ary appeal . . . a critical nomenclature for paralleling in analytic terms what a work of art itself performs in terms of the 'creative,' the 'imagi-native'" (CS ix). The lexicon "attempts to define the principles under-lying the appeal of literature" (CS 123). As he observes in "Applications of Terminology," "a writer is engaged in the producing of effects upon his readers. . . . He will manipulate their ideology, he will exploit his and their patterns of experience" (CS 190). Unlike Iser, Burke starts with the assumption that psychology, form, and ideology are interinanimating aspects of rhetoric.

As its subtitle indicates, "Lexicon Rhetoricae" seeks to codify, amplify, and correct "Psychology and Form." Nevertheless, it begins with the same assumptions: that form "is an arousing and fulfillment of desires" and that "a work has form in so far as one part leads a reader to anticipate another part [and] to be gratified by the sequence" (CS 124). The major amplification is to discuss form in terms of four aspects: "progressive form (subdivided into syllogistic and qualitative progression), repetitive form, conventional form, and minor or incidental forms" (CS 124).

Syllogistic progression follows the logic of linear development and "is the form of a perfectly conducted argument, advancing step by step. . . . We call it syllogistic because, given certain things, certain things must follow, the premises forcing the conclusion. In so far as the audience, from its acquaintance with the premises, feels the rightness of the conclusion, the work is formal" (CS 124). Qualitative progression, on the other hand, is subtler. "Instead of one incident of the plot preparing us for some other possible incident of the plot (as Macbeth's murder of Duncan prepares us for the dying of Macbeth), the presence of one quality prepares us for the introduction of another (the grotesque seriousness of the murder scene preparing us for the grotesque buffoonery of the porter scene" (CS 124–25). What we have "is a bold juxtaposition of one quality created by another, an association of ideas, which, if not logical, is nevertheless emotionally natural" (CS 39). Because such progressions "lack the pronounced anticipatory nature of the syllogistic progression," we recognize their rightness "after the event" (CS 125). The plot of an Agatha Christie novel, for example, depends almost exclusively upon syllogistic progression—its logic is that of a deductive argument—whereas the symbolic action of "The Waste Land" depends almost exclusively on qualitative progression—its psycho-logic is that of the association and juxtaposition of images and ideas.

Repetitive form is "the consistent maintaining of a principle under new guises . . . the restatement of a theme by new details" (CS 125). "A succession of images, each of them regiving the same lyric mood; a character repeating his identity, his 'number,' under changing situations; the sustaining of an attitude, as in satire; the rhythmic regularity of blank verse; the rhyme aspect of *terza rima*—these are all aspects of repetitive form" (CS 125). The recurrent tics and mannerisms of an Hercule Poirot or a Sherlock Holmes, for example, provide a source of pleasure that is distinct from the syllogistic progression of the plot and may partly explain why the stories featuring these protagonists in some manner transcend the psychology of information.

Conventional form "involves to some degree the appeal of form *as form*" and has an "element of 'categorical expectancy.' . . . Whereas the anticipations and gratifications of progressive and repetitive form arise *during the process* of reading, the expectations of conventional form may be *anterior to* the reading" (*CS* 126–27). One expects a sonnet by Shakespeare, for example, to be a lyric poem in iambic pentameter that is divided into three quatrains and a couplet, that together rhyme *abab cdcd efef gg*. This is not to say, however, that there is anything permanent about categorical expectancies and conventional forms. On the contrary, "categorical expectations are very unstable," and "the artist can, if his use of the repetitive and progressive principles is authoritative enough, succeed in bringing his audience to a sufficient acceptance of his methods" (*CS* 204). In fact, "the changes may very rapidly become 'canonized' in popular acceptance and the earlier convention may seem the violator of categorical expectancy" (*CS* 204). In *Waiting for Godot*, Samuel Beckett's failure to provide a purposeful flow of beginning, middle, and end violated the categorical expectancies of his 1953 audience but eventually became an integral part of the conventions of the Theatre of the Absurd. As far as the artist working in the present is concerned, conventional forms and categorical expectancies are simply rhetorical resources to be exploited; they may be used to fulfill or violate, satisfy or frustrate, sustain or modify the expectations of an audience.

Minor or incidental forms are aspects of a work "which can be discussed as formal events in themselves" — "such as metaphor, paradox, disclosure, reversal, contraction, expansion, bathos, apostrophe, series, chiasmus" (*CS* 127). "Their effect partially depends upon their function in the whole, yet they manifest sufficient evidences of episodic distinctness to bear consideration apart from their context. . . . A monologue by Shakespeare can be detached from its context and recited with enjoyment because, however integrally it contributes to the whole of which it is a part, it is also an independent curve of plot enclosed by its own beginning and end" (*CS* 127).

Progressive, repetitive, conventional, and minor forms necessarily overlap. As Burke points out:

> The lines in Othello, beginning "Soft you, a word or two before you go," and ending "Seized by the throat the uncircumcised dog and smote him thus *(stabs himself)*" well exemplify the vigorous presence of all five aspects of form, as

this suicide is the logical outcome of his predicament (syllogistic progression); it fits the general mood of gloomy fore-
bodings which has fallen upon us (qualitative progression);
the speech has about it that impetuosity and picturesqueness
we have learned to associate with Othello (repetitive form);
it is very decidedly a conclusion (conventional form); and
in its development it is a tiny plot in itself (minor form).
(CS 128)[5]

Sometimes, however, the forms may conflict, for "an author may create
a character which, by the logic of the fiction, should be destroyed; but
he may also have made the character so appealing that the audience
wholly desires the character's salvation" (CS 129).

Forms, for Burke, are ways of encompassing experiential and ideological complexities. Although art deals with "the constants of humanity . . . the recurrent emotions, the fundamental attitudes, the typical
experiences . . . art is also historical—a particular mode of adjustment
to a particular cluster of conditions" (CS 107). "A form is a way of
experiencing" (CS 143), and a writer necessarily manipulates readers'
ideologies in order to arouse, shape, and control their desires. In Burke's
lexicon, the term "ideology" is used descriptively; it is not a synonym
for "false consciousness."

By an ideology is meant the nodus of beliefs and judgments
which the artist can exploit for his effects. It varies from one
person to another, and from one age to another—but in
so far as its general acceptance and its stability are more
stressed than its particular variations from person to person
and from age to age, an ideology is a "culture." But there
are cultures within cultures, since society can be subdivided
into groups with divergent standards and interests. Each of
these subdivisions of a culture may possess its own characteristic ideology (contrast the ideology of a young radical in
the coal mines with the ideology of a retired banker touring
the Mediterranean), but in so far as they overlap they belong
to the same culture (both the radical and the banker, for instance, may despise the informer). Generally, the ideology of
an individual is a slight variant of the ideology distinguishing the class among which he arose. (CS 161–62)

Accepting the essential rhetoricity of all discourse, Burke acknowl-
edges that "the artist obtains his effects by manipulating our ideological
assumptions in many ways" (CS 162). Unlike Iser's, Burke's conception
of the repertoire of material drawn from literary traditions and social

systems is neither static nor monolithic, for "an ideology is not a harmonious structure of beliefs or assumptions; some of its beliefs militate
against others, and some of its standards militate against our nature.
An ideology is an aggregate of beliefs sufficiently at odds with one another to justify opposite kinds of conduct" (CS 163). A reader, to give
a simple example, may hold contradictory beliefs, say, in the desirability
of ecological balance and the beneficence of technological progress, and
the artist may exploit these ideological inconsistencies, pitting "the
assumptions of natural beauty" against "the industrialist's assumptions of progress—or vice versa" (CS 163). Moreover, artists themselves may unwittingly embrace profound ambivalences, embedding
contradictory assumptions into the structure and texture of their own
writing. Though form is undoubtedly the psychology of the audience,
the author's manipulation of ideological assumptions and readerly
expectations—whether those assumptions and expectations be categorical or text-specific—is an inordinately complex business, and at the
same time authors are manipulating others, they are inevitably manipulating themselves. Burke's conception of the fourfold nature of form
shows how formal motives generate verbal substance, constrain discursive practice, and condition reader response. The rhetoric of form not
only has a suasive impact upon the audience; it also has a suasive impact, conscious or unconscious, upon the author. While we are using
the formal, rhetorical, and ideological resources of language and literature, they are using us.

To account for the reading process, then, is to account for a manifold of factors. Though the defects of Iser's approach have been touched
on above, his phenomenology has the virtue of deploying the biactive
model and stressing the dynamism of the reading process. The theory is
weak, in my view, insofar as it is a *phenomenology* rather than a *rhetoric* of reading. Once one accepts the claim that form is the psychology
of the audience—and Burke, it seems to me, made good on that claim
nearly seventy years ago—then the value of a reader-response theory
resides in the resourcefulness and scope of its rhetorical lexicon, in the
relative proportions of blindness and insight to which its reflections, selections, and deflections give rise. It seems to me that "Psychology and
Form," "Lexicon Rhetoricae," and "Applications of Terminology"—
the riches of which have only been adumbrated—together compose a
version of reader-response criticism that is theoretically defensible and
practically useful. If one supplements these early essays from *Counter-
Statement* with the tools of discourse analysis to be found in Burke's
subsequent meditations on the grammatical, rhetorical, poetical, and
ethical aspects of language as symbolic action, one has a powerful machine for criticism indeed.

Notes

1. Burke's relationship to Aristotle is too complicated to explore here, but it is interesting to note that references to Aristotle from *Counter-Statement* (1931) through *The Philosophy of Literary Form* (1941) are incidental rather than substantive. From *A Grammar of Motives* (1945) through "Poetics, Dramatistically Considered" (1958), Aristotle is a ubiquitous presence, Burke having enjoyed "the advantage of friendly controversy with the 'Neo-Aristotlians'" during a term at the University of Chicago" (*CS* 218) in 1938 and in 1949–50. In 1942, he published "The Problem of the Intrinsic (as reflected in the Neo-Aristotelian School)," which is included as an appendix to *A Grammar of Motives*.

2. The first two terms are borrowed from Norman Holland. See his "Recovering 'The Purloined Letter': Reading as a Personal Transaction." There are, of course, many versions of reader-response criticism—Holland's psychoanalytical "transactive criticism," David Bleich's "subjective criticism," not to mention feminist, hermeneutical, structuralist-semiotic, sociological-historical, and so on. In her introduction to *The Reader in the Text,* Suleiman surveys six varieties of audience-oriented criticism.

3. As an example of predispositions laid down by the text itself, consider the frame narrator's metalingual instructions to the audience near the beginning of Conrad's *Heart of Darkness:* "The yarns of seamen have a direct simplicity, the whole meaning of which lies within the shell of a cracked nut. But Marlow was not typical (if his propensity to spin yarns be excepted), and to him the meaning of an episode was not inside like a kernel but outside, enveloping the tale which brought it out only as a glow brings out a haze, in the likeness of one of these misty halos that sometimes are made visible by the spectral illumination of moonshine." After Marlow begins to speak, the frame narrator knows that he and his companions are "fated . . . to hear about one of Marlow's inconclusive experiences." The reader is thereby conditioned to expect what the text will *not* offer: it will not offer a typical sea yarn or adventure story; it will not offer a kernel of significance that can be readily extracted from the text's symbolic action; it will not offer a conclusive experience. All stories predispose their readers in one direction or another, though not always in so overt a fashion.

4. I say "spurious" because all accounts of the reading process are *ex post facto* reconstructions of an interpretive process that is necessarily mediated by reflexive discursivity and that is never a direct transcription of immediate experience. Like all criticism, reader-response criticism is an art of prophesying after the event.

5. Taking no pleasure in cutting Othello down to size, I nevertheless note that Shakespeare's text actually reads: "I took by th' throat the circumcised dog, / And smote him—thus."

Bibliography

Burke, Kenneth. *Counter-Statement.* 1931. Berkeley: University of California Press, 1968.

——. *Language as Symbolic Action: Essays on Life, Literature, and Method.*
Berkeley: University of California Press, 1966.

——. "Poetics, Dramatistically Considered." Manuscript, 1958.

Fish, Stanley. *Doing What Comes Naturally: Change, Rhetoric, and the Practice of Theory in Literary and Legal Studies.* Durham: Duke University Press, 1989.

——. *Is There a Text in This Class? The Authority of Interpretive Communities.* Cambridge: Harvard University Press, 1980.

Holland, Norman. "Recovering 'The Purloined Letter': Reading as a Personal Transaction." In *The Reader in the Text: Essays on Audience and Interpretation.* Ed. Susan R. Suleiman and Inge Crossman. Princeton: Princeton University Press, 1980. 350–70.

Iser, Wolfgang. *The Implied Reader: Patterns of Communication in Prose Fiction from Bunyan to Beckett.* Baltimore: Johns Hopkins Press, 1974.

Poulet, Georges. "Phenomenology of Reading." Trans. Richard Macksey. *New Literary History: A Journal of Theory and Interpretation* 1.1 (Oct. 1969): 53–68.

The Reader in the Text: Essays on Audience and Interpretation. Ed. Susan R. Suleiman and Inge Grossman. Princeton: Princeton University Press, 1980.

6

Screening Symbolicity: Kenneth Burke and Contemporary Theory

Thomas Carmichael

> Any reader of modern French criticism will be astounded to realize that Kenneth Burke, in whose huge output many of the issues and methods currently engaging the French were first discussed, is unknown. Is this the result of ignorance, convenience, or deliberate ideological omission?
> —Edward Said, *The World, the Text, and the Critic*

> Kenneth Burke, it struck me, was one of those rare figures who had never made any of the mistakes—if we can call them that—that were made in contemporary literary theory.
> —Frank Lentricchia, interview by Imre Salusinszky

In the celebrated representative anecdote from *The Philosophy of Literary Form*, Kenneth Burke asks us to envision the source of the materials for drama and the logic of the "dramatic perspective" in a situated discursive moment:

> Imagine that you enter a parlor. You come late. When you arrive, others have long preceded you, and they are engaged in a heated discussion, a discussion too heated for them to pause and tell you exactly what it is about. . . . You listen for awhile, until you decide that you have caught the tenor of the argument; then you put in your oar. . . . However, the discussion is interminable. The hour grows late, you must depart. And you do depart, with the discussion still vigorously in progress. (110–11)

With its suggestion of our embeddedness within an "unending conversation," Burke's anecdote directs us toward both the historical situation of rhetoric and the ways in which all discursive practices are caught
up in an infinite play of signification, but it also serves to remind us of
the complex network of continuities and affiliations that links his position, particularly in *A Grammar of Motives* and *Language as Symbolic
Action,* with the project of contemporary theory.

As Jean-François Lyotard famously observes in *The Postmodern
Condition,* in "postindustrial society, [or] postmodern culture," "The
grand narrative has lost its credibility, regardless of what mode of unification it uses, regardless of whether it is a speculative narrative or a
narrative of emancipation" (37). Driven by a logic of performativity
and guided by an unshakeable "incredulity toward metanarratives,"
postmodern knowledge is characteristically provisional, local, and pragmatic, produced out of contemporary language games that proceed in
the absence of any metalinguistic authority (xxix). Lyotard's influential
reading of the condition of postmodernity is by now of course well-
known, but what Lyotard asserts more widely about all forms of contemporary knowledge is perhaps most accurate with respect to linguistically oriented cultural theory as it has developed over the past quarter
century. As Paul de Man once observed, the resistance to theory is "in
fact a resistance to reading," a resistance which in de Man's terms re-
capitulates the latent tension between rhetoric and grammar: "The resistance to theory is a resistance to the rhetorical or tropological dimension of language, a dimension which is perhaps more explicitly in the
foreground in literature (broadly conceived) . . . or—to be somewhat
less vague—which can be revealed in any verbal event when it is read
textually" (15, 17). For de Man, what is properly known as theory is
rhetorical and threatens a subversion of the grammatical, and it is the
grammatical, de Man argues, that "stands in the service of logic which,
in turn, allows for the passage to the knowledge of the world" (14).
What Lyotard presents as a crisis of legitimation is elaborated by de
Man at the level of the linguistic sign in his tactical demonstration of
the tropological subversion of any affinity between grammar and knowledge.[1] As both of these positions suggest, postmodern theory is resolutely skeptical theory. Burke resolutely anticipates this postmodern/
poststructural project, both its implications and its limitations, and
he does so most clearly through his ambiguous relation to the anti-
foundationalism upon which dramatism rests and which his subsequent
elaborations of symbolic action resist.[2]

In the field of contemporary theory, the figure whose work most
closely conforms to the position that I am attributing to Burke is Stanley
Fish, who argues in *Doing What Comes Naturally* that "epistemologies

are accounts of how we know what we know, not recipes for knowing" (21). In his relentless pursuit of an anti-foundationalist project, Fish at times appears to side with de Man's narrowly figural understanding of theory as rhetoric particularly when he suggests that anti-foundationalism commits one to an "epistemology in which the object to be described cannot be sharply distinguished from the descriptive vocabulary that seems appropriate to it" (143). However, Fish elsewhere signals more clearly his affiliation with Burke, particularly in the ways in which Fish's account of the interpretive community as the scene of these epistemological encounters echoes much of what Burke has to say about terministic screens and contexts. In his description of his own understanding of anti-foundationalist claims for critical self-consciousness, for example, Fish asserts that "each of us is a member of not one but innumerable interpretive communities in relation to which different kinds of belief are operating with different weight and force" (30). For Fish, the import of this assertion is twofold: it enables him to provide an account of how an individual's beliefs might change, and it also identifies theory with nothing more than the claims of practice. As Fish puts it, "theory's project—the attempts to get above practice and lay bare the grounds of its possibility—is an impossible one. Theory is a form of practice, as rooted in particular historical and cultural conditions as any other" (156). Earlier in *Doing What Comes Naturally*, Fish is more blunt about these inescapable conditions and limitations of theory: "all that will tremble when the hit parade of theory undergoes a change is the structure of philosophy departments. . . . Again, I am not denying that theory can have political consequences, merely insisting that those consequences do not belong by right or nature to theory, but are contingent upon the (rhetorical) role theory plays in the particular circumstances of a historical moment" (156, 28). Unlike de Man, who would insist that the rhetorical swerve of theory is really an admission of the prison house of language, Fish argues along with Burke that the claims of theory (and I am claiming that dramatism is very much theory in this sense) are inextricably contingent, always dependent upon a context that is both linguistic and extralinguistic although always already encoded. Faced with the absence of original ground or authority, anti-foundationalist theory seeks to address matters of fact, but, as Stanley Fish would remind us, always in a "language that is infected by partisan agendas and desires, and therefore colors and distorts the facts which it purports to reflect" (474). With its emphasis on the provisional, the contingent, and the local, and its suspicion of any transcendental claim or rhetoric of authority, while all the time recognizing the inescapability of interpretation, postmodern theory, or at least postmodern/poststructural theory in its Americanized form, comes to resemble the position that I will argue is largely Burke's own: anti-foundationalist, skeptical, and inevitably worldly if not finally literal about symbol-using.

Much of what we might consider to be Burke's proleptic contemporary position can of course be drawn from the "Five Summarizing Essays" of *Language as Symbolic Action*, but what we find there with respect to the definition of man and terministic screens also informs his considerably earlier articulation of the dramatistic view in *A Grammar of Motives*. And it begins there with the opening discussion: in his consideration of the "Paradox of Substance" in section two of part one, "The Antinomies of Definition," Burke demonstrates that "the intrinsic and extrinsic can change places," such that to define is always to contextualize and to uncover the absence of a solid ground for a claim to knowledge. And this for Burke leads us to "an *inevitable* paradox of definition, an antinomy that must endow the concept of substance with unresolvable ambiguity, and that will be discovered lurking beneath any vocabulary designed to treat of motivation by the deliberate outlawing of the *word* for substance" (*GM* 24). In part, this "outlawing of the *word* for substance" is simply a consequence of the recognition that all motivation arises out of the enculturated matrices of a "second nature"; as Burke remarks later in this discussion, "One might hypothetically grant that the treatment of motives in terms of 'action' and 'substance' is wholly fallacious, yet defend it as central to the placement of statements about motives. Men have talked about things in many ways, but the pentad offers a synoptic way to talk about their talk-about" (*GM* 33, 56). Burke's privileging of pentadic terms here is largely a provisional one, as it is later in the *Grammar*, and this is borne out in the first paragraph of "Scope and Reduction," in which Burke anticipates his own later attention to terministic screens. Vocabularies, Burke reminds us here, as he will later remind us in *Language as Symbolic Action*, are both selections and deflections of reality (*GM* 59).

This is of course the premise of Burke's later discussion of terministic screens, but what it indicates here in the *Grammar* is an original skepticism on Burke's part with respect to the ability of the verbal or terministic to hook onto the nonverbal. "Dialectically," Burke argues, "the context or ground of the *verbal in general* must be the *nonverbal in general*. But the ground of any particular verbal action must be a complex of verbal and non-verbal factors that can be defined in terms of varying circumference" (*GM* 103). In this respect, Burke's dramatism repeatedly insists upon the ways in which its own terministic schemes, its reductions of circumference, are inevitably inadequate misrepresentations, or at least are governed by only the rough calculus of appropriateness. Yet even this claim is in some sense attenuated by

Burke's emphasis upon the "dialectical principles of merger and division," which returns him at the end of the *Grammar* to the very antinomies of definition with which he began. While " 'events' themselves are often said to be 'constitutive of reality,' " dramatistically speaking we must more adequately say, as Burke does, that "in sum, one's initial act in choosing 'where to draw the line' by choosing terms that merge or terms that divide has an anticipatory effect upon one's conclusions" (*GM* 415). As Greig Henderson points out, Burke's dramatism rejects the foundationalist assumption that "immediate experience—brute and raw—is self-authenticating and provides a foundation for knowledge," and the concomitant principle that "truth involves a correspondence between unmediated, nonconceptual, and nonlinguistic data of experience and the mediated, conceptual, and linguistic scheme that represents them" (92, 93). Although Burke's reliance upon terms such as "adequacy" in discussions of circumference and reduction might seem to mitigate this assertion, the anti-foundationalist position that informs the *Grammar* is consistent with the foregrounding of the very problematic that this position entails in Burke's later work, particularly, as I have noted already, in the "five Summarizing Essays" from *Language as Symbolic Action*.

In his definition of man as the symbol-using animal, Burke commits himself in *Language as Symbolic Action* to the view that "much of what we mean by 'reality' has been built up for us through nothing but our symbol systems" and that while words are "a link between us and the nonverbal, [they] are by the same token a screen separating us from the nonverbal—though the statement gets tangled in its own traces, since so much of the 'we' that is separated from the nonverbal by the verbal would not even exist were it not for the verbal" (*LASA* 3, 5). As Burke subsequently remarks in "Our Attempt to Avoid Mere Relativism," "And now where are we? Must we merely resign ourselves to an endless catalogue of terministic screens, each of which can be valued for the light it throws upon the human animal, yet none of which can be considered central? In one sense, yes . . . " (*LASA* 52). The sense in which this is true for Burke is again in large part a consequence of the explosion of the human capacity to create a second nature. As he asserts in his 1978 essay, "Methodological Repression and/or Strategies of Containment,"

Once the human organism has developed, by physiological mutations, the ability to impose a strong anthropomorphic imprint upon the nonhuman "context of situation" in which humanity developed, the mere postulate that this aptitude for symbolic action is grounded in nonsymbolic (and by the

same token nonhuman) nature does not imply that such a
realm of symbolicity cannot be an originating force in its
own right. Its "ideas" (Logology would prefer to say its
"terms") are not merely "derived" from material conditions;
they are positively "creative" of material conditions. (414)

Although I have observed elsewhere that this suggestion intimates an
access to a "nonhuman 'context of situation'" that is logically prior to
and outside of human signification, Burke's notion that terms are creative entangles us once again in the problem he addresses in "Terministic
Screens": "In brief," Burke asserts, "much that we take as observations
about 'reality' may be but the spinning out of possibilities implicit in
our particular choice of terms" (*LASA* 46).[3] Even in the essay "Dramatism," which is admittedly troublesome for the case I am making and
to which I will return in this discussion, the dramatistic project is defined as a "theory of terminology," to which a nomenclature might as-
pire only "if it were specifically designed to talk, *at one remove,* about
the cycle of terms implicit in the idea of an act" ("Dramatism" 337;
emphasis added). This would seem to mark a clear separation of an act
or "the idea of an act" from any attempt to talk about it, and to represent Burke's embracing of an uncompromising anti-foundationalism
that could only be read as an anticipation of the narrowest forms of
deconstructive thought. But it is also clear that elsewhere and even in
the texts already cited in this discussion, Burke is often quick to point
out that this is not the whole story. There are many moments in Burke
that I might cite to demonstrate this claim, but perhaps the most effective way to make this case in the present discussion is to exploit the
principle of "coöperative competition" by considering Fredric Jameson's reflections on Burke.

In his 1978 essay, "Ideology and Symbolic Action," Jameson
charges that "Burke's too immediate celebration of the free creativity
of human language (in its broadest symbol-making sense) overleaps the
whole dimensions of our (nonnatural) determination by transindividual
historical forces," and this is consistently the crux of Jameson's knock
against Burke (422). As he remarks in a prior essay, "I will therefore re-
gret that Burke finally did not want to teach us history, even though he
wanted to teach us how to grapple with it . . . " ("Symbolic Inference"
523). Jameson's distinction between teaching us history and teaching us
how to grapple with it is designed to drive home his complaint that
dramatism is finally only another form of aestheticized reassurance in
which gesture, ritual, and the illusion of full subjectivity come to pre-
figure every act and every reading. But what Jameson urges in its place

ironically returns us to the conundrum Burke himself has literally grappled with since *A Grammar of Motives*. And that conundrum, expressed in Jamesonian terms, is this: while history is itself not merely a text, it is accessible to us largely only in textualized forms, or we approach it only through its "prior textualization"; nevertheless, history remains the absent cause that every text obscures and discloses. As Jameson puts it,

> The whole paradox of what we are calling the subtext can be measured by this, that the literary work or cultural object itself, as though for the first time, brings into being that situation to which it is also, and at the same time, a reaction. It articulates its own situation and textualizes it, encouraging the illusion that the very situation itself did not exist before it, that there is nothing but a text, that there never was any extra- or con-textual reality before the text itself generated it. ("Symbolic Inference" 511, 512)

But it is precisely the relationship between the verbal and nonverbal, the textual and contextual or extratextual that has propelled dramatism through its successive reformulations in symbolic action and logology, and if we accept Robert Wess's claim that positivism is the ghost in the machine of dramatism, then it is also at the heart of the conceptual engine of *A Grammar* ("Burke's 'Dialectic' " 6).[4] This question of the relation between the verbal and nonverbal rests, too, at the heart of every effort to discuss Burke and his relationship to contemporary theory and is the focus of most prior discussions of the epistemological and ontological in Burke.[5]

Burke himself refers to it first at the outset of the *Grammar* when he pauses to consider the intrinsic nature of things. He remarks, "For things *do* have intrinsic natures, whatever may be the quandaries that crowd upon us as soon as we attempt to decide definitively what these intrinsic natures are." He concludes this line of thought with the assertion that "The transformations which we here study as a Grammar are not 'illusions,' but citable realities. The structural relations involved are observable realities" (*GM* 56–57). He later qualifies his assertion of the reality of these structural patterns in his discussion of the "Agent in General" in *A Grammar,* when he suggests apropos of his consideration of Hume, "we can say that people interpret natural sequences in terms of cause and effect not because of something in the natural scene requiring this interpretation, but *because they are the sort of agents that see things in terms of necessary relations*" (*GM,* 187). This claim leads us directly, in my reading, toward the late articulations of the distinction between motion and action. If humankind is simply the sort of agent that looks for necessary relations, then, Burke maintains, "For the sake of the argument, I'm even willing to grant that the distinction between *things moving* and *persons acting* is but an illusion. All I would claim is that, illusion or not, the human race cannot possibly get along with itself on the basis of any other intuition. The human animal, as we know it, *emerges into personality* by first mastering whatever tribal speech happens to be its particular symbolic environment" (*LASA* 53). This would appear to leave the question of the correspondence between these intuitions and whatever might lie beyond them weakly in abeyance, and thus would appear to confirm what I have described as Burke's epistemological condition; however, this easy conclusion is confounded somewhat by Burke's claim in "(Nonsymbolic) Motion/ (Symbolic) Action" that although "the motion-action 'polarity' is unbridgeable," and "never the twain shall meet," there is "in every tribal idiom however rudimentary, . . . a wholly reliable basic correspondence between a thing and its name" (815). And this correspondence might be read as much more than simply basic and reliable if we accept the literal cast of Burke's descriptions of dramatism, in the essay of the same name, as the launching of an ontological description of the symbol-using animal. In "Dramatism," Burke asserts, "I make a point of insisting that the Dramatistic perspective is *not* a metaphor. . . . I claim that the proposition 'things move, persons act,' is *literal*," and later he remarks, "In this sense, man is defined literally as an animal characterized by his special aptitude for 'symbolic action,' which is itself a literal term" (331, 337). In the light of what I have suggested up to this point, both these claims might well give us pause. Taken at face value, it would appear that embedded in the seemingly ontological description of the human subject is an equal claim about the epistemological grounds of dramatism. I would, however, like to conclude by offering three proposals for reading these claims, each of which would properly caution us against seeking a quick exit from the rigorous epistemological skepticism that has been the consistent hallmark of Burke's project.

The first of these proposals is to read a literal dramatism as the anticipation and confirmation of what Greig Henderson has found in Burke's logology, "the necessity of imposing some sort of absolute value on language itself," in order to establish a "surrogate theology" that betrays, in Henderson's words, "a psychological need for a sense of permanence akin to a religious faith in the curative power of the word made flesh" (*Kenneth Burke*, 105). In this respect, a literal dramatism might be read as relinquishing without overcoming the exacting indeterminacy we find in *A Grammar*. The second proposal is to read Burke against himself, so to speak, in the differential terms suggested in Jacques Derrida's "Signature, Event, Context." Derrida reminds us that while communication depends upon a determined context, there is no sense in which we can ever ascertain an absolutely determinable context (310). Even, for example, to agree for a moment that human beings are literally symbol-using animals is, as Burke himself pointed out fifty years ago, to launch ourselves into "the quandaries that crowd upon us as soon as we attempt to decide definitively what these intrinsic natures are" (*GM* 56–57). In purely Derridean terms, the implications are also more dire, for the absence of an absolutely determined context is the sign that all communication takes place in the condition of writing, with its endless play of difference and deferral. As Derrida remarks, "This structural possibility of being severed from its referent or signified (and therefore from communication and its context) seems to me to make of every mark, even if oral, a grapheme in general, that is, as we have seen, the nonpresent *remaining* of a differential mark cut off from its alleged 'production' or origin. And I will extend this law even to all 'experience' in general, if it is granted that there is no experience of *pure* presence, but only chains of differential marks" (318). To stop here, however, would simply be to suggest that Burke's ontological turn inevitably contains its own subversion and that despite his efforts to retain the worldly dimension of the sign, his skeptical critique necessarily ensnares him in the web cast by the free-play of signification.

The third and final proposal I offer here is largely of Burke's own devising in as far as we can see Burke as participating in the tradition of what Richard Rorty would call an edifying philosopher as opposed to a systematic one. There is an implicit negativity in language, Burke tells us, and that negativity should alert us to the separation of language from the world, to the absence of an easy correspondence between ways of seeing and facticity. In this sense we are condemned to conversation, to the indeterminate scene of the representative anecdote with which this discussion began. However, Burke's necessarily incomplete project is not designed finally to bring us to a literal ground, but to bring us to the recognition that even in the claim that human beings are literal symbol-using animals there is the full awareness that the abstract literal is only a dead metaphor, and "metaphor," in Burke's own words, "is not literal" (*LASA* 12). As Richard Rorty has urged us, "we should not try to have a successor subject to epistemology, but rather try to free ourselves from the notion that philosophy must center around the discovery of a permanent framework for inquiry" (Rorty 380). I would extend both Rorty's assertion and Burke's ample skepticism to his own claims for literalness, and I would have us recall that in Burke's own words "we cannot use language maturely until we are spontaneously at home in irony" (*LASA* 12).

Notes

1. Paul de Man employs what he calls Burke's "well-known insistence on the distinction between grammar and rhetoric" in "Semiology and Rhetoric" (127). But de Man's account of this supposed "well-known" distinction overlooks the full complexity of the relation between grammar and rhetoric for Burke. This is effectively demonstrated in Henderson ("Dramatism and Deconstruction").

2. Consider, for example, the close proximity of my opening anecdote of the "endless conversation," which also encompasses Burke's definition of man, and Lyotard's choice of "language games as my general methodological approach." Lyotard's perspective here is that "language games are the minimum relation required for society to exist: even before he is born, if only by virtue of the name he is given, the human child is already positioned as the referent in the story recounted by those around him, in relation to which he will inevitably chart his course" (15).

3. I have borrowed here from my previous specific discussion of Burke and Jameson; see Carmichael.

4. For more recent observations on this question, see Wess, *Kenneth Burke* 70.

5. Not wishing merely to rehearse what has been said to date on this question, I will simply acknowledge here some useful discussions: Nelson, Williams, and Brock et al.

Bibliography

Brock, Bernard, et al. "Dramatism as Ontology or Epistemology: A Symposium." *Communication Quarterly* 33.1 (Winter 1985): 17–33.

Burke, Kenneth. "Dramatism." In *Communication: Concepts and Perspectives.* Ed. Lee Thayer. Washington, DC: Spartan Books, 1967. 327–52.

——. *A Grammar of Motives.* 1945. Berkeley: University of California Press, 1969.

——. *Language as Symbolic Action: Essays on Life, Literature, and Method.* Berkeley: University of California Press, 1966.

——. "Methodological Repression and/or Strategies of Containment." *Critical Inquiry* 5.2 (1978): 401–16.

——. "(Nonsymbolic) Motion/(Symbolic) Action" *Critical Inquiry* 4.4 (Summer 1978): 809–38.

——. *The Philosophy of Literary Form: Studies in Symbolic Action.* Baton Rouge: Louisiana State University Press, 1967.

Carmichael, Thomas. "Postmodernism, Symbolicity, and the Rhetoric of the Hyperreal: Kenneth Burke, Fredric Jameson, and Jean Baudrillard." *Text and Performance Quarterly* 11 (1991): 319–24.

de Man, Paul. *The Resistance to Theory.* Theory and History of Literature 33. Minneapolis: University of Minnesota Press, 1986.

——. "Semiology and Rhetoric." In *Textual Strategies: Perspectives in Post-Structuralist Criticism.* Ed. Josué Harari. Ithaca: Cornell University Press, 1979. 127.

Derrida, Jacques. "Signature Event Context." In *Margins of Philosophy.* Trans. Alan Bass. Chicago: University of Chicago Press, 1982. 307–30.

Fish, Stanley. *Doing What Comes Naturally: Change, Rhetoric, and the Practice of Theory in Literary and Legal Studies.* Durham: Duke University Press, 1989.

Henderson, Greig E. "Dramatism and Deconstruction: Burke, de Man, and the Rhetorical Motive." In *Kenneth Burke and the Twenty-first Century.* Ed. Bernard L. Brock. Albany: State University of New York Press, 1999. 151–65.

——. *Kenneth Burke: Literature and Language as Symbolic Action.* Athens: University of Georgia Press, 1988.

Jameson, Fredric R. "Ideology and Symbolic Action." *Critical Inquiry* 5.2 (1978): 417–23.

——. "The Symbolic Inference; or, Kenneth Burke and Ideological Analysis." *Critical Inquiry* 4.3 (Spring 1978): 507–23.

Lyotard, Jean-François. *The Postmodern Condition: A Report on Knowledge.* Trans. Geoff Bennington and Brian Massumi. Theory and History of Literature 10. Minneapolis: University of Minnesota Press, 1984.

Nelson, Cary. "Writing as the Accomplice of Language: Kenneth Burke and Poststructuralism." In *The Legacy of Kenneth Burke.* Ed. Herbert W. Simons and Trevor Melia. Madison: University of Wisconsin Press, 1989. 156–73.

Rorty, Richard. *Philosophy and the Mirror of Nature.* Princeton: Princeton University Press, 1979.

Wess, Robert. "Burke's 'Dialectic of Constitutions.'" Kenneth Burke Society Conference. New Harmony, IN, 1990.

——. *Kenneth Burke: Rhetoric, Subjectivity, Postmodernism.* Cambridge: Cambridge University Press, 1996.

Williams, David Cratis. "Under the Sign of (An)nihilation: Burke in the Age of Nuclear Destruction and Critical Deconstruction." In *The Legacy of Kenneth Burke.* Ed. Herbert W. Simons and Trevor Melia. Madison: University of Wisconsin Press, 1989. 196–223.

7

Pentadic Terms and Master Tropes: Ontology of the Act and Epistemology of the Trope in *A Grammar of Motives*

Robert Wess

> ... truth, though one, has no single expression ...
> —Richard McKeon, *Rhetoric*

"Four Master Tropes" ends *A Grammar of Motives* (503–17), but it seems less a final word than a new beginning. A pentad—act, agent, scene, agency, purpose—dominates the book, but in the end, a quartet of tropes appears. Each trope, moreover, is paired with a companion term that enhances its analytic significance:

metaphor and perspective

metonymy and reduction

synecdoche and representation

irony and dialectic

Burke devotes relatively few pages to these tropes compared to the chapters on his pentad, but one is left suspecting that he could use them to write another book. That the tropes appear not in a concluding chapter but in an appendix seems only to accentuate their marginality and thereby to suggest a range of possible interpretations.

Stephen Bygrave projects the tropes back onto *A Grammar of*

Motives, reading them as an unassimilated margin: "The Constitution needs to be grasped as a synecdoche and as an act. (These are from different terminologies, but they are the terminologies Burke veers between at the end of the *Grammar*)" (93). Cary Nelson, by contrast, glimpses in this margin an anticipation of a later Burke: seeing a shift from humanist to poststructuralist terminologies in Burke's career, Nelson singles out "Four Master Tropes" as marking the place where "almost without quite wanting to" Burke begins to shift from one to the other (161). For Lynn Worsham, finally, this margin is subversive. Worsham recognizes that while the pentad dominates *A Grammar of Motives*, act dominates the pentad, as Burke underlines in the first sentence of the chapter "Act": "our entire book illustrates the featuring of act" (227). With "Four Master Tropes," by contrast, attention shifts to epistemology, away from the pentadic terms in general and act in particular. In the first paragraph, Burke explains that his interest in these tropes is not "with their purely figurative usage, but with their role in the discovery and description of 'the truth'" (503), a point he immediately accentuates by introducing his companion terms for the tropes. It is this turn to epistemology that prompts Worsham to suggest that this text "subverts the grammatical and philosophical project of *A Grammar of Motives*" (74). In Worsham's view, a turn to epistemology in Burke constitutes an abrupt about-face. With the tropes we encounter, she proposes, "an apparent *shift in emphasis* from symbolic action to epistemology, in spite of the fact that Burke has consistently maintained an *exclusive interest* in terms derived from and productive of theories of action, not theories of knowledge" (74; emphasis added).

A "shift in emphasis" from action to epistemology would be a shift from ontology to epistemology, for in *A Grammar of Motives* Burke emphasizes that he uses the "Creation" as a prototypical model for the act to write an ontology of the act:

> Statements about both "Evolution" and "the Creation" are alike in this: despite their reference to matters of sequence, to "befores" and "afters," they are *ontological* statements, statements about *being*, about what *is*. . . .
>
> The Creation, considered as a prototype of action in our paradigmatic, or summational sense, involves "principles," and these are not historical or temporal "firsts," but logical firsts. They are the kind of "beginnings" that are always. . . .
>
> In sum: we are discussing the Creation not as a temporal event, but as the logical prototype of an act. (63, 64; emphasis in original)[1]

Worsham's phrase "exclusive interest" is misleading, however, because Burke doesn't depict act and knowledge as mutually exclusive, a polar opposition in which the inclusion of one entails the exclusion of the other. Rather, he argues consistently that one must start with action, make it primary, and then incorporate knowledge in a derivative role. For example, in 1942, he begins "The Study of Symbolic Action" with the proposal to view language as action rather than as knowledge but immediately adds, "'Knowledge' and 'action' are not antithetically related, however. . . . [P]oetry as a symbolic act may be said to lead into 'knowledge.' . . . [Begin with] the approach in terms of action, with considerations of knowledge figuring secondarily" (7). Similarly, decades later, in "A Dramatistic View of the Origins of Language," Burke again moves from action to knowledge as he charts, in support of his thesis that language originates in the negative, a series of carefully distinguished steps from the hortatory negative (act) to the propositional negative (knowledge) (*LASA* 421–25).

Further, as we will see, it is questionable whether it is even possible to divide ontology from epistemology in a mutually exclusive opposition, not just in Burke's discourse in particular but in any discourse in general. Worsham is correct that "Four Master Tropes" gives us an epistemology but not that Burke's epistemology subverts his ontology. The two are partners, with act serving as the senior member of the partnership.

Traditionally, ontology is closely associated with metaphysics. Indeed, in the *Cambridge Dictionary of Philosophy,* the entry for ontology is a cross-reference: "See Metaphysics," where the example of Aristotle illustrates that metaphysics may be identified with "the study of being *qua* being, i.e., of the most general and necessary characteristics that anything must have in order to count as a being, an entity *(ens).* Sometimes 'ontology' is used in this sense . . . '" (490). Ontology, furthermore, may be considered a whole of which epistemology is a derivative part:

> Metaphysics, most generally, the philosophical investigation of the nature, constitution, and structure of reality. It is broader in scope than science, e.g., physics and even cosmology (the science of the nature, structure, and origin of the universe as a whole), since one of its traditional concerns is the existence of nonphysical entities, e.g., God. . . . In its most general sense, metaphysics may seem to coincide with philosophy as a whole, since anything philosophy investigates is presumably a part of reality, e.g., knowledge, values,

and valid reasoning. But it is useful to reserve the investigation of such more special topics for distinct branches of
philosophy, e.g., *epistemology*, ethics, aesthetics, and logic,
since they raise problems peculiar to themselves. (489; emphasis added)

Cambridge's entry for epistemology sketches the traditional problem of
knowledge, adding reference to a few of the traditional solutions:

> *Epistemology* (from Greek *episteme,* "knowledge," and *lo-
> gos,* "explanation"), the study of the nature of knowledge
> and justification; specifically, the study of (a) the defining
> features, (b) the substantive conditions, and (c) the limits of
> knowledge and justification. The latter three categories are
> represented by traditional philosophical controversy over
> the analysis of knowledge and justification, the sources of
> knowledge and justification (e.g., rationalism versus empiri-
> cism), and the viability of skepticism about knowledge and
> justification. (233)

But even considered as a derivative part, epistemology is a necessary
part. For an ontology—that is, a specific ontological doctrine such as
idealism, materialism, or realism—would be itself knowledge of being.
An ontology necessarily entails epistemology, for to explain its own existence as a philosophical doctrine, an ontology would have to contain
an epistemology, even if only implicitly, to conceptualize the process by
which knowledge of being occurs. Aristotle, for example, provides an
epistemology for his ontology by theorizing a mind that becomes identical with its ontological object, becoming all things.[2]

Entailment works in the opposite direction as well, as the example
of Descartes's epistemology illustrates. Richard Rorty's account of the
Cartesian revolution contrasts Aristotle's epistemology to Descartes's.
Whereas Aristotle's mind identifies with its object, Descartes's remains
resolutely apart from it:

> The substantial forms of frogness and starness get right
> into the Aristotelian intellect, and are there in just the same
> way they are in the frogs and the stars—*not* in the way in
> which frogs and stars are reflected in mirrors. In Descar-
> tes's conception—the one which became the basis for "mod-
> ern" epistemology—it is *representations* which are in the
> "mind." The Inner Eye surveys these representations hoping
> to find some mark which will testify to their fidelity. (45)

In separating mind (which knows) from matter (which is known), Descartes's epistemology presupposes an ontology: the Cartesian dualism. Rorty suggests that Descartes's distinction between mind and matter is "like a distinction between two worlds" (52).

Consider one of these worlds, the world of matter, as it appears in *Meditations on First Philosophy* in Descartes's famous analysis of wax in two states: (1) fresh from the hive and (2) melted down to a hot liquid: "Does the same wax remain after this change [from (1) to (2)]? We must confess that it remains; none would judge otherwise. What then did I know so distinctly in this piece of wax? It could be nothing of all that the senses brought to my notice, since all these things which fall under taste, smell, sight, touch, and hearing, are found to be changed, and yet the same wax remains" (154). The wax remains the same in the sense that its substance enables it to remain the same through changes in sensory appearance (154–55). The key epistemological point is that this substance is comprehended through the mind: "But what must particularly be observed is that its perception is neither an act of vision, nor of touch, nor of imagination . . . but only an intuition of the mind" (155). In conceptualizing his epistemology, in other words, Descartes makes an ontological commitment to a substance that can be thought but not sensed as he makes mind rather than sense his primary epistemological agency.[3]

The examples of Aristotle and Descartes thus suggest that ontology and epistemology entail one another. One may be subordinated to the other in either direction—Aristotle privileges ontology; Descartes, epistemology—but conceptualizing one entails assumptions about the other. The two are partners rather than mutually exclusive antagonists.

Before considering the form such partnership takes in Burke, we need to consider "the linguistic turn" in modern thought and the rhetoricizing of philosophy that can accompany it, as the example of Burke himself illustrates. In the context of this turn, where we have problems getting beyond or through language that philosophers like Aristotle and Descartes seem not to have encountered, what form do the problems of ontology and epistemology take?

This turn's problematization of our access to the nonverbal may be approached from the standpoint of Richard McKeon's aphorism in our epigraph.[4] In it, McKeon encapsulates an idea, occasioned by his reading of Cicero, that proved seminal in his own rhetoricizing of philosophy: "truth, though one, has no single expression" (204).[5] While more complete illustrations of this aphorism will come later, I can introduce it with an example as simple as a date. Any date would do, but let's take August 27, 1997, the date I'm writing this sentence. It has become common to speak of linguistic or cultural constructs such that even August 27, 1997, could be termed a "construct." It may seem odd to call a date a construct since it seems to refer to something that undeniably happened—we know we live one day at a time—not something constructed through language and cultural practice. But consider 1997 —why that number? The experience in 2000 of living through the end of "the" second millennium will be the effect of a construct based on counting years from the birth of Christ. To call August 27, 1997, a "construct" is not to say it is a pure fabrication, only that our culture chooses to chart time with a particular calendar. The choosing, a historical process, is the constructing. A historical contingency, one construction can be displaced by another. A new calendar was invented during the French Revolution, for example, one that counted anew beginning in 1792, which would make 2000 merely 208, many lifetimes short of "the" first millennium; this calendar also rewrote the months, renaming them and renumbering the days, an allusion to which appears in Marx's title *The Eighteenth Brumaire of Louis Bonaparte*.[6] From an ecological standpoint, to consider another possibility, one might argue that for the world culture that may be emerging in our time we need a new calendar that counts years from the beginning of life on earth— marginalize Easter and centralize Earth Day. In short, the occurrence we identify with the expression "August 27, 1997" may be expressed in other ways. Any expression is a construct, a choice of this way rather than that way. The occurrence may be analogized to the "truth" in McKeon's aphorism; the multiplicity of possible calendars, to the absence of definitive expression: the occurrence, though one, has no single calendric expression.

Put roughly, McKeon's aphorism may be said to keep the practical or subjective side of discourse distinct yet inseparable from the theoretical or objective side. Multiple calendars, by which subjectivities situated historically address practical problems, may differ significantly yet each must chart the earth's rotation and orbit objectively enough to work well enough to achieve the practical purposes of its users. The experience of living through the end of a second millennium is and is not an effect of a cultural fiction. There is no definitive calendar of calendars, but that doesn't mean all calendars are empty fabrications. While keeping reference to "truth," McKeon's aphorism still puts us in a rhetorical rather than a philosophical world by refusing the possibility of the definitive expression of truth.

The absence of such definitive expression is the premise of Paolo Valesio's "ontology of rhetoric" (21)—Valesio is also of interest to Burkeans because he frequently cites Burke. By virtue of this absence, Valesio concludes that there is in all discourse an "inevitable *stylization* (simplification, 'biased' structure, eristic use, or any other term of this kind that one would care to employ) that is the ontological basis of rhetoric" (31). To illustrate, he quotes at length from *The Philosophy of Literary Form,* where Burke shows how, simply by posing strategic questions, one can even stylize a discussion, orienting it in this direction rather than that one, as by taking a poll about a statesman's "integrity" one makes his integrity an issue rather than something that goes without saying: "Even those who come to his defense must, in this very act, themselves help to emphasize the element of doubtfulness" (*PLF* 67). From Valesio's standpoint, one could say that Aristotle and Descartes stylize the ontology/epistemology relationship differently, orienting in different ways consideration of ontological and epistemological issues. Behind Valesio's principle of stylization, one may even glimpse a *locus classicus* in the rhetorical tradition, namely, Aristotle's observation that you can praise or blame a man by stylizing the "same" qualities differently: "rashness will be called courage, extravagance generosity," or vice versa (*Rhetoric* 1367^b 2).

Thomas M. Conley, in his comprehensive *Rhetoric in the European Tradition,* suggests that McKeon's project may be analogized to "Cicero's method of *controversia,* in which . . . there is a merger of the uses of philosophical discourse and rhetorical method. To call for such a merger is to insinuate a revolutionary change by virtue of which philosophizing becomes an activity in which 'places' (*topoi* or *loci*), and not intuitions or sense verification, are the primary means by which modes and meanings in nature and art are illuminated" (289). Topoi, as Eugene Garver notes in his authoritative study of Aristotle's *Rhetoric,* "are the rhetorical substitute for principles, doing the job that principles do in scientific argument" (78). When philosophy is rhetoricized, there are only topoi, no principles based on "intuitions or sense verification."

Our earlier discussion of the ontology/epistemology relationship illustrates how rhetoric transforms philosophy. We treated this relationship not as a truth with a definitive expression but as a topos with multiple expressions, such as Aristotle's and Descartes's, which are in Rorty's account in competition with one another. Ontology and epistemology each need the other. There is room to conceive their relationship in different ways, but conceiving one without the other seems to be impossible, a constraint that is inescapable, not something that an individual thinker may dispense with at will. This constraint requires that ontology and epistemology be married (one truth), implicitly if not explicitly, but the marriage can take different forms with different partners (no definitive expression).

This kind of constraint is in some sense objective albeit not in the sense that has evolved out of the tradition that Descartes and Locke inaugurated in the seventeenth century. Writing on Locke, John Dewey observes, "What characterizes sensation and observation, and hence experience, is, in Locke's thought, their coerciveness. They are forced upon us whether we like them or not; if we open our eyes and ears we cannot help receiving certain 'simple ideas'" (14). The ontology/epistemology topos is coercive but its coerciveness does not operate through sense. Nor does it operate through Descartes's mind, for the topos is not clear and distinct, as Descartes's rationalism requires, but ambiguous, structuring the different meanings Aristotle and Descartes give ontology and epistemology. The coerciveness of this topos operates not through subjective faculties of sense or mind but as an objective condition of discourse. It is impossible, we've suggested, to conceive (1) the process of knowing without assumptions about the thing to be known or (2) a thing to be known without assumptions about how we come to know it. Thing (ontology) and thought (epistemology) implicate one another—the truth of the marriage of ontology and epistemology. This truth's coerciveness operates in and through discourse, regardless of whether the writer is aware of it, as a condition of its intelligibility. The rhetorical complication is that this same truth can be expressed and made intelligible in different ways. In its ambiguity, it is a rhetorical rather than a philosophical truth, not the kind of truth that coerces Locke's sense or Descartes's mind.

Further, since the rhetorical truth of this marriage can be expressed in different ways, it can't be identified with Aristotle's, Descartes's, or any other discourse.[7] It appears, rather, through conflicts among discourses, like the conflict Rorty depicts between Aristotle and Descartes. The ontology/epistemology topos is simultaneously a part of and apart from both Aristotle's and Descartes's ontology/epistemology: the topos is the sameness by virtue of which we comprehend differences between Aristotle and Descartes as different versions of the same thing. Such fusion of sameness and difference takes us much closer than our calendar example to the heart of McKeon's aphorism. The topos exhibits a truth beyond discourse, but our only access to it is through differences among discourses.

Our access to rhetorical truth, then, is through the process of interrogating conflicting discourses. Burke encapsulates this process in his well-known representation of

> the "unending conversation" that is going on at the point in history when we are born. Imagine that you enter a parlor. You come late. When you arrive, others have long preceded you, and they are engaged in a heated discussion, a

discussion too heated for them to pause and tell you exactly
what it is about. In fact, the discussion had already begun
long before any of them got there, so that no one present is
qualified to retrace for you all the steps that had gone before.
You listen for a while, until you decide that you have caught
the tenor of the argument; then you put in your oar. Someone answers; you answer him; another comes to your defense; another aligns himself against you, to either the embarrassment or gratification of your opponent, depending
upon the quality of your ally's assistance. However, the discussion is interminable. The hour grows late, you must depart. And you do depart, with the discussion still vigorously
in progress. (*PLF* 110–11)

Locke's sense and Descartes's mind are both epistemological agencies
independent of the conversation. For Burke, neither agency is available
because exiting from the conversation is impossible. As Burke insists,
"it is in this 'unending conversation' that the assertions of any given
philosopher are grounded. *Strategically*, he may present his work as departing from some 'rock-bottom fact' (he starts, for instance: 'I look at
this table. I perceive it to have . . . ' etc.). Actually, the very selection of
his 'rock-bottom fact' derives its true grounding from the current state
of the conversation" (*PLF* 111). One prepares to put one's "oar" into
the conversation not by escaping from it but by going to the library to
immerse oneself in it.[8]

Such considerations suggest how topoi can substitute for philosophical first principles (not necessarily everything that has ever been
called a topos; the rhetoricizing of philosophy is selective). A topos appears in discourse, naming an objective constraint, a subject matter that
is in some sense "out there," but this naming is ambiguous, as different
discourses give it different meanings. With the idea of the topos, finally, we can anticipate the form the ontology/epistemology partnership takes in Burke. The topos has two sides: (1) truth; (2) variant expressions of this truth, none definitive. A discursive site in the unending
conversation, the topos mediates between truth (ontology) and our access to it (epistemology).[9]

Burke's pentad names the subject matter of his *"controversia,"* to bor-
row Conley's term for Cicero's method and McKeon's modern analogue. Traditionally, we associate ontology with terms like those Burke
links to pentadic terms, as in scene/materialism and agent/idealism to
name two examples (*GM* 128). The pentad is at one with all ontologies
in that it allows them all to have their say. But in being inclusive, it is

not at one with any of them in their claim to definitive expression of the truth, not even act/realism, the category for dramatism, if one identifies act/realism with a philosophy like Aristotle's. Aristotle's ontology of the act is one thing; Burke's is quite another—we'll return to this difference in the conclusion.

Ontologies in the traditional sense see themselves demonstrating truth definitively, whereas the pentad transforms them into "assertions" in the Burkean *controversia:*

> [T]here is an internal development that causes the nature of philosophy as an assertion to be lost in the problems of demonstration. . . .
>
> But with the pentad as a generating principle, we may extricate ourselves from these intricacies, by discovering the kinds of *assertion* which the different schools would exemplify in a hypothetical state of purity. Once this approach is established, problems are much less likely to conceal the underlying design of assertion, or may even serve to assist in the characterizing of a given philosophic work. (*GM* 131–32)

Burke's pentad exemplifies McKeon's aphorism more fully than any of our previous examples. "In treating the various schools as languages," Burke proposes, "we may define their substantial relationship to one another by deriving them from a common terminological ancestor" (*GM* 127). Burke does present his pentad as a grammar, "a common terminological ancestor," but that should not lead to the conclusion that it is a formalism without semantic reference. For a purely formalistic grammar, one can look to Noam Chomsky's *Syntactic Structures.* Consider Chomsky's test for grammaticality:

(1) Colorless green ideas sleep furiously.

(2) Furiously sleep ideas green colorless.

Chomsky argues that while both, from a semantic standpoint, are equally nonsensical, the first, unlike the second, is nonetheless "grammatical" (15). Chomsky thus reduces grammar to syntax, a pure form without semantic content that can evidence itself even in nonsense. Burke's pentadic grammar, by contrast, expresses the truth of the act albeit in multiple pentadic forms.

In the relations among his pentadic terms, Burke finds patterns of reciprocal entailment like that in the ontology/epistemology topos. While he notes repeatedly that a rounded terminology should cover all five terms, actual pentadic analysis typically works with two terms at a time—the ratios such as scene/agent, scene/act—and can proceed in either direction. Burke observes, "We originally said that the five terms allowed for ten ratios; but we also noted that the ratios could be reversed, as either a certain kind of scene may call for its corresponding kind of agent, or a certain agent may call for its corresponding kind of scene, etc. The list of possible combinations would thereby be expanded to twenty" (GM 262). Relations in the ratios—the Burkean topoi— are objective constraints. There is great latitude allowing different discourses to instantiate ratios in different ways, but such latitude is limited by the objectivity of the constraint. This is not an objectivity, however, that eventuates in definitive expression. There is no verbalization of the scene/agent ratio, for example, that could be privileged against all others as the final truth about the scene/agent relationship. Each topos, capable itself of being a site of a Burkean conversation, opens a path to all five terms.

Burke remarks in a later text that when he first began working with the pentad, he thought of the five terms as related simply by "and," only realizing later "their analytic familyhood (in the sense that the idea of an act implied the idea of an agent; the idea of an agent acting implied the idea of a scene in which the act takes place; there can be no act without recourse to some means, or agency; and there can't be such a thing as an act without a purpose)" (Dramatism and Development 22). The whole cluster, Burke suggests in the same passage, adds up to "a 'Cycle of Terms' Implicit in the idea of an 'Act,' based upon [his] anti-Behaviorist equation, 'Things move, persons act'" (21)—we'll return in the concluding section to Burke's polemic with behaviorism.

Act is the truth behind the pentad, appearing not directly in a definitive expression but indirectly in multiple pentadic expressions, which together cooperate in a "collective revelation," as Burke phrases it (GM 340). Through the analytic tool of the pentad, Burke exposes the version of pentadese that a discourse speaks, whether its writer knows it or not. He writes, in other words, from a position inside the conversation to expose multiple pentadic differences among the conversants. Just as the ontology/epistemology topos is simultaneously a part of and apart from both Aristotle's and Descartes's discourses, the pentad is simultaneously a part of and apart from the discourses of the conversants. The pentad is the sameness by virtue of which we recognize the discourses as different versions of the same thing.

For Burke discourses are acts and the pentad constitutes the conditions that make action intelligible. Discourses are intelligible—that is, grammatical—to the extent that they express through the pentad the conditions of their actionhood. Just as an ontology needs an epistemology to explain how it can be known, a discursive act needs the pentad to explain its enactment. Evidence of pentadic expression— compiled throughout *A Grammar of Motives,* particularly in "The Philosophic Schools" (127–320)—argues that the pentad is indeed a condition of discursive grammaticality. Particularly revealing is evidence that a discourse may make room for the truth of the act even against its own apparent overt purposes. Lucretius's materialism, for example, is a universe filled with atoms, but these atoms have a tendency to "swerve," and by virtue of this swerve there is space for action, including Lucretius's discursive act (160).

The ontology of the act expressed through multiple pentadic variants exhibits itself in the unending conversation of history. This conversation is the site where Burke's ontology marries his epistemology. "Four Master Tropes" charts the features of this epistemology that distinguish it from traditional epistemology, exemplified in figures like Descartes and Locke, although, as we'll see, this text needs to be modified in one respect to theorize fully the epistemology of the unending conversation.

"Four Master Tropes" introduces into Burke's discourse his term "representative anecdote": *"A terminology of conceptual analysis, if it is not to lead to misrepresentation, must be constructed in conformity with a representative anecdote—whereas anecdotes 'scientifically' selected for reductive purposes are not representative"* (GM 510).[10] Coming near the end of section three, this passage divides the essay into its two main stages: the first laying the groundwork for conceptualizing the representative anecdote, the second beginning with the two-sentence paragraph concluding section three: "What then, it may be asked, would be a 'representative anecdote?' [*sic*]. But that takes us into the fourth pair: irony and dialectic" (511). Irony/dialectic, while serving as an example of a representative anecdote, also brings Burke's formulation of his epistemological process to its culmination, as the irony/dialectic pair proves to comprehend the most distinctive characteristics of his epistemology. Burke alerts us in stating his epistemological project in his opening paragraph that he is interested in the areas of overlap by virtue of which "the four tropes shade into one another. Give a man but one of them, tell him to exploit its possibilities, and if he is thorough in doing so, he will come upon the other three" (503). In concluding with irony/dialectic, Burke brings the cooperation among the tropes and their companion terms to its conclusion.

Irony/dialectic serves as a norm against which Burke defines a series of deviations that are in effect all escapes from the unending conversation, not real escapes—real escape is impossible—but illusory escapes. Altogether, Burke defines three such deviations.

The first is relativism: *"Relativism* is got by the fragmentation of either drama or dialectic. That is, if you isolate any one agent in a drama, or any one advocate in a dialogue, and see the whole in terms of his position alone, you have the purely relativistic. And in relativism there is no irony" (512). In other words, relativism results when one discourse in the conversation is seen not as one act in dramatic or dialogic competition with other acts but as a monologue that is the only discourse in town. The pentad, as noted earlier, allows one to restore the act of assertion constitutive of a philosophy. Restoration is needed as philosophies tend to see themselves engaged in the demonstration of a monologue rather than in the assertion of a perspective ironically qualified by other perspectives in a conversation. The unending conversation, in short, is the proper counterpart to the Burkean truth that expresses itself through multiple expressions, no one of which is definitive. In Burke's epistemology, then, relativism is paradoxically needed to avoid relativism, since relativism is avoided only insofar as a discourse is placed in the context of the conversation, where it is considered relative to other discourses that qualify it ironically/dialectically. It's the monologue that purports to speak a definitive truth that lapses into relativism, since the monologue's guise of objectivity conceals the relativity of its perspective.

Relativism is typically conceived in opposition to absolutism. But for Burke, the oppositional counterpart to relativism is to be found, rather, in the conversational dialogue of competing assertions of multiple perspectives. Insofar as such assertions are

> encouraged to participate in an orderly parliamentary development, the dialectic of this participation produces (in *the observer who considers the whole* [emphasis added] from the standpoint of the participation of all the terms rather than from the standpoint of any one participant) a "resultant certainty" of a different quality, necessarily ironic, since it requires that all the sub-certainties be considered as neither true nor false but *contributory* (as were we to think of the resultant certainty or "perspective of perspectives" as a noun, and to think of all the contributory voices as necessary modifiers of that noun). (513)

The "certainty" Burke envisions in his epistemological process thus differs radically from the certainty philosophy traditionally roots in "intuitions or sense verification," as Conley phrases it. The epistemological tradition coming down from Descartes conceives the epistemological process as an interaction between an isolated human subject and an objective world "out there." The process is universal, common to all subjects, but epistemological certainty occurs in individuals one at a time.[11] Burke, by contrast, locates "certainty" in the conversation, as its "resultant." This "certainty" is the counterpart to a "truth" that has no definitive expression.

There is one ambiguity in the above quotation, in the parenthetical reference to "the observer who considers the whole." This "observer" appears to be in a superior position, above the conversation. Yet it is precisely this kind of superior position that Burke identifies as a second mode of illusory escape from the conversation. Allen Tate's reading of Eliot's *The Waste Land* provides the text Burke uses to demonstrate this error. Tate defines irony as "permit[ting] to the spectator an insight superior to that of the actor," citing in particular the poet's superiority to the clerk in the seduction scene (514). The irony in Burke's epistemological process disallows such superiority. "True irony, humble irony," Burke argues, "is based upon a sense of fundamental kinship with the enemy as one *needs* him, is *indebted* to him, is not merely outside him as an observer but contains him *within*, being consubstantial with him" (514). (Perhaps behaviorism is the "enemy" Burke needs; more on this possibility later.) Tate's position of superiority is in effect a privileged position apart from the conversation—like Locke's and Descartes's epistemological agencies (sense, mind)—whereas for Burke there is no such position. Burkean irony arises as each assertion in the conversation modifies others, just as they modify it. Hence, the reference to the "observer who considers the whole" appears contradictory. Consideration of the third mode of illusory escape can help to identify the source of this contradiction.

This mode is defined as the "simplification of literalness" (516). The temptation to lapse into this illusion arises from the fact that a drama often features a character who is *"primus inter pares"* such that while all the characters may be viewed as ironically modifying one another, this one character seems to take a step beyond them to serve as the summation of the drama's whole development. Two examples: "This is the role of Socrates in the Platonic dialogue, for instance—and we could similarly call the proletariat the Socrates of the Marxist Symposium of History, as they are not merely equal participants along with the other characters, but also represent the *end* or *logic* of the development as a whole" (516). The "simplification of literalness" occurs when this summarizing character is privileged to the point of being cut loose from his/her ironic ties to other characters: "The character is 'adjectival,' as embodying one of the qualifications necessary to the total definition, but is 'substantial' as embodying the conclusions of the development as a whole. Irony is sacrificed to 'the simplification of literalness' when this duality of role is neglected (as it may be neglected by either the reader, the writer, or both)" (516). Literalness is the effect of sacrificing the "adjectival" to the "substantial" to reproduce the traditional epistemological claim to a neutrality above the conversation. This third mode of illusory escape suggests that the "observer who considers the whole" slips into "Four Master Tropes" because here Burke envisions a conversation within the framework of a single text.

By contrast, the conversation in the unending conversation, quoted earlier, is among interacting texts.[12] In this conversation, we are always in the middle, competing with other assertions, but destined to leave with no end in sight and forced to begin without knowing from whence the whole process started. Burke's representative anecdote of a parlor conversation comes perhaps as close to the outside of the conversation as one can get, but this anecdote concedes the impossibility of comprehending beginning and end. Without origin or closure, this conversation turns dialectical structures such as Platonic dialogues or Marxist historical narratives into assertions qualified by others in the unending interaction among them. *The Philosophy of Literary Form*'s conversation may thus be read as less dialectical, since there is no development to a summation, but more ironical, as it radically eliminates any possibility of an "observer who considers the whole" from a position outside the conversation. We may, like Burke, take a stab at comprehending the whole but we do so from a position inside the conversation.

Traditionally, we tend to think of knowledge as a state of mind in individuals—a "mirror of nature," as Rorty reminds us (12)— that results from an epistemological agency (sense, mind, and so forth) interacting directly with an objective world. Burkean knowledge, by contrast, is not in an individual in permanent possession of a knowledge fixed once and for all, but, rather, in symbol-users equipped to converse today better than yesterday and maybe even better tomorrow. Burkean knowledge resides in the capacity, acquired by going to the library, to put our "oar" into the unending conversation into which we are born. Studying multiple expressions of a truth that has no definitive expression equips us to converse, to write. There was a time when I would not have been able to write the present essay, and I look forward to the day when I can write a better one—your critique could help me get there sooner than I might if left solely to my own devices. We can get better because there is something "out there" that we can learn about, but we can never rest because we can never express it definitively for all time.

Burke's epistemology, then, differs radically from traditional epistemology, exemplified in figures like Descartes and Locke, that presupposes a position of neutrality apart from the unending conversation. Simply by deploying tropes to theorize epistemology, Burke alerts readers that they are in for an epistemology of a different stripe. Beginning with metaphor and defining it as "seeing something *in terms of* something else" (*GM* 503), Burke posits an absolute freedom of verbal action insofar as there is no limit on the perspectives one might invent with combinations of "something" and "something else." From the standpoint of traditional epistemology, such freedom of action would start one down the road toward a relativism that would be the end of epistemology. But for Burke, just the opposite is the case:

> It is customary to think that objective reality is dissolved by such relativity of terms as we get through the shifting of perspectives (the perception of one character in terms of many characters). But on the contrary, it is by the approach through a variety of perspectives that we establish a character's reality. If we are in doubt as to what an object is, for instance, we deliberately try to consider it in as many different terms as its nature permits: lifting, smelling, tasting, tapping, holding in different lights, subjecting to different pressures, dividing, matching, contrasting, etc. (504)

Metaphor opens up multiple perspectives, but these qualify one another ironically to yield, as we've seen, a "resultant certainty" (513). Taken together, metaphor and irony theorize the core of the epistemology of the unending conversation. Joining metaphoric freedom of action and ironic constraint of interaction, this epistemology of the trope is an epistemology of the act.

Metonymy and synecdoche, the other two tropes, are used in "Four Master Tropes" in a polemic with behaviorism to define the concept of representative anecdote. Metonymy "convey[s] some incorporeal or intangible state [something] in terms of the corporeal or tangible [something else]" (506). "Reduction" serves to define this translation to the level of the tangible. Synecdoche, by contrast, is "representation," defined as a two-way street in which the "something" and the "something else" can change places. The prototype for such reciprocity, Burke suggests, is the microcosm/macrocosm relationship: "where the individual is treated as a replica of the universe, and vice versa, we have the ideal synecdoche, since microcosm is related to macrocosm as part to whole, and either the whole can represent the part or the part can represent the whole" (508). Such reciprocity appears in Burke's unending conversation, since the parlor conversation is the microcosmic counterpart to the macrocosm of the historical process. By contrast, behaviorism's use of animal behavior as its anecdote is metonymic reduction rather than

synecdochic representation, showing that anecdotes scientifically selected for "reductive" purposes are not "representative" (510). What
complicates matters is that metonymic reduction to the tangible appears in poetry as well. Burke thus draws a distinction between uses of
metonymy; behaviorism's error resides not in metonymy as such but in
its distinctive use of it (507).

Burke's polemic with behaviorism is enacted recurrently in his discourse because it effectively contrasts dramatistic emphasis on action to
behavioristic emphasis on motion. This action/motion distinction is
not, of course, a mutually exclusive opposition: symbol-using animals
are, for Burke, bodies in motion, but their symbol-using prowess adds
a level of action that cannot be reduced to motion—the behaviorist's
error.

As suggested earlier, in commenting on Burke's definition of "true
irony," behaviorism may be the "enemy" Burke is "indebted to," even
"consubstantial with," to apply terms from the definition (514). Explicit evidence of consubstantiality even appears in the retrospective
prologue Burke wrote for the second edition of *Permanence and Change,*
in a section where he distances himself from his frequent use in this
book of hypothetical animal experiments featuring behavioristic stimu-
lus-response conditioning (l–li): "To look over a book twenty years after it was first written is to discover that the author has been imaginative despite himself. That is, he has contrived to put himself in the role
of a character not his own. He has imagined someone who stoutly
averred things that he now would state quite otherwise. The book
which he thought of as a monologue when he wrote it, has thus become
in relation to his later books more like one voice in a dialogue." By
Burke's own account, then, there are two Burkes, with differing views
on the motion/action issue, coexisting consubstantially through the
irony/dialectic of dialogue. It's an odd dialogue, of course, since the
early Burke never gets to talk back to the later one. To fill the gap, we
might add a reviewer of *A Grammar of Motives* who argues that the
book "reduces intellectual history to matters of transformation, placement and position—in short, to the very terms of motion that the five
key dramatist terms were designed to prevent" (Rosenfeld 317).

Particularly interesting from the standpoint of Burke's ongoing
polemic with behaviorism is a remarkable passage in "Terministic
Screens": "I should make it clear: I am not pronouncing on the metaphysics of this controversy. Maybe we are but things in motion. I don't
have to haggle about that possibility. I need but point out that, whether
or not we are just things in motion, we think of one another (and especially of those with whom we are intimate) as *persons.* And the difference between a thing and a person is that the one merely *moves* whereas

the other *acts*" (*LASA* 53). Burke thus deliberately foregoes any appeal to "intuitions or sense verification" to settle the motion/action issue with philosophical finality. Instead, he puts the issue on the rhetorical level of human interaction, the unending conversation. It is on this level that Burke battles materialistic reductions of human behavior to motion as he typically argues his case by imagining a scenario whereby his antagonist is exposed before other conversants in the conversation as lapsing into self-contradiction. For example, in *A Grammar of Motives,* he proposes, "The very man who, with a chemical experiment as his informing anecdote, or point of departure, might tell you that people are but chemicals, will induce responses in people by talking to them, whereas he would not try to make chemicals behave by linguistic inducement" (59). Two decades later, in "Terministic Screens," he continues to rely on the same scenario: "Even the behaviorist, who studies man in terms of his laboratory experiments, must treat his colleagues as *persons,* rather than purely and simply as automata responding to stimuli" (*LASA* 53). In his polemic with behaviorism, Burke thus typically imagines himself engaged in an argument he is confident he can win. He thereby finds the anchor he needs for his affirmation of action, but he does so as a rhetoricizer of philosophy, a part of the unending conversation, not as a philosopher apart from it.

Burke's act/realism, as suggested earlier, should not be confused with Aristotle's. Aristotle's act puts the universe together once and for all time, as an unmoved mover prompts beings of every kind to actualize the potentiality built into their natures.[13] Aristotle's philosophy sees itself as a monologic, definitive expression of truth. Burke's act, by contrast, puts everyone into an unending conversation, where ontology and epistemology meet in a process whereby discourses like Aristotle's have their day before being displaced by others.

Aristotle theorizes modes of being in an eternal present, whereas Burke theorizes acts extending from the past into the future. On a certain level, Burke anticipates the future and thereby, unlike Aristotle, cannot be displaced by it, for Burke's act is paradoxically the permanence in change. Act theorizes the creative dimension of experience whereby the new—by definition irreducible to antecedent experience—can change future experience: "each act contains some measure of motivation that cannot be explained simply in terms of the past, being to some extent, however tiny, a *new thing*" (*GM* 65). To return to an earlier example, a change in calendars could alter our experience of time, as suggested by the difference between Easter and Earth Day. Newness, however, is paradoxically always the same: all new things must be alike in sharing the property of being different from the old. Acts are alike (permanence) and different (change).

Burke's act is best considered against the backdrop of his breath-taking cameo of the human condition:

> We in cities rightly grow shrewd at appraising man-made institutions—but beyond these tiny concentration points of rhetoric and traffic, there lies the eternally unsolvable Enigma. . . . [F]or always the Eternal Enigma is there, right on the edges of our metropolitan bickerings, stretching outward to interstellar infinity and inward to the depths of the mind. And in this staggering disproportion between man and no-man, there is no place for purely human boasts of grandeur, or for forgetting that men build their cultures by huddling together, nervously loquacious, at the edge of an abyss. (*PC* 272)

Aristotle's act unites everything from the heavens to the human mind. It is the linchpin of the universe, which would unravel without it. Burke's act theorizes only the loquaciousness at the edge of the abyss. The dissolution of this act, from the standpoint of the universe, would be little more than a hiccup. Apart from the conversation, Aristotle's act is transcendental. A part of the conversation, Burke's act is transhistorical.

Notes

1. Burke, of course, characterizes his later shift from dramatism to logology as a shift from ontology to epistemology, a self-characterization that prompted a debate in which some Burke scholars see the shift from dramatism to logology going in the opposite direction, from epistemology to ontology. My own views on Burke's self-characterization and this ensuing debate appear in Wess, *Kenneth Burke* 234–39. What is said there is qualified by the present text to the extent that my argument here is that ontology and epistemology always go hand in hand, implicitly if not explicitly, such that one might look for a shift from a dramatistic ontology/epistemology to a logological ontology/epistemology.

2. See *De Anima* (On the Soul), 429a13–24. As Sir David Ross puts it, for Aristotle "the character of mind is to have no character of its own but to be characterised entirely by what at the moment it knows; if it had a character of its own, that would interfere with the perfect reproduction of the object in the knowing mind. . . . Thus in knowledge mind and its object have an identical character, and to know an object is to know one's mind as it is in knowing the object" (182).

3. We have simplified matters, of course, in focusing mainly on one half of Descartes's dualism, where mind knows itself (substance 1) as well as matter (substance 2), and functions in a complex relationship to God. Our aim in this section is simply to introduce, as a perspective on Burke, the proposal that

ontology and epistemology entail one another such that constructing one involves marrying it to the other.

4. Coincidentally, Burke and McKeon were lifelong friends. In his authoritative study of Burke and the 1920s, Jack Selzer records: "One of Burke's tutors at the time was Richard McKeon, then a young graduate student working on a dissertation on Spinoza. McKeon had befriended Burke on their ferry rides from New Jersey to Columbia. . . . Wrote Burke [in a 1921 letter]: 'The one bright spot in my intellectual life is Richard McKeon, whom I see every couple of weeks, and who is a consolation to me because he *knows* things'" (41).

5. McKeon couples this aphorism with another, occasioned by reading Plato: "truth, though changeless, is rendered false in the uses to which it is put" (204).

6. Marx's title alludes to the coup of November 9, 1799, November 9 being the eighteenth Brumaire according to the new calendar. See "French Revolutionary Calendar," *The New Columbia Encyclopedia*, eds. William H. Harris and Judith S. Levey (New York: Columbia University Press, 1975) 1014; and Karl Marx and Frederick Engels, *Collected Works*, vol. 11 (New York: International Publishers, 1979) 11:642.

7. The problems with Descartes's dualism—"by common consent, not properly sorted out" ("Descartes, René," *Cambridge Dictionary* 196)—may be a sign that Descartes failed to marry epistemology and ontology altogether successfully, that is, failed to express this truth.

8. In his *Discourse on Method*, Descartes tells the story of how he did just the opposite, forgetting the books he spent his youth reading in favor of an epistemological method that relies solely on his own mind. Burke brings us full circle as he depicts listening to the conversation as the condition of entering it.

9. One of the curious features of the current intellectual landscape is that while signs of the revival of rhetoric are everywhere, topoi continue to receive relatively little attention, especially considering their centrality in the rhetorical tradition. The postmodernism now commonly cited to define our era may be characterized as a rhetoric that is partially aware of its rhetoricity insofar as it knows that it cannot avail itself of, as Conley phrases it, "intuitions or sense verification," but has yet fully to avail itself of topoi. As a result, postmodernism has had a propensity to sever itself from objective constraints altogether, resulting in rhetorical idealism in contrast to the rhetorical realism available in Burke and McKeon. On a personal note, I might add that my book's subtitle— "rhetoric, subjectivity, postmodernism"—was Cambridge's idea and used only at its insistence. The first sentence of my preface translates Cambridge's subtitle into my own: "In the narrative in these pages of Kenneth Burke's career, the themes of rhetoric, subjectivity, and postmodernism are concentrated in the term 'a rhetoric of the subject.'"

10. This term's debut, to the best of my knowledge, is this appearance in "Four Master Tropes," published in 1941 before its reprinting in *A Grammar of Motives*.

11. In *Discourse on Method*, Descartes deploys Burke's scene/agent ratio to frame his epistemology of the individual albeit an individual bearing the universal. He recounts that he moved in the right epistemological direction on a

cold winter day in Germany: "I remained the whole day shut up alone in a stove-heated room, where I had complete leisure to occupy myself with my own thoughts" (87). Alone, he resolves, "as regards all the opinions which up to this time I had embraced, I thought I could not do better than endeavour once and for all to sweep them completely away" (89). In their place, "accept . . . nothing more than what was presented to my mind so clearly and distinctly that I could have no occasion to doubt it" (92).

12. *The Philosophy of Literary Form* appeared in 1941, the same year as "Four Master Tropes." Another, earlier version of the conversation conceives it moving in a definable direction, more like the irony/dialectic model in "Four Master Tropes" than the "Unending Conversation" without origin or telos in *Philosophy of Literary Form*: "And when a new thinker is born, to carry on some one historic line of thought, it is as though a man had come into a room, found people there discussing some matter, and after he had listened long enough to get the drift of their conversation, had begun putting in remarks of his own, accepting *their* remarks as the basis of *his* remarks, 'proving' his points on the strength of the points which the other speakers had taken for granted" (ACR 102).

13. See *Metaphysics,* ch. 12: (1) "Since 'being' has two senses, everything changes from potential being to actual being, for example, from potentially white to actually white" (1069b16–17); (2) "That by which it [being] is changed is the first mover, that which changes is the matter, and that to which it is changed is the form" (1070a1–2); (3) "[T]here is something which causes motion without being moved, and this is eternal, a substance, and an actuality. And this is the way in which the object of desire or the intelligible object moves, namely, without itself being moved" (1072a25–28). Note that just as the *Grammar of Motives* reviewer Rosenfeld sees motion in Burke's action, one might ask if there is motion in Aristotle's action. There is a motion/action distinction but perhaps not a definitive expression of it.

Bibliography

Burke, Kenneth. "Auscultation, Creation, and Revision: The Rout of the Esthetes—Literature, Marxism, and Beyond." In *Extensions of the Burkeian System.* Ed. James W. Chesebro. Tuscaloosa: University of Alabama Press, 1993. 42–172.

———. *Dramatism and Development.* Barre, MA: Clark University Press, 1972.

———. *A Grammar of Motives.* 1945. Berkeley: University of California Press, 1969.

———. *Language as Symbolic Action.* Berkeley: University of California Press, 1966.

———. *Permanence and Change: An Anatomy of Purpose.* 1935. Rev. 3d ed. Berkeley: University of California Press, 1984.

———. *The Philosophy of Literary Form: Studies in Symbolic Action.* 1941. 3d ed. Berkeley: University of California Press, 1973.

———. "The Study of Symbolic Action." *Chimera* 1 (Spring 1942): 7–16.

Bygrave, Stephen. *Kenneth Burke: Rhetoric and Ideology.* London: Routledge, 1993.

Cambridge Dictionary of Philosophy. Ed. Robert Audi. Cambridge: Cambridge University Press, 1995.

Chomsky, Noam. *Syntactic Structures.* London: Mouton, 1965.

Conley, Thomas M. *Rhetoric in the European Tradition.* London: Longman, 1990.

Descartes, René. *The Philosophical Works of Descartes.* Ed. Elizabeth S. Haldane and G. R. T. Ross. Vol. 1. Cambridge: Cambridge University Press, 1967.

Dewey, John. "An Empirical Survey of Empiricisms." *Studies in the History of Ideas* 3 (1935): 3–22.

Garver, Eugene. *Aristotle's* Rhetoric: *An Art of Character.* Chicago: University of Chicago Press, 1994.

McKeon, Richard. *Rhetoric: Essays in Invention and Discovery.* Ed. Mark Backman. Woodbridge, CT: Ox Bow Press, 1987.

Nelson, Cary. "Writing as the Accomplice of Language: Kenneth Burke and Poststructuralism." In *The Legacy of Kenneth Burke.* Ed. Herbert W. Simons and Trevor Melia. Madison: University of Wisconsin Press, 1989.

Rorty, Richard. *Philosophy and the Mirror of Nature.* Princeton: Princeton University Press, 1979.

Rosenfeld, Isaac. "Dry Watershed." Review of *GM. Kenyon Review* 8 (1946): 310–17.

Ross, Sir David. *Aristotle.* London: Methuen, 1949.

Selzer, Jack. *Kenneth Burke in Greenwich Village: Conversing with the Moderns.* Madison: University of Wisconsin Press, 1996.

Valesio, Paolo. *Novantiqua: Rhetorics as a Contemporary Theory.* Bloomington: Indiana University Press, 1980.

Wess, Robert. *Kenneth Burke: Rhetoric, Subjectivity, Postmodernism.* Cambridge: Cambridge University Press, 1996.

Worsham, Lynn. "Kenneth Burke's Appendicitis: A Feminist's Case for Complaint." *Pre/Text* 12.1–2 [1991]: 67–95.

Part Three

Transcendence and the Theological Motive

8

The Many Voices of Kenneth Burke, Theologian and Prophet, as Revealed in His Letters to Me

Wayne C. Booth

Hail to
That Undefinable *Definiendum*
the Infinite Wordless Universe
with the Countless
Universes of Discourse

that Story can make of it . . .
　　　　　　　　—Kenneth Burke, letter to Wayne Booth

I feel anxious here, naturally enough, just as Kenneth Burke often reported of himself before giving a talk. The anxiety comes mostly from
the presence of you Burkeans who no doubt know more about him than
I do. But it also comes from the sheer difficulty of ever doing justice to
this complicated polymath. The shameful fact is that for several decades in my young scholarly life I neglected him grossly. I was taught
by "Chicago-schoolers" who claimed that Burke, like too many other
twentieth-century thinkers including the New Critics, was not worthy
of prolonged attention because he had been trapped in the prison house
of language-centered dogmas. What's more, we "neo-Aristotelians"
knew enough not to be captured by anyone who seemed to revel in
parataxis.

　　When I finally began in the sixties to read him seriously, I became
increasingly—inevitably—impressed. I taught several graduate courses
that centered entirely on him and Ronald Crane as complementary—

perhaps contradictory—pluralists, and I finally wrote what I intended to be the first fully empathic, fully *comprehending* account of his whole project. I was even tempted to call it—so confident did I feel—"Kenneth Burke from the Perspective of Kenneth Burke" (Booth, "Kenneth Burke's Way of Knowing"). As I celebrated his dramatistic "dancing," I was certain that he would say to himself, "At last I have found one reader who has really understood me."

His unhappy response, the article "Dancing with Tears in My Eyes," almost drew tears from mine. Those of you who know Burke's way of responding to critics could easily have predicted something like that response. But you could not have predicted what he actually said about it in a letter of January 2, 1979, addressed to "Dear Ever-Wax." Sometimes he started his letters to me with "Dear Ever-Waxing Wayne," never, I'm glad to say, with "Dear Waning Wax." Once he referred to me as "wax birth, or some such." Anyway, here's how he qualified his deep annoyance.

> Starting the n-year right, I wanna make it clear that my bleats are but professional, not poisonal. I have plenty of friendliness and admiration envers vous, and hope to go on saying so.
>
> Your mistake in starting from the dramatistic pentad rather than from the principles of form in the *lexicon rheto-ricae* was due to a hangover from Ronald Crane's brain-washing of you before you had a brain.

Then, after a bit more remonstration, he wrote:

> Peace, peace! While I call Crane the Stalin of pluralism.
>
> Avec universal Liebe,
> KB

Was I devastated by the critique of my misunderstanding? I was. But I went on reading him, teaching his works, quoting him in many a public talk, attempting to probe more deeply into what continued to feel a bit mysterious, unfathomable, shifting under my feet. When a few years later I attempted a kind of perspectivalism of my own, I felt that the way to honor the validity of Burke's objections would be to print them in the book along with some pluralistic "placement" (Booth, *Critical Understanding*).

As you might predict, the response was, while friendly, clearly that of one who felt grossly misunderstood and mistreated. I'd done him wrong again, honoring him as one of three major pluralists, but placing him between Crane and M. H. Abrams, instead of at the beginning or at the climactic end where he belonged.

VII/25/79

Dear WeBst*r,

Or do I know you long enough to call you by your given name, Dear Dan?

Oh, if only somebody had told me about Crane's scrupulous "scholarship" as attested on your p. 87![1] That's a crooked or incompetent deal, if there ever was one. I point out that Wordsworth suggested the Albatross. And for the good reason that it bolstered up my case! Coleridge wanted simply a guilt-laden wanderer (whose boat was the main vehicle of the withdrawal symptoms). I hold that there are three. . . . [In] my role as a "pluralist," I saw that by Gawd that strand is there, and is clearly traceable.

As for "scholarship": Before I came to Chicago, I had had a job as a ghost writer for [and there follows a page-long claim that he had scholarly knowledge about drugs].

You are supposed to be an expert on me. But you're racing all over the world, so you just didn't have the time to study me. More obviously, the proper way to build me after Crane would have been to feature my . . . [and he lists works I had failed to discuss]. You shd. also have discussed my ways of wrestling with "equations." . . .

Then, and only then, you should have introduced my Pentad (not "pentagon," dawlink, that's a bit on the flamboyant side). You could have shown how it was . . .

And on he goes, with suggestion after suggestion. I wrote several drafts of a rather defensive but apologetic reply, including the point that "pentagon" had been meant as a pun, and two weeks later he wrote as follows:

8/12/79

Well, but here is a humiliated confession: I completely missed the pun in [your] "pentagon." The word itself so relates to my personal "psychosis" that I saw in it nothing but connotations of disrespect. That was indeed ironic! I'd have enjoyed it hugely; for also it ties in with my vexation with my need to "hex" the damned thing, (that is, raising them [the five key terms] to six.)

Maybe it's this way: as a logological pluralist [placed by you] in the middle, I couldn't deserve [from you] an adequate statement of my case ad intra, for it wd. look too much like a brand of "dualistic monism." So I'm caught in the middle, not like our savior between two thieves, nor like my intermediate section on "perspectives by incongruity" in *Permanence and Change,* but like my adopted and adoptive state of New Jersey, which gets trampled on by the traffic to and from New York.

Meanwhile, heck, forgive me if (I was feeling gloomy those days anyhow, and still largely am, through no fault of yours) I seemed to be enrolling myself too much among the primi donni. In a letter to Denis Donoghue I slavishly quoted your closing sentence,[2] (Hillis Miller, by the way, wrote a quite generous item anent the sickly selph for a biographical piece in *Int. Encyc. of Soc. Sci.*)

Now my point in beginning here with his thorny responses is not, as he might have felt, to put Burke down as an egotist. Rather it is more a putting down of my younger self: I never got him right, and I don't even expect to do so here. The invitation to address him once more led me to the first full rereading of his letters to me, starting in November 1971, when he was already seventy-four, and I was astonished at how many different "Kenneth Burkes" I was meeting in those letters, many of them "voices" never encountered in his publications.

As I then read back through that pile, I was forced to address again the questions raised by Bill Rueckert in his fine essay on the many voices he has found in Burke's writings ("Some of the Many Kenneth Burkes," *Encounters With Kenneth Burke).* I became absorbed not only in the question of what rivaling voices I would find but even more in the tougher one: "Is there any one voice that unifies the huge chorus? Does the full drama get written, with any kind of discernible center?"

It should surprise no one here that I came to no one decisive answer. Though we are all socially constructed through the manifold voices we take in, Burke was an amazing, perhaps unique instance of a multivoiced genius, one who could transform each of the manifold voices that had constructed him into new and marvelous inventions. I shall of course finally ask us to listen to the one voice that *to some degree* harmonizes at least eight others.[3] Burke wrote a good deal of music in what I find it hard to describe as his "spare" time. I like to think that he would not jump on me for employing now metaphors of the kind he himself often offered, asking, "Just what *tunes* did the 'real' Burke ultimately *dance* to with greatest enthusiasm or deepest engagement?" Relying partly on Rueckert's listing, but moving beyond it toward a choral harmony, we may seem for a time to be simply underlying the thesis of another paper at this conference: Burke as devotee of "the aesthetic."[4] But—as his God repeats again and again at the end of *The Rhetoric of Religion:* "It's more complicated than that."

I've already given perhaps more than enough of the self-reproaching egotist who was never fully satisfied not just with my efforts but with *anyone's* efforts to sum him up: what he has called his "sickly sylph" (sometimes it was "selph"). I'm mildly shocked, though, by just how often he spends time and energy complaining about the stupidities of other critics. Usually the claims are like the one I just read: the "assholes" haven't bothered to read all or most or any of his work. In "As I Was Saying," for example, Burke answers René Wellek's charge that his purpose "remains obscure," by saying: "the obscurity is due to his [Wellek's] piecemeal method of reporting."

Another typical response was to Fredric Jameson's critique:

September 16, 1978

> Hence of course my genuine astonishment at Jameson's procedure in his report on me and ideology. . . . And I have considerable morbid curiosity in seeing how in Gottes Namen he can write on ideology and form in ways that by-pass my lexicon in C-S *[Counter-Statement]* and my socioanagogic line in RM *[A Rhetoric of Motives]* since both aspects strike me as quite in line with literary Marxism. My term "logology" was needed for putting together my two slants on ideology in those books.

From then on for some reason he always refers to Jameson as "your champion." Had I actually praised Jameson in one of my letters?

Such responses could be condemned as simply petty, and Burke himself sometimes condemns them as "poisonal." But the closer I look at the laments and accusations the more they seem to me an inevitable result of the very nature of his lifetime project. For him, every idea connects to every other idea, and since none of his critics could even come close to grasping conclusions that Burke himself was still working out, nobody could possibly get him right, let alone cover all of his bases.

Still, there was a KB who was unusually vocal about the distress everyone feels when criticized or misunderstood. What might be called his "competitive pain" reached a peak in our letters when, in October of 1981, we editors of *Critical Inquiry,* supported in our judgment by a reading from Bill Rueckert, turned down his piece on "Sensation, Memory, Imitation/and Story." I'll return at the end to our rejection, which I now see as a mistake.

Here's how he responded:

> Naturally, [when I got your rejection] I poured myself a drink, then waited a few minutes, and sure enough, the answer came through, I sat me down and typed

> Hail to
> That Undefinable *Definiendum*
> the Infinite Wordless Universe
> with the Countless
> Universes of Discourse
>
> that Story can make of it.
> Then I confided to Whomever, "if Billions R**ck*rt or John
> Wayne B**th, or any of them farts can write more statu-
> esque-like than that . . . " and I feel better now.

Note how he turns the anger and hurt into a creative moment. More important, as I look forward to my final voice today, is the hint of the religious inquirer, as he turns what could have been simply a curse against "them farts" into an address to the "Undefinable," the Infinite Wordless Universe, with the Countless Universes of Discourse, confiding all that to "Whomever," with a capital W.

Sometimes a different voice comments on the problem of *why* his letters reflect so much vitriol, and what to do about it.

April 14, 1980

> As for my letters, let 'em linger. I'm not interested in their being around while I still am. Incidentally, I forget whether I told you: my letters will do me dirt the way Nixon's tapes did him. Most of my "friendly" letters were written at cock-tail hour. If I write many, by the later ones the adrenaline is working. I had a deal with Libbie [his wife] whereby I'd not seal them until the next morning, when I'd glance through them before mailing. She was right: many I didn't send. And I'd make amends by being more friendly or demure. But often I filed the unsent one along with a duplicate of the one that passed. So I am undone. For I don't have the time or inclination to weed out all that [vitriolic] stuff.

Thus Voice One often merges into this quite different Voice Two, the writer who, while still suffering from competitive angers, turns the blame upon himself:

February 8, 1973

> It's good to hear that Dick McKeon still holds forth, and holds out, so valiantly. I must admit, I see no reason for him to be "afraid" of me, though I keep on finding reasons for me to be afraid of myself. Even if there be a heaven, and I were able to get there (two tremendous if's indeed!), even

with infinity in which to catch up on my required reading, I could neer catch up with Dick. I write, as a means of escaping such awful obligations.

The self-criticism of Voice Two is seldom blatant, usually following an outburst about unfair treatment, as in his response on New Year's Day, 1980, to the special issue of *RANAM*.[5]

January 1, 1980

... There is no more awsome [*sic*] silence than an occasion of that sort [referring to the absence of his real voice in the article], here made absolute in that I got but three copies. Two kinds of operation, to recover from differently [one a hernia operation, the other the *Ranam* issue], "operation autour de l'auteur." At least many of the pages are on the slope of solace (some by Bob Garlitz in ptikla); but as I experience it, we're all in the same silence, together [about one's real work and its real importance]. Your pedagogical and editorial ties protect you against the possibility of those vexations, even if all else did go wrong. They are my home. 1/1/80

Those vexations are indeed *his home*. Throughout the letters I find lines like this: "But I feel guilty (heck, I always feel guilty in some way ...)" (February 4, 1981: "2 A.M., Drinking"). "My God-given morbidity makes me grow damned uneasy with regard to the state of total non-communication"—that of a neglectful editor (October 6, 1981).

You will have noticed that Voices One and Two are seldom boring because they usually are rivalled by Voice Three, what he sometimes himself calls "the comedian": the witty, genuinely humble jester who simply enjoys joking about everything, whether putting down other critics, putting down himself, or inventing new versions of his own schemata or of Christianity or of the whole of creation. Some of it is just plain irresistible wordplay, as in his: "Thanks one whole lot for thy promptitudinosity" (January 19, 1978), or his occasional reference to the book he called *Attiturds Towards History*.

As he grew ever older, Voice Four increasingly intruded, that of an old man lamenting his aging and thinking about death, but the witty Voice Three was still usually kept alive. I have been reading many other authors about aging, death, and dying, and I've found nobody who manages to talk about dying more spiritedly.

In 1973, after I'd expressed sympathy about his health and his grief about Libbie's death, he wrote ever-waxing Wayne a three-pager about his projects, and then turned to health.

November 22, 1973

You also seemed to have misgivings about the prognosis for
my current state of mindandbody [*sic*]. When I assured you
that I'm "still kicking," I had both meanings in mind. But I
do watch me with a mean eye. For instance, all of a sudden
I wasn't sure whether it's Anatole or Anatol. In the course of
checking, I incidentally discovered that the reference book I
sought had disparooed (which is French for "disappeared").
So I have to deal with things like that, too.

Then, since it was Thanksgiving, he added a sarcastic poem "on
giving thanks" and a wonderfully ironic one, introduced with the comment, "as for me poisonally":

But for These Lucky Accidents

Were I not tall and suave and handsome
were I not famed for my glamourous Byronic love-affairs
had not each of my books sold riotously
had not my fists made strong men cringe

did not my several conversions enlist
further hordes of followers
and did not everything I turned to
make me big money

despite my almost glorious good health
of both body and mind
how in God's name
could I, through all these years,

have held up
and held out
and held on?
    And thanks for kind, encouraging words—yes. And at
least Burpian brands of irony can tell for sure how wayne
promises wax.
    Friendliest greetings.

Onwards, Outwards, and UP,
KB

That aging voice was given more and more platform space as the
years went by:

July, 1977:

Dear *Ever-waxing:*

Du bist mir ans herz *gewachsen—and* cordial greetings to youenz all.

Bejeez, you make it worth while for a guy to be hanging on into his eighties, a-gettn lonesomer and lonesomer.[6]

Three years later he seemed overwhelmed as he wrestled with age and death. He was often miserable—but he kept on managing to sound as wittily thoughtful as always:

April 14, 1980

Damn it all—I gotta bow out. Somethinks wrong, I ail. Still not diagnosed, but decidedly would not want to fare far forth. . . . Meanwhile, it's possible that my ills may be but psychological. But I have been undergoing purely physical examinations. [Note the motion/action-body/symbol pairing at work here.] . . . I have, many times in my life, run into twists with purely "symbolic" modes of motivation. And though we're told that you can't teach an old dog new tricks, in our eighties the ways of senescence improvise new dealings with the line betw. senility and senectitude.

Meanwhile I continue to find myself an engrossing source of data.

As we might expect, the complaints diminished considerably as honors and attention from the world began to arrive in deserved quantities, after his decades of feeling unappreciated. When he received the National Medal for Literature, as well as further teaching offers and an invitation to read his poetry for *one grand,* he wrote:

April 17, 1981

So although quite problematical physically, I'm a bit on the levitation side attitudinally. . . . I guess if one hangs on long enough into one's eighties people decide to be sorry for an old slob.

And three years later he repeated his play with the word senility:

February 12, 1984

. . . Incidentally, do you think it's just my 86-years that make(s) me find the "death" lyric so "perfect" (i.e. "finished")? I

write you in a state of senescence that sloped by nature toward senility while opting hard for senectitude. Hoila!

Sometimes these first four voices can seem to me now in conflict
with a persistent Voice Five, one who sounds like an engrossed scholar
pursuing nothing but a universalizing attempt to understand everything. In 1971 a couple of my students, Robert Kirschten and Donald
Barshis, wrote him asking for his theory about how people become not
just rhetors but rhetoricians—what these days I call, weakly trying to
imitate his neologistic style, rhetorologists. He answered them at length:

May 5, 1971

You're wondering how we become rhetoricians. An enter-
priser who has been working on some of my stuff asks how I
became a dialectician. Maybe we should make up a word and
say that we begin by babbling, which is "polymorphously
proverse," [*sic*] then get narrowed down by contingencies . . .
a neologism that logologizes.

Incidentally, within about a fortnight we shall open the
dam, and not close it again until next spring. During that
portion of the year, we find it more diplomatic to refer to
Lake Bottom as "Lake Fulfillment," thereby taking advantage of an Empsonian ambiguity, since the temporary alias
can stand for either the entelechial exfoliation of the cycle
of terms implicit in the idea of lake as a bottom, or as the
promise of a rebirth when the dam is closed again next
spring.

Such scheming was taught me by Ignatz de Burp, author of "The Anaesthetic Revelation of Herone Liddell,"
a thinly veiled autobiographic figure who says (*Complete
White Oxen* 309): "I live by dodges, and so do my symptoms."

The voice of this unrelenting scholarly inquirer—this perspectival-
ist, this dialectician, this dramatologist—the voice humorous or solemn
or angry, has been interpreted in two quite different directions, because
it exhibits two quite different tones: What I might call Voice Five-A is
that of the *skeptical* prober who sees humanity primarily as inventor/
discoverer of the skeptical negative, and thus as a creature inevitably
caught up in misguided, sacrificial, competitive, destructive entelechial
warfare salvageable only by—well, by the efforts of people like Kenneth
Burke. This Burke can be seen as a man who uses the negative as what

knocks down every aspiration toward perfection, even though the aspiration toward perfection is irresistibly built into our natures. Obsessed with the knowledge that every perspective is limited, that no language is adequate to more than a slice of things, Burke delights in intellectual killings of the kind that he hopes will someday cure actual warfare.

If we listen to his project in this way, as a universal inquiry into inevitable limitations, his putting down of everybody, including himself (Voices One and Two), sounds akin to the very best of the deconstructionists: to put it in terms that he would probably have rejected, *every* statement can be deconstructed to show how it can lead to aporias. Thus if we listen selectively we can hear Burke as the first full-fledged deconstructionist.[7]

I won't trouble to quote the many passages in his letters, as in his published works, that sound to me like something Hillis Miller or de Man or Derrida might write. I'll assume that readers here will know a lot about that aspect of his work; what's more, we now have a full treatment of it in Robert Wess's recent book (especially 158–71). I find it interesting that many of us who read him in the forties and fifties rejected him in terms that sound very much like the objections by many traditionalists these days to the work of the postmodernists: we feared then that his paratactic probings of everything were giving away the rational store.

Some critics these days, however, see Burke's project as not *sufficiently* postmodern, poststructuralist. His letters to me could be said to provide them with evidence, in a voice I'll call Five-B, still the relentless scholar but one who would be troubled by the comparison I just made. This is the voice not of the system-smasher but the confident *system-builder,* the voice of a man who believed not just that there is indeed some truth worth pursuing, but that he was pursuing it in the one proper way. It is the voice of a man who could jokingly say he wanted to live long because he always wanted the last word (in the new language, Burks). This voice he himself even called the "absolutist" whenever he was seeking to divorce himself from what he saw as deconstructionist relativism or behaviorist reductionism. In 1979, in that letter complaining about my article, he offered me what he called

> . . . my confession to the effect that in some respects I'm almost an "absolutist." For instance, as vs. the behaviorists, I absolutely *insist upon* a *dualistic* position. And with regard to any and all other isms, I *insist upon* the motion/action pair as the groundwork of a *secular* nomenclature for the discussion of human relations.

He could often be dogmatic like that when he encountered post-modernists who seemed to him to sell out the reality of the body, of real motion underlying all symbolic action. In March of 1982 he wrote from Emory University about a recent conference:

> To me the prize [scandalous] exhibit of all was Scholes on Derrida [saying things like]: "For spoken language to exist, human sounds must be organized into a system of phonemic differences. If we assume that these differences have priority over perception, then we must accept that we are indeed in a prison house of language. This is why Derrida says, "I don't know what perception is and I don't believe that anything like perception exists." etc.

He then presents a chart of sensation/memory, imitation/story, along the lines of the article that *Critical Inquiry* had rejected. (See "Sensation, Memory, Imitation/and Story"). For our primal ancestors, he writes, before words came into the world, there was "sensory perception" in the technical sense that some things "tasted good" and some things didn't.

> If Derrida is so slick he can't believe that "anything like perception" (of that sort) existed and still does, O.K., let him take it to bed with him. . . . [T]hat guy [Scholes] should be put in prison until he *says* "I want out."

It is this voice, the almost-absolutist, who interests me most today —the vigorous, astonishingly learned man who was seeking, with the one right method, a unified view of all human pursuits: the system-builder who became increasingly wedded to his body/mind, motion/action, sign/symbol, animality/symbolicity distinctions. If we ask why it was that the competitor-voice kept putting critics down for getting things wrong, and for looking at only a part of his oeuvre, we can see that beneath all the fragments there was a man almost desperately attempting to put it all together in a grand view of everything: not the mere language theorist that my mentors tended to dismiss but the frustrating and frustrated critic who could not get everybody, including Derrida, to see the difference between the taste of an orange and the words "the taste of an orange." Everybody got it wrong, because everybody latched onto only one fragment, whereas the true KB was attempting the noble, if impossible, task of putting it all together. We'll return to that voice as Voice Seven.

How different that overconfident one is from Voice Six, the voice of the poet we have already heard speaking: the man attempting not to pin down the world but to evoke wittily or feelingly a lived piece of that world, with all its resistance to any formulation in prose. Indeed I suspect that anyone describing his work up to at least the mid-thirties would have summarized it under this "Aesthetic Voice." His letters would often include poems cooked up on the spot, or copies of poems that he later published. Some of them could be described as a bit windy, unpoetic, prosaic, even "scholarly." KB himself confesses at one point, sending me a copy of a wonderful poem about the loss of his wife, that the distinction for him between prose and poetry is after all muddy.

November 5, 1977

I doubt whether I ever started out to write a poem on the typewriter, though I often revise one on the machine; and some of the notes that I take by hand might turn up eventually on either the verse or prose side. But I lamely admit that that's far from an ideally professional way of distinguishing verse from prose. Basically, my notion is this: given any work at all, it will yield to analysis as poetry, rhetoric, self-portraiture, philosophy, science. Usually it yields more fully to one such classification rather than another. But the distinctions need not stay put. Consider, for instance, the difference between the Bible as doctrine and the Bible as "literature." We all know this sort of thing, yet we forget it, as you made me forget it.

The poem, by the way, that I both wanted to read and dodged, goes thus:

Postlude

When something goes, some other takes its place,
Maybe a thistle where had been a rose;
Or where lace was, next time a churchman's missal,
"Erase, efface," Life says, "when something goes."

Her death leaves such a tangled aftergrowth,
By God I fear I have outlived us both.
. . . I so much wanted to risk those lines—yet I knew I'd make a damfool of myself. Them internal rhymes, nsech. I have loyally vowed that they're the best lines I'll ever have been able to write.

But that's the trouble with us comedians; all comedians are most tearfully sentimental. In any case, I'm most sentimentally grateful to youenz guys . . .

I could go on adding voices—Burke the physician, curing the world's
ills; Burke the ecologist (as you may know, his ecological explorations
have by now produced a large following: in the thirty-six dissertations
I've located seeking to relate him and religion, a large proportion emphasize ecology as if it were his center.) But I turn now to the voices that
interest me most, at this stage of *my* life: two closely related voices,
Seven and Eight, the voices of Burke the religious inquirer.

First, then, Voice Seven, the voice that uses Voice Three, that of
the wit, to play with religious phrasing and terminology, with no discussion of actual religious belief—indeed usually no admission that he's
coming even close to addressing religious questions. As every reader of
The Rhetoric of Religion knows, Burke again and again claims that his
logology can neither prove nor disprove religion or the existence of
God, and I have found nowhere any statement in which he admits to
being anything other than an agnostic who had long since moved beyond childhood experiences with churches, including Christian Science.
But if you read his work with religion in mind, you find from the beginning an astonishing amount of reliance on religious language and
history. Some of this is perhaps merely verbal echoing of his religious
upbringing. The letters are full of biblical phrasings, but of course that
is true of the writing of most good writers, even the most aggressive
atheists. But there's an astonishing amount of direct reference to God,
some of it obviously only playful, some of it ambiguous. As I read the
following, help me decide whether Burke is, in your definition of God,
addressing God:

> *February 7, 1976*
>
> . . . only God can know how much I may be sacrificing when
> I fail to cash in on this sure thing for myself.

> *May 13, 1977*
>
> And you phoned me on my God-luck day of all days (Wow!
> I thought I meant "good". Give me enough Friday the thir-
> teenths, and I'd own the world.)
>   Forgive me for being so superstitious.

> *May 31, 1977*
>
> The makings of please are in the infant which, as it devel-
> ops from speechlessness into talk and even talk-about-talk,
> learns to transform its spontaneous cry into a mode of com-
> munication. It began by crying because it had a bellyache,
> and it learned to cry as a way of summoning mamma. Thus
> I would see religion as grounded in prayer, supplication—an

infant experience that confronts the basic "speaker/speech/spoken-to" design from the speaker gate . . .

Ennihow, such considerations may indicate why I felt that it wd. be speculatively relevant to start my hymnal deductions from "we in our weakness cry unto thee." Proceeding thence to the Latin amplifying of thee, and thence to the "mediatory" stage of Christ as the transition from topics of power to topics of weakness. Viewed thus, at least the chorale is well-formed.

January 16, 1978

Would C[ritical] I[nquiry] want this companion piece (which I have recently revised)? 'Tis but three sentences, a bit longish, but designed as an invocation for a meeting of logologers, and intended to indicate how deeply pious we are, after all. And sure you'll agree: if a guy ain't pious enough to scare himself, he . . . well, what the heck?

January 29, 1978

Meanwhile, here's what makes me feel that Big Shot may still be on my side:

Were I not down here [in Florida] now, the chawnstes [*sic*] are that by now some organ of mine would have been expertly excised in the light of my symptoms. . . .

Ennihow, 'tis a sunny Sunday morning, and I wish the same even to [you] Mormans [*sic*]; and may we all be enterprising, as one thing leads to another. I write you as an ex-Christian-Scientist, with love to all.

January 2, 1979

Eennyhow, apparently there is a God—for youenz guys, and not us, are getting the worst of the bad weather.

In fact, almost always when he is worrying about aging, ill health, or dying, he will move quickly to religious language—and sometimes even to religious questions:

April 12, 1980

Gad, is it a brain-lesion? I can imagine how an unwanted x-ray of the brain (circa 3 1/2 years ago) could have *begun* what now attains fulfillment (Ah! most glorious word: "Teteletai," I think the Greek is, but I can't check on it, for someone seems to have "borrowed" my Greek N.T.; *consummatum*

est, before our legendary savior mythically bowed his head
and died; *es ist vollbracht,* as per one of Bach's *passions*—
the Greek, I think, wd. be a reduplicated future perfect). But
heck, a guy like I'm could be excused for feeling a bit "sacrificial" if he proves to be the victim of *unwanted* scientific
prowess, e'en as he now welcomes the powers of applied science to check on these matters of its own excesses.

I feel so damn-tangled, I'm almost ready to *welcome* a
sugar-augury that would settle for incipient diabetes. And in
any case, we're dealing with a *physiological* condition, regardless of its source. . . .

KB.

"Source" is not capitalized. Source is not at this point discussed. And it
is usually surrounded with "if," as in the quotation I gave earlier:

February 8, 1973

Even if there be a heaven, and I were able to get there (two
tremendous if's indeed!), even with infinity in which to catch
up on my required reading, I could neer catch up with Dick.

In my view, even those "if's" demonstrate that what we've seen him call
the "Big Boss" or "Whomever" is always in the wings.

That leads us to Voice Eight, which I want to claim harmonizes
them all—though of course in an immeasurably contrapuntal chorus.
This is the voice we know from *The Rhetoric of Religion,* the one that
openly and systematically probes into religious questions, the logologist
—the man who increasingly in his later years unites questions about
religious language with questions about other perfectionist quests and
worries about the triumphs of technology, ecological decline, aging, and
death—and always about the incompleteness of his corpus.

Dealing with this voice we come to that grand unanswerable question that I originally intended to constitute my whole talk: "What were
Burke's deepest unspoken beliefs about God and creation?" Obviously
I cannot hope to answer that question firmly, but what I cannot doubt
is that genuinely religious questions—according to my own conception
of genuine religion—were at the center of his thinking. The miracle-
flaunting Gods of his youthful religious training had been killed off by
science and modernism. For a time in the early thirties, he embraced
what might be called the God of aestheticians, "Beauty"; some of his
essays then sound almost like a defense of art for art's sake. The young
aesthetician was a man who *thought* he had found a new, superior
religion—beauty, form. But he then soon discovered that that was not
enough, and turned briefly to left-wing politics. When that also proved

insufficient, he took up what might be called the lifetime project of disguised theology.

It is still true that if to be religious requires that one embrace some sort of church, Burke remained irreligious. If religion requires unambivalent belief in an intervening providential lord, Burke is again out—most of the time, even though, as you've heard, the question is often on his mind. But if religion is what I think it is, a belief in a mysterious but real cosmic creative power; if it is belief in the power of the so-called nature that made us as we are in all our complexity; if it is the power that confusingly but genuinely commands of us that we pursue its nature, as Burke did, and the relation of that nature to ours—dictating, for example, hard honest thought, decent treatment of our fellows, and so on to the list of Burkean virtues; or if it is what Matthew Arnold calls "something eternal, the enduring power, not ourselves, that makes for righteousness" (57); or if it is, in more current terms, whatever center in the so-called scientific universe gave us the gift of life and along with it the irresistible urge to improve life—if, if, if, if—then Kenneth Burke is a modern prophet engaging in a postmodernist, postpositivist revival of religious inquiry. His probing of our origins in nature and our ways of transcending the world of motion; his battles against the behaviorists and his defense of free agency; his probing of our satanic commitments to victimization and sacrifice and our manifold efforts to escape them; his marvelous grappling with the central issues of Genesis and Augustine's work; his echoing again and again of intellectual moves that traditionally had been made only by theologians, particularly when they constructed the ontological proof for the existence of a God ultimately incomprehensible—all of these drives show that religious questions and cautiously labelled "religious" answers were in his bones, aching to come out into the open.

That ache expressed itself most fully in his echoes of the ancient ontological proof for the existence of God. Burke knew—indeed was obsessed with the knowledge—that

- once we speak, we express value,
- once we express value, a distinction between the good and the not good, we imply a hierarchy of values according to which that judgment makes sense,
- any hierarchy of values necessarily entails a supreme value term at the top, a god-term validating the steps in the hierarchy.

What he left only implicit is the "top" term of the ontological proof: the notion that true perfection at the top requires genuine existence: if you think of a God "at the top" who exists only as a concept, that God

is inferior to any God who truly exists. Thus you must either give up
the entire hierarchy, since the capstone does not exist, or embrace the
perfect God who exists and validates the pyramid. Anselm claimed that
after thinking hard about this issue, "only a fool could deny the existence of God." As Burke might have put it but never did, "only fools
could ever deny, once they have climbed the pyramid implied by their
chosen value system, that the pyramid really exists, with a genuine
Value Structurer at the top."

Though Burke saw the many ways in which such hierarchy building
can lead to a perfectionism that destroys, he was driven by the convic-
tion that if we are ever to achieve loving peace, if we are ever to destroy
war, indeed if we are ever even to formulate a defensible way of talking
about the world, we must ask the very questions about that hierarchy
that the best religious questioners have always been asking. He thus
joined, always in a sense reluctantly, the great theological traditions.

I would sometimes try to push him on why he kept separate the two
grand ontological pyramids, the substantive hierarchy of good vs. not-
so-good, leading to God, and the linguistic hierarchy of value-laden
terms, leading only to god-terms. I argued that some versions of his ontological proof for the inescapable triumph of god-terms could be inserted into Anselm or Descartes without disrupting their texts. Why not
make the leap, I would ask, from one pyramid to the other, where the
taste of the god-term becomes not just the language of god-terms but
the realities of a religious belief (however carefully qualified, as mine
is)? Why not move from the lower-case "g" to a full embrace of the
Capital? He always dodged the full affirmation, though he sometimes
came close to it.

But he would usually turn to that other question, about whether his
logology is too tightly tied to Christian thinking. For example:

March 18, 1980

> . . . Somewhere . . . (I seem to have lost the reference)
> you seem to feel that my logologizing of theology is too local
> to *Christianity.* Though the stress upon the motif of "origi-
> nal sin" as "inherited" from the "first" man is a major "stra-
> tegic" device in "rationalizing" the grandest case of infanti-
> cide conceivable (much grander than its O.T. forerunner in
> Abraham's willingness to sacrifice Isaac for the good of the
> cause), I don't see that my way of interpreting the story of
> the integral relationship between the "creation" and the
> "fall" should be any different if I were a pre-Christian rather
> than a post-Christian interpreter of the relation btw. "narra-
> tive" and "logical" terms for motivational "priority." (Yet it

is true that, as the OED tells us, "logology" first meant the doctrine of Christ as "the Word," then later got its analogical secularization as a synonym for "philology.")

One thing is certain here. The *Hellenic* stress upon the divinity of "the Word" (as per the Book of John, and the sectarian haggles around the role of the "Judaizers" as to whether that book should be admitted into the canon), the specifically *Christian* emphasis upon "the Word" did sharpen our awareness of "the Word" as motive. But I can't see how, given *any logolizing of* any myth in *any* theological structure, my *essential* point about temporal and logical priority would be any different. Smattera fack, the issue is discussed in gm *[Grammar of Motives],* written long before my essay on "the first three chapters of Genesis." True, I had been engrossed with Augustine's Latin as early as my days as a masturbating adolescent. And to them, as knows . . .

My claim here, then, moving toward a still open-ended conclusion, is that *The Rhetoric of Religion* belongs on every genuine religious inquirer's bedside shelf, not just as an inquiry into language but as a disguised inquiry into genuine religious belief. Indeed, if I were in charge of the next printing of his book, I would want to add some polite clarifications, after the last page of the foreword, where Burke says, "In this book we are to be concerned not directly with religion, but rather with the *terminology* of religion; not directly with man's relationship to God, but rather with his relationship to the *word* 'God.' " "Whatever else it may be, and wholly regardless of whether it be true or false, theology [like logology] is preeminently *verbal.* It is 'words about God' " (vi). My new foreword would add, in italics or boldface, the following, signed by "Waxing Wane":

> Actually, in contrast to this assertion, Burke was distressed by any thinker who reduced all reality to language. Consider for example his annoyance about deconstructionists like Derrida who, in Burke's reading, deny the plain fact, the hard substantive reality, that a child learns to distinguish real tastes before he or she learns any words for distinguishing tastes. Any careful reader of the whole of what he called boikswoiks will discover that in his gut, as in his heart, KB knew that he was grappling not just with language about reality but with the reality of value distinctions and their mysterious source at the top. His reality was permeated with the presence of a mysteriously shifting, unfixable totality so

complex, so full of conflicts between what look to us like both affirmations and negations, that no human language can ever encompass him/her/it/them. What you will find in this volume are rich and sometimes confusing reasons for being skeptical about everyone's totalizing enterprise— except, of course, his own: the theorizing of the dialectician/logologist/theologian.

Burke's kind of totalizing is not arrogant but humble, because even as he tries to harmonize all his competing voices, he knows, as the Lord says again and again in the great dialogue with which he ends the book, "No, it's more complicated than that."

What this book of his tends too often to obscure is a further distinction that he often worked with. Once we move from body/motion to mind/action, via the distinction between "taste of the orange" and words *about* the taste of the orange, we encounter a further step: the difference between merely pointing with words to something not "present" and *telling a story* with those words, still about what is not present. Burke sometimes actually calls the symbolic world of words about the "taste of the orange" the world of spirit.

I would instead save that word spirit or spiritual for the additional world we enter when telling stories, or sharing a painting, or composing or listening to music, or worshipping or engaging in genuine prayer. In stories, in any medium, we escape from both the body world and the word-bound symbolic action world into a new world freed from our ties to ordinary time. We move up and out of the temporal order into a new order that requires a new term, perhaps something up-to-date but still Burkean, like *"virtual symbolic action,"* or "transcendence of time." In other words, there are, as he always implies but too rarely notes, two domains within his domain of symbolic action: symbolic *naming,* "the taste of the orange," and symbolic *story-making* that uses the words: "Yesterday I peeled an orange, hoping for the usual wonderful taste, and out popped a genie with a magic wand and . . . "

Abandoning that "preface," which of course would have annoyed him, I conclude with a bit of prophecy after the event: if we editors of *Critical Inquiry* had been smart enough to see what Burke was grappling with in that short essay we rejected (see "Sensation, Memory, Imitation/and Story"), we might have urged him toward combining what he had written about individual literary works into that third step in his trilogy, never completed. We could have helped him produce a revised version of "Sensation/Memory/Imitation/and Story," in which he had accompanied each of the four stages with a dramatic gong, the last one ringing more and more like what I see as a religious hymn. What he wrote went like this:

gong	gong	gong	gong
sensation	memory	imitation	story

The "gong" of story (like the gong of music that filled his non-publishing life) resonated with religious tones. It thus seems to me inescapable that Burke's lifetime project was a religious one—perhaps searching for a replacement for the childhood orthodoxies he had rejected, perhaps . . .

Well, I must leave it to you to speculate about the motives of the grand rhetorologist who replied to my religious urgings like this:

June 5, 1979

Dear Web-ster—and wadda stir!

Naw, I'm still hangin on. . . .
No need to *convert* a nonbeliever like I'm. St. Paul tells us that there would be no theology without language. And my theories tell me that theology is the "perfect design of grace." Why, then, should a shrewd logologer frustrate the "natural" rites of speech? Why just talk to himself when he could address "Big Shot"? And when he hears himself talk, that would be the equivalent of Paul's pronouncement that "faith comes from hearing."

As ever, towards freedom,
KB

Is not Prophet Burke saying here that there's no need for a missionary type like Waxing Wane to try to convert a nonbeliever, *because* KB's already converted?—converted, that is, to his religion, the true religion, and not to any standard version? Is he not saying that beneath and beyond the dark inhospitable sky that masked his loneliness lived a man who saw that sky as divinely hospitable?

Notes

This is a revision of a talk given at the Kenneth Burke Society meeting in Pittsburgh in 1996. Because so much of it is quoted from Burke's own letters in their informal style, I have preserved my own oral style throughout. The argument is extended, in somewhat more theoretical terms, in "Kenneth Burke's

Religious Rhetoric: 'God-terms' and the Ontological Proof," forthcoming in *Rhetorical Invention and Religious Inquiry: New Perspectives,* ed. Walter Jost and Wendy Olmsted.

1. "A scholar before he was a critic, Crane never lost his scholarly passion for attending to the 'facts' a[s] found in the text or in its historical setting. His scorn for readers who misreported details terrified his graduate students and colleagues; legend has it (no doubt falsely) that many an author quit the profession after reading Crane's short tongue-lashing in *Philological Quarterly.* It seemed to hurt him personally that Kenneth Burke could build a case about how the albatross stands for Coleridge's drug habit, when there is no evidence that Coleridge even had the habit at the time of composing 'The Rime of the Ancient Mariner'—and besides it was Wordsworth who had suggested the albatross in the first place!" Booth, *Critical Understanding* 87.

2. Does he mean this sentence? "There was only one Burke, and I could not hear him, monist that I [then] was"? Booth, *Critical Understanding* 127.

3. Rueckert has only six: Burke the aphorist, the comedian, the dialectician, the logologer, the dramatist, and the poet. So obviously, in Burkean terms, I win!

4. Denis Donoghue, "The Aesthetics of *Counter-Statement.*" Paper presented at the Third Triennial Conference of the Kenneth Burke Society, Pittsburgh, May 1996.

5. Special issue of *Recherches Anglaises et Americaines (RANAM),* 12, Charles Susini, ed. Strasbourg: Association Strasbourgeoise des perioisques de sciences humaines, 1979.

6. Proofreading this talk for the umpteenth time (December 1997, May 2000), I suddenly note my omission of one more voice: the "street-kid" or "ignoramus" who uses expressions like "bejeez" and "a-gettn." But to move in that direction would require me to add the juggler with German, French, Latin, and Hebrew. He was especially fond of throwing languages together, as in his frequent "Avec universal Liebe."

7. Several critics have noted how prescient Burke was in "predicting" postmodernism. See Lentricchia and Wess. But others have emphasized differences, some on Burke's side (Henderson 99), some on Derrida's.

Bibliography

Arnold, Matthew. *Literature and Dogma: An Essay Towards a Better Apprehension of the Bible.* London: n.p., 1873.

Booth, Wayne C. *Critical Understanding: The Powers and Limits of Pluralism.* Chicago: University of Chicago Press, 1988.

——. "Kenneth Burke's Way of Knowing." *Critical Inquiry* 1 (1974): 1–22. Rev. reprint, with Kenneth Burke's response, in Booth ch. 3.

Burke, Kenneth. "As I Was Saying." *Michigan Quarterly Review* 11 (Winter 1972): 1–27.

——. *Complete White Oxen: Collected Short Fiction of Kenneth Burke.* Berkeley: University of California Press, 1968.

——. *Counter-Statement.* 1931. 3d ed. Berkeley: University of California Press, 1968.

——. "Dancing with Tears in My Eyes." *Critical Inquiry* 1 (1974): 23–31.

——. *A Rhetoric of Motives.* 1950. Berkeley: University of California Press, 1969.

——. *The Rhetoric of Religion: Studies in Logology.* 1961. Berkeley: University of California Press, 1970.

Burks, Don M. "KB and Burke: A Remembrance." *Kenneth Burke Society Newsletter* 9.1 (Dec. 1993): 6.

Garlitz, Robert. "The Sacrificial Word in Kenneth Burke's Logology." *Recherches Anglaises et Americaines (RANAM)* 12 (1979): 33–44.

Henderson, Greig E. *Kenneth Burke: Literature and Language as Symbolic Action.* Athens: University of Georgia Press, 1988.

Lentricchia, Frank. *Criticism and Social Change.* Chicago: University of Chicago Press, 1983.

Rueckert, William H. *Encounters With Kenneth Burke.* Urbana: University of Illinois Press, 1994.

——. "Some of the Many Kenneth Burkes." In *Representing Kenneth Burke.* Ed. Hayden White and Margaret Brose. Baltimore: Johns Hopkins University Press, 1982. 1–30. Also reprinted in Rueckert, *Encounters* 3–28.

Wess, Robert. *Kenneth Burke: Rhetoric, Subjectivity, Postmodernism.* Cambridge: Cambridge University Press, 1996.

9

Sensation, Memory, Imitation/and Story

Kenneth Burke

A reference (by Brown) to "Kant's notion of knowledge as mediated by the categories of mind" involves Kant's distinction between "percepts," or "intuitions of sensibility" (as per his "transcendental aesthetic") and the "categories," or "concepts of the understanding" (as per his "transcendental analytic"). The body's senses in themselves are a primary medium of awareness, giving us, in our nature sheerly as animals, reports of external conditions. But such sensory "percepts" could be called "immediate," in contrast with the kind of "mediation" that comes to fulfillment in the "conceptual" objectifications of scientific knowledge. Kant also has a third stage, a "dialectic" that deals with "ideas" of "reason." Unlike the "concepts" of the understanding which are "constitutive," these terms have no objective counterparts; (they say "What do" rather than "What is") they involve "regulative" *beliefs* which cannot be scientifically proved or disproved; yet one should act "as if" they are true. His top ones of this sort are God, the soul, freedom, and immortality.

Logology of secular cast would somewhat resemble yet depart from that lineup thus: In keeping with the distinction between nonsymbolic motion and symbolic action, along with the "principle of individuation" implicit in the centrality of the nervous system, we take it that as regards the body's contact with its environment, it is aware of impressions, as recorded by the senses, in terms of sound, sight, taste, "here" rather than "there," "before-after," heavy, light, moments sometimes painful, sometimes pleasurable, etc. These are a medium of "appearances" which could be called (our style) a kind of translation, the figurative use of the term referring to the fact that certain kinds of goings-on "out there" can be experienced ("interpreted" by the senses in terms of sight or sound or as at a particular location, etc.), but only if the organism that "naturally" sees and hears ("from within itself") does not suffer sensory privation whereby it is blind or deaf, etc. (We need not be concerned with Zen-like quandaries as to whether thunder is noising when there is no ear thereabouts to hear it.) Given the centrality of the nervous system, regardless of how everything merges into everything else, a physical sensation is "immediately" the experience of one organism and no other's, as my toothache is mine not yours.

But besides being *immediately* experienced, sensations may be remembered; besides *seeing* an "appearance," an "image" of something, we may *remember* such an experience. And the corresponding *duplications* of all sensations could be called "images." (A Platonist would say that a word for such a duplication is the duplication of a duplication.) Hume called such remembrances "less lively impressions," in an empiricist philosophy the attempt to dodge which drove Kant to the ingeniously intricate weavings of a "transcendental" epistemology such that even stylistic challengers like Nietzsche and Marx could be classed as offshoots of Kant, via offshoots of Schopenhauer and Hegel respectively.

To sensation and memory, add imitation. And since humans are the kind of organism that lives by locomotion, we should also include here the kind of response to others that may *counter* the motions of others. This view of imitation includes both doing exactly what others are doing and, for instance, fleeing because some other is attacking. Mead would have called it "taking the attitude of the other," and acting accordingly. (Some Zen tricks are possible here, too. If the proverb "the burnt child dreads the fire" implies a "memory" of the sensation, might it then follow that Pope's proverbial proposition, "Just as the twig is bent the tree's inclined," implies that the tree's inclination is a "behavioral" form of memory? And since his line rhymes with "'Tis education forms the common mind," might we go on to observe that, inasmuch as education is a form of conditioning, if a stick is broken, it has been conditioned to respond in a way it will never forget? But we must hurry on.)

The main point is that sensation and memory as here considered differ in one notable respect from imitation as a form of physiological motion. Such sensation and memory are in the nature of "reports" about the individual body's relation to the conditions of the environment in which, on the basis of its sensory reports, it finds its way about. The term "limitation," as extended to cover the field of locomotive response in general, implies not just a way of swimming with the current, but also a way of going against it—for as Bergson taught us to realize, our *sympathy* with where things *hurt* (or taste good?) can guide our choice of where to hurt some other (and thus what to eat, at the edible's expense?).

Logology inclines to assume that, if our primordial ancestors had but gone on thus, sans words, *we'd* still not be any farther from *their* natural responses to a natural environment than *they* were; and there would be no other kind of environment for us, their descendants, to live in now (in contrast with the technologically formed equivalent of exceptional genius which the stupidest of us now is, when going to a supermarket with some money to "freely" buy some "goods"—and in a long, industrious life one could not remotely chart the great complexity of "unnatural" processes and relationships that come to a focus in a sales transaction at the check-out counter).

This all had its beginnings when the primitive powers of imitation could be expended in a direction not possible to sheerly physiological modes of awareness (sensation, memory) and corresponding modes of imitation. The human animal's *departure* from nature (in the purely physiological dimension) owes its origin to the fact that a so-called natural language (developed largely by imitation as the child learns the idiom of its tribe) introduces a wholly different kind of duplication. It is the difference, say, between the immediately physiological experience that something *feels hot* and an expression such as "that feels hot," as conveyed in one or another conventional, arbitrary symbol-system.

At that point enter the resources of *story,* resources constituting a realm of motivation in their own right, involving transformations local to any one medium, and in the large developed by modes of analogical extension, itself an aspect of imitation that Bentham called "fictions."

"Immediately" our range of experience (and corresponding knowledge) is confined to the order of "appearances" as reported by the body's senses and memories of such. But the peculiar symbolic medium of communication which, apparently, no other animal on earth "naturally" masters, *mediates* a vast world of accumulated knowledge, fragments of which largely constitute our "Orientation," our "adjustments," our notions of "reality," our "taking the attitude of the other," though none of it has the *immediacy* of sensation. It comes from the world of *story,* the realm of *entitlements.*

The taste of an orange is a sensation. The words, "the taste of an orange," tell a story. They are in the realm of symbolic action, a realm that duplicates the realm of nonsymbolic motion but is not reducible to it (though not possible without it). By this resource, which adds narration to speechless nature, there arise in time stories of the Supernatural, or astrology, astronomy, alchemy, chemistry, geology, biology, geography, history, myths and rituals, ideologies and routines, etc. (beginning with gossip and the news; all animals, and even inanimate things, have modes of communication in purely physical ways; but only human animals can gossip, tell one another stories).

In brief the *wordless* "universe" which can tell no stories gets fragmentarily translated in countless "universes of discourse" made possible by the *public* nature of the medium in which the individual wordless human body is born with the ability to learn by imitation. And the human powers of imitation in this mode of *mediation* are such that many members of the human kind are now monkeying around with things like atom bombs and recombinant DNA—and what a story! . . . and though the day will come when, as was before human speech got started on this planet, things will again go on and on, as processes unmentioned, wholly devoid of story, the resources of story are such that we can say: "What is now going on will forever go on having gone on exactly as it is now going on—and so throughout all eternity" (having gone on as they once did go on in a line with whatever we mean or think we mean by "eternity"—a storytelling word which has grammatical dimensions of its own, with a corresponding range of personal attitudes involving in our idiom first person, second, third, singular, and plural; and be they right or wrong, all attitudes are real so far as concerns their grounding in the constitution of the body).

10

Kenneth Burke and Mary Baker Eddy

Michael Feehan

During an interview for *All Area* in 1983, Kenneth Burke was asked a rather standard question about the writing of *Permanence and Change*, "But weren't you rebounding from a kind of naive Marxism in that book?" ("Counter-Gridlock" 18).[1] Burke returned a wild curve. "You know what I was rebounding from? This is a drastic confession. You wouldn't believe this. There's an awful lot of that book that was really secularizing what I learned as a Christian Scientist. All this psychogenic illness stuff . . . there's no other secular book in the world where you find so much of that published at that time. I got that from Mary Baker G. Eddy, and I secularized it! ("Counter-Gridlock" 19). The interviewer responded with a secularization of his own, "That's a revelation." Then everyone silently agreed to drop the subject. I'd like to revive it here.[2]

For most students of Burke, the *All Area* interviewer's presumption that *Permanence and Change* was written in response to the Marxists fits comfortably with the received stories of Burke's development through the twenties and thirties. In a 1989 article with the perfectly apt title "Kenneth Burke's 'Secular Conversion,'" Don Paul Abbott tells that received story. "A significant change occurred in Burke's thinking between the publication of *Counter-Statement* and the writing of *Permanence and Change*, which Charles Glicksberg describes as a 'sudden leap from a corrective philosophy of science to a militant Marxist gospel'" (39). The following discussion will require some revisions in that received story.

All readers of Burke are aware of his many secularized terms: piety, secular prayer, secular conversion, god-terms, the Demonic Trinity, and so on. Hugh Dalziel Duncan, in his introduction to the second edition of *Permanence and Change*, goes so far as to call dramatism "a naturalistic, linguistically oriented, secular variant of Christianity" (xxxviii). Indeed, in the late phase of Burke's work, secularizing appears everywhere, from *The Rhetoric of Religion* to the late essay "Theology and Logology" and the short story "The Anaesthetic Revelation of Herone Liddell."

Still, Burke's crack about Christian Science suggests a more serious questioning. Can we find in *Permanence and Change* employments of this "secularizing" that are explicitly drawn from Mary Baker G. Eddy's work, and if so, how important are those "secularizings" for understanding *Permanence and Change*? In what follows, I hope to show that the secularizing goes to the heart of *Permanence and Change*: The pivotal secularizing term for *Permanence and Change* is "piety," a term that allows Burke to move effortlessly back and forth between religious and commercial cultures, without trivializing either of those realms of motives. Most importantly, Burke employs in *Permanence and Change* methods of analysis he learned from Eddy's *Science and Health (SH)*. Burke's process of secularizing Eddy can be seen most clearly by comparing the language of *Permanence and Change* to that of "Auscultation, Creation, and Revision," the book that Burke completed, but did not publish, just before embarking on *Permanence and Change*. "Auscultation, Creation, and Revision," which focuses on issues central to the American Marxist community of the early 1930s, employs language that is more clearly of religious origin than the language of *Permanence and Change*.

The role of piety in *Permanence and Change* is best expressed in a 1989 article by Thomas Rosteck and Michael Leff:

> In Burke's idiosyncratic lexicon, piety is transferred from the religious orbit where it normally appears and applied to a secular context. The term still retains an ethical valence, since it represents a principle of coherence, a standard against which to judge all aspects of speech and behavior. Yet, Burke extends the term so that it encompasses any impulse toward order and system. Piety thus functions to sustain the coherence of a perspective, but it now attaches itself to all levels of human experience, to the mundane as well as the divine. Moreover, while the function of piety remains constant, in substance pieties are diverse, since their content shifts in accordance with changing perspectives. (327–28)

Rosteck and Leff identify as the focal point of Burke's secularizing the association of the religious term "piety" with the rhetorical term "propriety." Burke makes this connection explicitly in *Permanence and Change:* "Every system of exhortation hinges about some definite act of faith, a deliberate selection of alternatives" (235). Crucially, Burke does not want this connection between religion and rhetoric to deflate the idea of piety to "mere rhetoric." He does not want religious feeling to be equated with something so simple as rules of etiquette. Rather, he intends to raise the idea of propriety to the level of genuine religious devotion. "Where you discern the symptoms of great devotion to any kind of endeavor, you are in the realm of piety" (83). Perhaps to bolster the apparent importance of the piety-propriety identification, Burke suggests that this identification comes from Santayana. "Santayana has somewhere defined piety as loyalty to the sources of our being" (71). Whether or not Santayana actually foreshadowed Burke's thinking, we see in the phrase "the sources of our being" that Burke wants us to take his new version of piety as equally consequential with its uses in religious discourse.

To "piety" and "propriety," Rosteck and Leff add *Permanence and Change*'s key methodological term, "perspective by incongruity": Piety creates permanences, that is, it "functions to sustain the coherence of a perspective" (327). However, our pieties cannot remain unchanged as we move through the world. Rosteck and Leff find in Burke a two-step conversion process: (1) reduction of scale and (2) construction of a new order (330). (We will see a two-step process again in Eddy's work.) "The midpoint in this progression constitutes what Burke calls 'a perspective by incongruity'" (330). But these incongruous perspectives are not merely static; they are causal, the function "which pries apart established linkages" (330). However constant the function of piety, changing perspectives create diversity by introducing new contents, subordinating or exiling old contents.

Rosteck and Leff miss one other important factor, "pliancy," the term that in *Permanence and Change* deals with adequacy of scope. Pliancy concerns the relations among piety, propriety, and perspectives by incongruity. "There is, of course, a further factor involved here: the matter of *interaction*. Certain of one's choices become creative in themselves; they drive one into ruts, and these ruts in turn reënforce one's piety" (78). Piety and propriety are orientations we can live in; perspectives by incongruity can break open those orientations whenever the need for some new orientation arises. But pieties can become ruts that trap us, prevent us from turning onto new roads. We require as a corrective a capacity to slide from one rut system to another whenever the pious rut we're presently following proves inadequate to our situation. Burke calls this capacity by many names, most succinctly "pliancy." If our pieties are sufficiently broad in scope, they allow us to resee or rethink our pieties without suffering a complete breakdown of our orientation. As we will see later, Burke limits this capacity of pliancy through his concept of "recalcitrance," the socializing power of the bodily world.

That Rosteck and Leff overlook the term "pliancy" cannot be surprising, because Burke used that particular term only rarely in *Permanence and Change,* though the concepts operative in that term pervade the book. Indeed, it was only with the 1984 afterword to the third edition that Burke made clear the importance of pliancy to understanding *Permanence and Change.* Burke compares Bentham's attempts to revise the language of the law with the practice within traditional debating clubs of assigning adversarial positions only in the last minutes before a contest begins. Burke says that the contestants' ability to align themselves with one side or the other on a moment's notice should be called "the pliancy of attitudinizing." This pliancy provides a valuable exercise program for our critical faculties, "a way of keeping in shape" (311). Through pliancy, especially through the "lyrical or dramatic" pliancy that Burke proposes, we can practice developing new pieties and proprieties during times of relative calm so that we will be better prepared for times of cultural storm.

The connection between *Permanence and Change*'s concept of pliancy and the ideas of Mary Baker G. Eddy will become clear if we add to the study of *Permanence and Change* a study of the two books Burke completed just before writing *Permanence and Change: Towards a Better Life* and "Auscultation, Creation, and Revision."

In *Towards a Better Life,* we see how a single individual who lacks pliancy can go to pieces. Indeed, the final section of the book, "Testamentum Meum," enacts the psychological disintegration of the main character, John Neal, by presenting a list of fragments of thoughts recapitulating the whole novel, without ever quite completing any one idea. The idea of pliancy appears as a problem of language: "there comes a time when one must abandon his vocabulary. For rigidness of words, by discovering a little, prevents us from discovering more" (216). Rigidness, being stuck in ruts, prevents change, while broadenings of vocabulary or of perspective make new orientations possible.

About three quarters of the way through *Towards a Better Life,* John Neal tells a story of "a man" who unfeelingly drove a good woman away from him only later to realize how completely that woman had sustained him. "He found that she alone had upheld him, for there was no pliancy in him that had not come from sources within this woman" (183). Pliancy holds us up; rigidity breaks us down. John Neal, already dangerously rigid himself, is threatened by the absolute rigidity of a "dummy policeman," a figure in wood that he regularly sees on a pedestal near his apartment: "There is nothing particularly unpleasant in the thought of him except its constancy. And I can assure you: he is so unchanging, that to think of him repeatedly is to feel the mind inexorably rigid. To consider him against one's wishes is like maintaining a constant muscular tension" (187). The act of thinking about rigidity becomes itself a form of rigidity.

One hope suggests itself. As John Neal becomes progressively more obsessed with the dummy policeman, even to the point of attempting conversation with him/it (190), a method for passing beyond the rigidity appears through the obsession itself. "Besides, any rigid thing, if watched intently will seem to stir" (193–94). That is, criticism, close analysis as the occupational psychosis of the critic, may provide the suppleness for new pliancies.

This line of thinking, "the pliancy of our attitudinizings," is better known under the guises it took in Burke's later work—in dramatism: adequacy, representative anecdote, and circumference; in logology: terministic screens. Studies of motivation and language must begin with a sufficiently broad conception of the subject matter of analysis because only an adequate scope, an adequately flexible set of terms, will provide us with the basis for breaking through received values to the creation of new values. In "Auscultation, Creation, and Revision," this idea of pliancy appears in Burke's argument against antithetical thinking (the "Saul-Paul" conversion pattern) and in favor of thinking through difference ("Goethe's chambered nautilus" conversion pattern).[3]

In "Auscultation, Creation, and Revision," Burke argues that Paul's sudden, complete conversion epitomizes the rigidly narrow program of changing perspectives that Burke is working to supplant. "The logical basis of the Saul-Paul reversal seems to stem from the thesis-antithesis-synthesis schema as borrowed from Hegel and revamped by Marx" (97). A logic of reversal, of antithesis, will always fall short of pliancy, will always trap us into "error of limitations," the state of being "closed to many important factors" (85). "We might seek to rate our schools by our 'error of limitations' concept, showing that some works took more factors into account than others—but we should eliminate entirely the notion of the 'error per se' contained in the Saul-Paul reversal" (96). When Saul was blinded, becoming Paul, the pieties that impelled Saul to persecute Christians became "error per se" to Paul. That is, the new orientation, by directly reversing the old orientation, outlawed the old pieties. Burke argues for the more flexible logic he calls "error of limitations." "There is a way of widening and deepening convictions until they are found to touch upon matters which at first seemed quite unrelated to them—and one may pursue these linkages along courses of their own, seeking to fit into a larger whole the particular concerns which started one on a particular hunt" (140). Broadenings of scope can show us how other people's pieties may be joined with our own to create new, more inclusive orientations.

Approaching the issues through the vocabulary of religion, Burke distinguishes between the sudden Saul-Paul conversion and "the Goethean 'chambered nautilus-coral island' complexity" (133). In secular terms, Burke distinguishes between logics of antithesis and logics of difference.

> And as simple Antithesis drops from the field of poetry and politics alike, we find that the Saul-Paul reversal would entail the renouncing of too much that must be kept. A Difference will bring new identifications, but these will lie across the old in such a way that much of the old is necessarily retained. "Rebirth" thus becomes Goethean, "growth by accretion," not a matter of mere negation, but the discovery of a broader frame for that which we already have, a discovery too *unpredictable* for us to be guided toward it by the mere automatic guidance of a schematic *opposite*. (172)

A critic, to create a fully pliant theory of conversion, must avoid antithesis. "In other words, the first thing he must drop as totally inadequate to his purposes will be the note of *Antithesis,* so ably suited for convincing the convinced, and so thoroughly unsuited to anything else" (169).

In arriving now at the work of Mary Baker G. Eddy, we might do well to begin with a wonderfully Burkean irony of doubling. Where Burke, in 1938 secularized Eddy, it is quite reasonable to see Eddy's own work as a "sacralization" of the secular system of Mesmerism. This point is neatly made in a discussion by Stefan Zweig of the first public announcement of Christian Science. "[T]his June 6, 1875, marks a turning point in the history of Mary Baker Eddy and in that of Christian Science. Herewith what had been a method of healing and an individual philosophy was transformed into religion" (185). Eddy began with the methods of Mesmerism and translated them into a new brand of Christianity.

Eddy had suffered throughout her life from a series of illnesses, always involving some form of paralysis. These illnesses may have been "nerves" or "hysteria" or "lack of faith," as you will. The critical passage of Eddy's life came during the Civil War years when she began collapsing into a paralysis that threatened to become total. Eddy consulted a Mesmerist named Phineas Quimby whose hypnosis succeeded in completely curing Eddy. She had just begun writing pieces for various local newspapers extolling Quimby's methods when, in 1866, Quimby suddenly died. Eddy suffered a complete relapse and quickly slid toward death. At that point, she discovered, recognized, invented—as you will—a connection between her cure under Mesmerism and Christianity. "When apparently near the confines of mortal existence, standing already within the shadow of the death-valley, I learned these truths in divine Science . . . " (*SH* 108; lines 19–21).[4] The Bible told Eddy that her seeming cure by Quimby could not have actually been caused by Quimby, since only God can heal us. Quimby could only have been a tool of God, a practitioner of misdirection through whom God's work could proceed effectively in an increasingly godless world. Therefore, since Quimby did not cause the cure, Quimby's death could not revoke the cure. Eddy's paralysis disappeared and she began writing the work that became *Science and Health*, a book that would defeat death itself.

In looking at Burke's secularization of Eddy, we begin with an embarrassment of riches. Eddy's three key terms, science, health, Christ, are mirrored in Burke's writing throughout his career, and especially in the three books we've been looking at: Eddy calls her book *Science and Health*; Burke is concerned with the threat posed by an overblown scientism; and Burke is constantly searching for ways to cure what ills us, especially in the matter of scapegoating, the fate of Christ. Burke's god-term "motive" suffuses Eddy's book. Most strikingly, Eddy spends much of her time providing interlinear translations between scriptural language and the language of Christian Science.[5] The concepts of conversion, translation, and transformation appear as interchangeable for both Eddy and Burke.

However, we have not gone beyond mere juxtapositions; we have yet to reach a point where we can see the secularizing of Eddy's work as constitutional of *Permanence and Change*. To get to that point, we need to look at the two writers' programs: Eddy's literal program for religious conversion and Burke's analogical program for converting orientations. Burke himself invites us to take method as a concept that transcends the competition between faith and reason. "But might we not avoid the whole question as to whether man is a rational or an irrational being by saying simply that man is *methodical*? Man is methodical, even methodological" (234). Furthermore, the concept of method so used may be seen as explicitly a secularization: "Might we, noting the suspiciously close connection between the *hodical* and the *methodical*, be once more encouraged to look for a unitary technique, called in religious verbalizations the *way* and in scientific verbalizations the *way after*? Might we assume a constancy of message throughout history precisely to the extent that the biologic purposes of the human genus had remained constant . . . ?" (234). Then, what method does Eddy propose?

For Eddy the process of becoming a Christian Scientist involves two stages:

1. The discovery of this divine Science of Mind-healing, through a spiritual sense of the Scriptures and through the teachings of the Comforter, as promised by the Master.

2. The proof, by present demonstration, that the so-called miracles of Jesus did not specially belong to a dispensation now ended, but that they illustrated an ever-operative divine Principle. The operation of this Principle indicates the eternality of the scientific order and continuity of being. (123; lines 20–29)

I will call these two phases of method reversal and faith. For each phase, I will first present Eddy's approach, then show Burke's secularization in *Permanence and Change* (and ACR). As we have already seen, Burke's guiding principle for secularizing Eddy's term "reversal" will be pliancy. Burke's guiding principle for secularizing Eddy's term "faith" will be the coupling of the terms "lex continui" and "recalcitrance."

Reversal. Eddy says, "If you wish to know the spiritual fact, you can discover it by reversing the material fact, be the fable *pro* or *con*,— be it in accord with your preconceptions or utterly contrary to them" (*SH* 129; lines 7–11). Eddy's reversals deal primarily with the inaccuracies of commonsense judgments about the physical world. "In viewing the sunrise, one finds that it contradicts the evidence before the senses to believe that the earth is in motion and the sun at rest. As astronomy reverses the human perception of the movement of the solar system, so Christian Science reverses the seeming relation of Soul and body and makes body tributary to Mind" (*SH* 119; lines 25–31). Christian Science is expressly concerned with reversals of common sense, because only by reversals of our most immediate daily experience can we see through to God's plan. "Divine metaphysics reverses perverted and physical hypotheses as to Deity, even as the explanation of optics rejects the incidental or inverted image and shows what this inverted image is meant to represent" (111; lines 14–18). The reversals proposed by Christian Science make it possible for us to see human existence in its properly spiritual character. "With its divine proof, Science reverses the evidence of material sense. Every quality and condition of mortality is lost, swallowed up in immortality. Mortal man is the antipode of immortal man in origin, in existence, and in his relation to God. (215;

lines 22–26). The way to God, the key to scripture, resides in literally reversing the evidence of the senses. Our entrapment in material bodies actively prevents our recognizing the true natures of both God and humans.

Eddy begins using reversals in *Science and Health,* the foundational book of Christian Science, in the first chapter, "Prayer," exhibiting the method before explaining it. (Burke waits until the middle of his book before introducing his impious version of piety). Eddy argues that public prayer, spoken prayer, serves only to ingratiate the speaker to some group. (Burke's piety is a form of socialization). Prayer cannot affect God: "God is not moved by the breath of praise to do more than He has already done, nor can the infinite do less than bestow all good, since He is unchanging wisdom and Love" (2; lines 4–11). The only valid purpose for prayer is to achieve what Eddy calls "harmony": "Prayer cannot change the Science of being, but it tends to bring us into harmony with it" (2; lines 15–16). Harmonious prayer consists in actions that evince gratitude for God's necessary goodness and a desire to be a part of that goodness. Harmonious prayer requires no outward sign, no speech. The more noise we make about our gratitude and desire, the less time we spend acting for God, in God's image.

Burke's first such reversal in *Permanence and Change* appears in the appropriation of Veblen's "invention is the mother of necessity" (5). In explicating his "Incongruous Assortment of Incongruities," Burke makes reversal the key to analogical argumentation: "Conversely, where the accepted linkages have been of an imposing sort, one should establish perspective by looking through the reverse end of his glass, converting mastodons into microbes, or human beings into vermin upon the face of the earth" (120). Burke follows Eddy in arguing that a simple reversal of our tools will bring valuable new insights. Burke goes beyond Eddy by adding the term "linkage." Any term can be linked with any other term; linkages can reach out in any direction; linkages provide virtually infinite pliancy for discussing motives, from atoms to sausages to political parties. "In a general way, we might say that events take character by a 'linkage of outstanding with outstanding.' . . . The accumulation and interworking of such characters is an orientation. . . . A sign, which is here now, may have got a significance out of the past that makes it a promise of the future" (14). Linkage recognizes that reversals aiming at new orientations cannot operate by total rejections of the past, but must gather outstanding aspects of the past to interconnect outstanding aspects of the present in order to fulfill the promised future. Burke's term "linkage," when coupled with the concept of analogical extension, creates the concept of pliancy.

Faith. Once we have reversed our terms, beliefs, perspectives, we must go on to ask why this reversed world is worth believing in. Eddy answers that Christian Science reversals reveal God's truth. Christian Science reversals will return Christianity to the path that Christ had originally set, but that has become lost because later generations of teachers could not or would not take Christ's message literally. Eddy's master reversal is called the "Divine Principle."

> Remember, brain is not mind. Matter cannot be sick, and Mind is immortal. The mortal body is only an erroneous mortal belief of mind in matter. What you call matter was originally error in solution, elementary mortal mind,—likened by Milton to "chaos and old night." One theory about this mortal mind is, that its sensations can reproduce man, can form blood, flesh, and bones. The Science of being, in which all is divine Mind, or God and His idea, would be clearer in this age, but for the belief that matter is the medium of man, or that man can enter his own embodied thought, bind himself with his own beliefs, and then call his bonds material and name them divine law. (*SH* 372; lines 1–13)

For Eddy, all physical existence is illusory. The only reality is spirit; everything we know through the senses must be wrong. These claims will seem merely silly unless we recognize these claims as God's truth. Eddy's mission is to prove that the Divine Principle is literally and absolutely true. *Science and Health* attempts to establish a way of reading, a method of translation, through which the Bible will be recognized as God's own speaking of the Divine Principle. For example, in the first chapter of *Science and Health*, "Prayer," Eddy provides a primer on translation, an interlinear rewriting of the Lord's Prayer:

> Our Father which art in heaven,
> *Our Father-Mother-God, all harmonious,*
> Hallowed be Thy Name,
> *Adorable One.*
> Thy kingdom come,
> *Thy kingdom is come; Thou art ever-present . . .*
> (*SH* 16; lines 26–31)

This excerpt gives the flavor of Eddy's rhetoric and an introduction to her program for translation: The first line introduces the feminist undercurrent of Eddy's revisionist Christianity, insisting on "Mother" as an aspect of God. The third line extrapolates from the Divine Principle to the idea of time: If the physical world is all illusion, then time is also illusory and God's plan is already complete. The translation continues in this vein, introducing and extrapolating further issues in Christian Science; however, a later translation exercise provides a broader introduction to Eddy's methodology.

In the chapter "Science, Theology, Medicine," in distinguishing her own vision from those of orthodox religious and orthodox healing cultures, Eddy charts the general pattern for Christian Scientific translations:

SCIENTIFIC TRANSLATION OF IMMORTAL MIND

GOD: Divine Principle, Life Truth, Love, Soul, Spirit, Mind.
MAN: God's spiritual idea, individual, perfect, eternal.
IDEA: An image of mind; the immediate object of understanding.—*Webster.*

SCIENTIFIC TRANSLATION OF MORTAL MIND

First Degree: Depravity.
PHYSICAL. Evil beliefs, passion and appetites, fear, depraved will, self-justification, pride, envy, deceit, hatred, revenge, sin, sickness, disease, death.
Second Degree: Evil beliefs disappearing.
MORAL. Humanity, honesty, affection, compassion, hope, faith, meekness, temperance.
Third Degree: Understanding.
SPIRITUAL. Wisdom, purity, spiritual understanding, spiritual power, love, health, holiness. (*SH* 115–16; lines 12–3)

Eddy here presents a systematic translation device that will allow its Christian Science user to recognize and thus avoid any language that, while purporting to be religious, actually misdirects our attention away from the spiritual realm toward the material. (We will see later how Burke deals with the material-spiritual distinction, in a discussion of Eddy's conception of Christ.) Here, we should look at Burke's direct secularizings of the term "faith."

In "Auscultation, Creation, and Revision," Burke says that he found a literal secularizing of faith in a book by Charles Barron, publisher of *Barron's.* Burke says, "And faith obviously is at the bottom even of something so apparently 'realistic' as business" (59). Then Burke allows Barron to speak. "It is really faith acquired or inherited that does the big things in the world. John D. acquired faith from his Bible-reading mother, and borrowed all the money he could to store oil when it was going to waste and considered of no value. He had faith in the value of the author of that oil . . . People who have no faith may be terror-stricken and swept off their feet before unknown and unmeasured adversaries" (59–60). Burke resumes his discussion with a flourish: "Then it is no accident that our word for 'credit' comes from the Latin 'to believe'" (60). Borrowing and believing interchange happily in a world of commerce; etymology provides good leads for spotting verbal intersections between the religious and the secular.

In *Permanence and Change,* Burke illustrates this process in an account of the historical development of our credit-based economy from the perspective of a "rephrasing of the Faith." Modern, free-enterprise markets, requiring "such diaphanous things as forecasts, prospects, futures," reorient merchants to the extent that "[a]ctual physical properties are hardly more than signs to be interpreted. A railroad approached, not in terms of tracks, engines, roundhouses, repair plants, and working force, but through data as to its capital structure! . . . Here, that deeply religious concept which once flourished as Providence does indeed seem to have been secularized, with all its spirituality intact, in strangely Ariel-like notions as to yield" (41–42). Pieties, even when they are shifted to a realm as shifty as that of the robber barons, retain their quality of "devotion to the sources of our being."

The faith that Eddy proposes revolves around three dominant terms: "science," "health," and "Christ."

Science. Eddy appropriates the term "science" to her new version of Christianity. "The terms Divine Science, Spiritual Science, Christian Science, or Science alone, she employs interchangeably, according to the requirements of the context" (*SH* 127; lines 9–12). The test for validity in this new science is "demonstration"; the method of accounting is mathematical. "My conclusions were reached by allowing the evidence of this revelation to multiply with mathematical certainty and the lesser demonstration to prove the greater" (*SH* 108; lines 12–15). This conception of science seems closer to classical rhetoric than to the processes of experimentation, replication, and verification of what even in 1866 had become the basic system of modern scientific investigation. For Eddy, proof in Christian Science comes by way of demonstration, by a setting before the eyes—in an irony Eddy never faces—through "sensible evidence." "This great fact [the demonstrable effectiveness of Christian Science] is not, however, seen to be supported by sensible evidence, until its divine Principle is demonstrated by healing the sick and thus proved absolute and divine. This proof once seen, no other conclusion can be reached" (*SH* 109, 6–10). The evidence of healing that Eddy actually provides in her book, in an appendix titled, "Fruitage," is testimony—one hundred pages of statements about healing events, each statement ending with a set of initials and the name of a city. We hear nothing more about the persons purportedly giving these testimonials.

Whatever actions may take place during events of Christian Science healing, readers of Eddy's book have only the printed words in lieu of "demonstration."

Burke's use of the term "science" in *Permanence and Change* is historicist, science being the third great stage of development. "Magic as the schema which stressed mainly the control of natural forces, religion stressing the control of human forces, and science stressing the control of the third productive order, the technological" (59). Magic and science can be thought of as constituting one category, as in Frazer's *The Golden Bough,* because "both magic and positive science assume a uniformity or regularity of natural processes, and attempt to harness these processes by the discovery of the appropriate formulae" (59). For religion, however, "[t]he laws of the universe are not immutable; an *arbitrary principle* is introduced. . . . Not the incantations or laboratory formulae of control, but the petitions of prayer were requisite" (60). God's power to change the laws of physics at whim make both magic and science impossible under this conception of religion. From this perspective, then, Eddy must count as a scientist: She rejects prayer as useless and she sees the world as immutable, subject to one unchanging principle. She differs from orthodox scientists only in her assertion that the subject matter of the other sciences does not exist.

Health. Eddy wants to "treat disease," but she does not want to "cure" illness. Under the Divine Principle, there simply cannot be any illness, and no death. "I have set forth Christian Science and its application to the treatment of disease just as I have discovered them. I have demonstrated through Mind the effects of Truth on health, longevity, and morals of men . . . " (*SH* 126; lines 22–26). Once we fully understand Eddy's discovery of mind, truth, science, and Divine Principle, we pass irrevocably beyond illness and death.

> The effect of mortal mind on health and happiness is seen in this: If one turns away from the body with such absorbed interest as to forget it, the body experiences no pain. (261; lines 8–11)

> Detach sense from the body, or matter, which is only a form of human belief, and you may learn the meaning of God, or good, and the nature of the immutable and immortal. Breaking away from the mutations of time and sense, you will neither lose the solid objects and ends of life nor your own identity. Fixing your gaze on the realities supernal, you will rise to the spiritual consciousness of being, even as the

bird which has burst from the egg and preens its wings for
a skyward flight. (261; lines 21–30)

Eddy devotes several hundred pages to attacks against various competi-
tors—Mesmerism, Animal Magnetism, Spiritualism, and the like—
each of which seeks to remedy some physical maladjustment between
body and spirit. Eddy insists that she is not speaking in metaphors, that
she is not engaging in hyperbole, that she means quite literally that nobody in fact inhabits a body, that there is no material existence and that
therefore all sensations of illness and all fears of death are illusory.
Those people who think that they are ill or dying have come under attack by Satan. Faith in God's goodness, which Eddy finds revealed
in the Divine principle, returns us to the truth that our existence is
wholly mind-spirit and, therefore, cannot ever come under the control
of bodily infection. Nobody needs to be cured; we only need to be converted.

   Permanence and Change can well be seen as Burke's act of taking
on Eddy's concerns for curing and conversion by reversing them or up-
ending them. Just as *Towards a Better Life* literally argues for hypo-
chondriasis, *Permanence and Change* argues that we should court "perspectives by incongruity" as a way of keeping intellectually fit: Regular
reversals of orientation both show us what the mirror world looks like
and keep our reversal muscles in trim. Artists keep in trim by doing
their art. "Rebirth and perspective by incongruity are thus seen to be
synonymous, a process of conversion, though such words as conversion
and rebirth are usually reserved for only the most spectacular of such
reorientations, the religious. . . . The artist is always an evangelist, quite
as the religious reformer is" (154 n. 1). The artist's experience may
compare to Paul's; thus, "we find the two aspects of the poet's certainty:
The poem is a sudden *fusion, a falling together of many things formerly
apart*—and the very force of this fusion leads one to seek further experiences of the same quality" (158). But we may also look to accretion-
like processes by which an artist becomes proficient in technique, processes like those undergone by Christ. "Christ seems to have developed
into a slowly increasing mastery of a *method*, much as an artist might
develop his technique with the years. He was concerned with matters
of strategy, of presentation, apparently being certain from the start
that his point of view was 'correct.' " (155). One might wonder how
Christian thinkers—Eddy, for instance—might respond to the idea of
Christ's self-education in the arts of rhetoric.

   Of course, here we are standing at the methodological heart of *Permanence and Change,* the theory of analogical extension through the

lex continui: "whereby we move step by step from some kind of event, in which the presence of a certain factor is sanctioned in the language of common sense, to other events in which this factor had not previously been noted. The thinker attempts to establish a continuity for arriving at conclusions which might seem abrupt and paradoxical if the two ends of his series were juxtaposed abruptly, without the interpolation of a gradient" (142). Analogy moves by graded series from term to term, transforming our received orientation into something new, something rife with unexpected by-products. When we accept some new orientation, we are converted; we have found a new piety. Thus, *Permanence and Change*'s secular logic of lex continui can be seen to draw directly on "Auscultation, Creation, and Revision"'s religious logic of conversion by accretion.

Christ. For Eddy the story of Jesus explains the Divine Principle through "our divine Exemplar" (*SH* 5; line 31). Jesus enacted the Divine Principle while he lived as human, and the gospels inerrantly portray those enactments. Unfortunately, the truth of Jesus' message has been lost to Christian teaching during the centuries since Jesus returned to heaven. "How true it is that whatever is learned through material sense must be lost because such so-called knowledge is reversed by the spiritual facts of being in Science" (*SH* 312; lines 1–4). Over two millennia, the priests have reversed the truth; now Eddy's reversal of that reversal brings us back to the source. We rediscover the original meaning of the Incarnation. "Born of a woman, Jesus' advent in the flesh partook partly of Mary's earthly condition, although he was endowed with the Christ, the divine Spirit, without measure. This accounts for his struggles in Gethsemane and on Calvary, and this enabled him to be the mediator, or *way-shower*, between God and men. Had his origin been wholly apart from mortal usage, Jesus would not have been appreciable to mortal mind as 'the way'" (*SH* 30; lines 5–13). Jesus took on flesh in order to become "appreciable" to humans as "the way." In a cursory reading, Eddy seems uncontroversial, but the crucial concepts here are "Mary's earthly condition" and "mortal mind." In the context of Christian Science, this version of the Incarnation, while recognizing the necessary function of the flesh, denies that Christ ever was material, even when he inhabited a human body. "God never ordained a material law to annul the spiritual law. If there were such a material law, it would oppose the supremacy of Spirit, God, and impugn the wisdom of the creator. Jesus walked on the waves, fed the multitude, healed the sick, and raised the dead in direct opposition to material laws. His acts were the demonstration of Science, overcoming the false claims of material sense or law" (*SH* 273; lines 21–28). Granted that we humans believe our flesh to be real, granted that we respond deeply to Christ's mission because he took on the sufferings of the flesh, still the Divine Principle guarantees both that neither we nor Christ ever were physical and that our sufferings are always only spiritual. Jesus suffered the pains of the flesh and then overcame them, overcame even death itself, in order to show us that all our fleshly sufferings are illusory, that our "earthly condition" is really only a test of faith.

Though we might spend a good deal of time discussing the various purifications of scapegoating to be found in *Science and Health* and *Permanence and Change*, it is Eddy's devaluation of the Incarnation that will take us farthest in studying Burke's methodological appropriation of Eddy. Readers of the "Boik-woiks" know all too well Burke's lifelong insistence on the body as the source of human individuation. "Our calling has its roots in the biological, and our biological demands are clearly implicit in the universal texture" (256). Burke's secularizing of Eddy is first of all a rejection by reversal of Eddy's version of the Incarnation, insisting on the body as the ground of human motives. In discussing the appeal of Charlie Chaplin's style, Burke borrows the vocabulary of religion. "His expressions possessed an almost universal significance, since they were based on the permanent certainties of the body, the eternal correlations between mental attitude and bodily posture" (52). Burke went so far in *Permanence and Change* as to call for a "Metabiology" (from Shaw's *Back to Methuselah: A Metabiological Pentateuch?*), a beyonding of biology.

The methodology associated with bodily certainty is "recalcitrance." When the communicating animal begins to make fictions to interpret the world, the world immediately begins to make counterstatements. "We must 'altruistically' take into account the order of difficulty that goes with the order of our intentions. The factor of recalcitrance may force us to alter our original strategy of expression greatly" (255). Orientations may be forced to change when they fail to fit in with the physical world. Our fictive points of view may create utterly new possibilities for understanding and acting in the world. "But the 'discoveries' which flow from the point of view are nothing other than revisions made necessary by the nature of the world itself" (257). Though our gift of language allows us to invent an infinite variety of possible orientations, the physical world necessarily limits our ability to simply ignore the physical world.

Burke sometimes talks about the logic of recalcitrance as a process of revision, as in the quotation above, sometimes as a system or "orders": "The universe 'yields' to our point of view by disclosing the different orders of recalcitrance which arise when the universe is considered from this point of view" (257). *Permanence and Change* presents the individual human body as the ground for orientations, the sources of certainty. As we grow up, our bodies are infused with various pieties that tell our bodies *"what properly goes with what"* (74). The weight of the physical world, its recalcitrance, may force us to change some or all of our pieties.

Burke's insistence on the body, pieties, and recalcitrance allows him to affirm an orientation that would otherwise be merely silly: D. H. Lawrence's "insisting that growing crops make the sun shine." Burke can accept this reversal, because it recognizes that human relations are necessarily motivated: "[W]hat we have left is an insistence that a purposive or teleological factor must be reaffirmed in our attempts to understand man's relation to his environment" (230). Once we introduce symbol users, it becomes impossible to ignore those symbol users' impulse to seek the most thorough ramifications of their symbols.

When we find ourselves involved with an orientation so far outside the range of common sense as Lawrence's, or Eddy's, we can take that orientation as noncontroversially true about the experience of its defenders, but we will not stop there. Burke's concept of recalcitrance will force its way into the discussion, demanding revisions. "The objection to Lawrence's statements is that they have not undergone the scope of revision required by the recalcitrance of the material which would be disclosed were we to extend them into all walks of investigation. They have not been *socialized,* as the cooperation of an entire historic movement might have caused them to be in the past or might again cause them to be in the future" (256). Whenever a given individual teaches a new orientation, that individual enters the realm of rhetoric, the realm of socialization, where recalcitrance reigns.

Burke can feel quite comfortable with secularizing Mary Baker G. Eddy because he makes some critical adjustments to her methodology: Replacing the Saul-Paul conversion with lex continui, insisting on the body as necessary ground, and establishing recalcitrance as the force that prevents our losing sight of the material world.

For Burke personally, the key secularization appears in his identification of conversion with translation, an identification that also pervades the work of Eddy. For instance, in June of 1932, Burke wrote to Malcolm Cowley, "I can only welcome Communism by converting it into my own vocabulary. I am, in the deepest sense, a translator. I go on translating, even if I must but translate English into English" (*Selected Correspondence* 202). In *Permanence and Change,* translation is proposed as the way to peace. "[T]he psychology of *translation* that is implicit in our concept of recalcitrance could lessen sectarian divisions by prompting a man to remember that his assertions are necessarily *socialized by revision,* an attitude which might make for greater patience" (265).

Notes

1. Burke's contests with orthodox Marxists have been discussed numerous times; see Lentricchia. For the impact of 1930s American Marxism on Burke's writing, especially the changes from ACR to *Permanence and Change,* see Crusius, Jay, and Henderson.

2. Burke's most extensive discussion of Christian Science appears in a pair of large footnotes in *Attitudes Toward History* 44–47 and 322–25.

3. Greig Henderson notes the irony of Burke's setting aside the vocabulary of ACR: "With remarkable poststructuralist prescience, Burke advocates difference rather than antithesis, suggesting that the most effective way to undermine and subvert a hegemonic discourse is from within" (180). Burke also dropped the term "free play": "The mind, to grasp meanings of this sort, must have a kind of 'expansiveness' or 'stretchableness.' . . . It is because the mind has this free play . . . that we can lay before it some *new* meaning . . . " (134).

4. All editions of Eddy's *Science and Health* are published in the same format, with line numbers in the margins of each page, so that any quoted passage may be found efficiently: i.e. a quotation appearing on page 372, beginning on line 1 and ending on line 13 will be cited (372; lines 1–13).

5. Burke and Eddy play similar kinds of word games. For instance, Eddy has a chapter titled "At-One-Ment;" Burke uses that same pun in a chapter title in ACR.

Bibliography

Abbott, Don Paul. "Kenneth Burke's 'Secular Conversion.'" *Horns of Plenty* 2 (Winter 1989): 39–52.

Burke, Kenneth. *Attitudes Toward History.* 1937. Rev 3d ed. Berkeley: University of California Press, 1984.

———. "Auscultation, Creation, and Revision." Chesebro 42–172.

———. *Permanence and Change.* 1935. Rev. 3d ed. Berkeley: University of California Press, 1984.

———. *The Selected Correspondence of Kenneth Burke and Malcolm Cowley: 1915–1981.* Ed. Paul Jay. Berkeley: University of California Press, 1990.

———. *Towards a Better Life.* 1932. Berkeley: University of California Press, 1966.

Burke, Kenneth, and Malcolm Cowley. "Kenneth Burke and Malcolm Cowley: A Conversation." *Pre/Text* 6 (Fall/Winter 1985): 181–200.

Chesebro, James W., ed. *Extensions of the Burkeian System.* Tuscaloosa: University of Alabama Press, 1993.

"Counter-Gridlock." *All Area* 2 (Spring 1983): 4–33.

Crusius, Timothy. "Kenneth Burke's *Auscultation:* A 'De-struction' of Marxist Dialectic and Rhetoric." *Rhetorica* 6 (Fall 1988): 355–79.

Eddy, Mary Baker Glover. *Science and Health: with Key to Scriptures.* Boston: Christian Science P. Soc. 1875, 1906.

Henderson, Greig E. "Aesthetic and Practical Frames of Reference: Burke, Marx, and the Rhetoric of Social Change." Chesebro 173–85.

Jay, Paul, ed. "Kenneth Burke and the Motives of Rhetoric." *American Literary History* 1.3 (Fall 1989): 535–53.

Lentricchia, Frank. *Criticism and Social Change.* Chicago: University of Chicago Press, 1985.

Rosteck, Thomas, and Michael Leff. "Piety, Propriety, and Perspective: An Interpretation and Application of Key Terms in Kenneth Burke's *Permanence and Change.*" *Western Journal of Speech Communication* 53 (Fall 1989): 327–41.

Zweig, Stefan. *Mental Healers: Mesmer, Mary Baker Eddy, and Freud.* New York: Viking, 1932.

Contributors

Index

Contributors

Wayne C. Booth is a professor emeritus in the Department of English at the University of Chicago. He considers Kenneth Burke, along with Mikhail Bakhtin, a major influence in complicating and deepening the critical education he received from the so-called Chicago School. His most recent book is *For the Love of It: Amateuring and Its Rivals* (1999). He has been for years attempting a book comparing the rhetorics of religion and science (faith and reason), but he has now been talked into attempting a book about how and why biography deceives us, for good and ill.

Thomas Carmichael is an associate professor in the Department of English at the University of Western Ontario. He is a coeditor of *Constructive Criticism: The Human Sciences in the Age of Theory* (1995) and of *Postmodern Times: A Critical Guide to the Contemporary* (2000). He is also the author of a number of articles on contemporary American fiction, literary theory, and postmodern culture.

Michael Feehan received his Ph.D. from Ross Winterowd's rhetoric-linguistics-literature program at the University of California in 1979. A teacher of rhetoric, writing, and literature at Memphis State University and University of Texas at Arlington from 1979 to 1992, he is the author of a dozen articles, most of them relating to Kenneth Burke. He is presently working as a staff attorney for the Bureau of Legislative Research of the General Assembly of Arkansas.

Greig Henderson is an associate professor in the Department of English at the University of Toronto. The author of *Kenneth Burke: Literature and Language as Symbolic Action* (1988) and a contributor to *Extensions of the Burkeian System* (1993) and *Kenneth Burke and the Twenty-first Century* (1999), he has also published articles on literary theory and modern literature. He is currently president of the Kenneth Burke Society.

William H. Rueckert is a professor emeritus in the Department of English at the State University of New York at Geneseo. He is the author of *Kenneth Burke and the Drama of Human Relations* (1963, 1982), *Glenway Westcott* (1965), *Encounters with Kenneth Burke*

(1994), and the editor of *Critical Responses to Kenneth Burke, 1924–1966* (1966). With Angelo Bonadonna, he has finished a collection of Burke's post-1966 essays entitled *On Human Nature: A Gathering While Everything Flows* (forthcoming). His final Burke project, "A Symbolic of Motives" Reader, will reconstruct Burke's original text as he wrote it between 1950 and 1955. Rueckert was the first president of the Kenneth Burke Society from 1990 to 1992 and is the author of numerous essays on American criticism and culture.

Robert Wess received his Ph.D. from the University of Chicago and is an associate professor in the Department of English at Oregon State University. A recipient of the Distinguished Service Award from the Kenneth Burke Society, he is the author of *Kenneth Burke: Rhetoric, Subjectivity, Postmodernism* (1996) as well as articles on various theoretical and literary topics.

David Cratis Williams is an assistant professor of speech communication in the Department of Philosophy and Liberal Arts at the University of Missouri, Rolla. Editor of *Argumentation Theory and the Rhetoric of Assent* (1990) and *The Cratis Williams Chronicles: I Come to Boone* (1999), he was a contributor to *The Legacy of Kenneth Burke* (1989) and is the author of several articles on rhetoric and public argument.

Index

Rhetorical Philosophy and Theory Series

The Rhetorical Philosophy and Theory Series aims to extend the subject of rhetoric beyond its traditional and historical bounds and thus to elaborate rhetoric's significance as a metaperspective in provocative ways. Rhetoric has become an epistemology in its own right, one marked by heightened consciousness of the symbolic act as always already contextual and ideological. Otherwise known as the rhetorical turn, this dialectic between rhetoric and philosophy may lead to views transcending the limits of each and thus help us better understand the ethical problems and possibilities of producing theory.

The Rhetorical Philosophy and Theory Series seeks quality scholarly works that examine the significance of rhetorical theory in philosophical, historical, cultural, and disciplinary contexts. Such works will typically bring rhetorical theory to bear on the theoretical statements that enfranchise disciplinary paradigms and practices across the human sciences, with emphasis on the fields of rhetoric, composition, philosophy, and critical theory.

Queries and submissions should be directed to David Blakesley, Editor, Rhetorical Philosophy and Theory, Department of English, Purdue University, West Lafayette IN 47907.